Choosing the Language of Transnational Deals

Practicalities, Policy, and Law Reform

Patrick Del Duca

ABA Section of
International Law
Your Gateway to International Practice

AMERICAN BAR ASSOCIATION
**Defending Liberty
Pursuing Justice**

Cover design by ABA Publishing.

Page Layout by Quadrum Solutions (www.quadrumltd.com)

The materials contained in this book represent the opinions and views of the authors and/or the editors, and should not be construed to be the views or opinions of the law firms or companies with whom such persons are in partnership with, associated with, or employed by, nor of the American Bar Association unless adopted pursuant to the bylaws of the Association.

Nothing contained in this book is to be considered as the rendering of legal advice, either generally or in connection with any specific issue or case; nor do these materials purport to explain or interpret any specific bond or policy, or any provisions thereof, issued by any particular franchise company, or to render franchise or other professional advice. Readers are responsible for obtaining advice from their own lawyers or other professionals. This book and any forms and agreements in this book are intended for educational and informational purposes only.

Library of Congress Cataloging-in-Publication Data

Del Duca, Patrick L.
   Choosing the language of transnational deals : practicalities, policy, and law reform / Patrick Del Duca.
       p. cm.
   Includes bibliographical references.
   ISBN 978-1-60442-937-4
1. Contracts—Language. 2. Export sales contracts—Language. 3. Contracts (International law)—Language. 4. Language and languages—Law and legislation. I. Title.
   K843.D45 2010
   346.0201'4—dc22
                                2010011599

DEDICATION

At the beginning of my career as a lawyer, I had the privilege to work for a year as a law clerk to Prof. Antonio La Pergola, then a justice of Italy's *Corte Costituzionale*. From my first introduction to him over dinner on a Roman summer evening, marked by the calls of cicadas in the umbrella pines (and an intense saffron-yellow risotto attributed origins in Prof. La Pergola's native Sicily), and throughout the remainder of his distinguished career, I witnessed his passion for the law as an instrument to promote respect for differences, while establishing frameworks for diverse communities to relate productively to each other. Whether his focus was Sicily, Italy's Regions, Europe's regions, Italy's place in Europe, American federalism, Latin America, constitutional justice in central Europe, or the constitution of the European Union, his work as a scholar, a political leader in the most noble sense of the calling, and as a judge of the Italian Constitutional Court and the European Court of Justice, was and remains a continuing example of the best that lawyers can conduct. I hope that this manuscript transmits the intelligence of his outreach to the world and his profound respect for the potential of law and legal frameworks to shape the world for the better.

About the Author

Patrick Del Duca, a member of the California bar, has assisted clients with transnational commercial and financial deals throughout his career. His languages are English, French, Italian, Portuguese and Spanish.

He is trained in common law, having earned a JD degree from Harvard Law School, and civil law, having earned a *laurea in giurisprudenza* from the *Università di Bologna* law faculty. He received a Ph.D in law from the European University Institute in Florence, Italy, after defending a dissertation addressing administrative and constitutional law issues of European Community, French, Italian, and United States law relative to relations among levels of government in the field of air quality regulation. He earned a *Diplôme des Etudes Approfondies en Economie Publique des Transports et de l'Aménagement du Territoire* from the Université de Lyon II, Faculté de Sciences Économiques. He is a graduate of Harvard College. He was a Rotary Graduate Fellow in France, and a Fulbright Scholar in Italy.

At the beginning of his career, he served as a law clerk for Judge Alfred T. Goodwin of the United States Court of Appeals for the Ninth Circuit, and then for Justice Antonio La Pergola of Italy's *Corte costituzionale.*

From early in his career as a practicing lawyer, he has taught law as an adjunct professor. He teaches predominantly United States students (and some students from other countries pursuing LLM degrees) at UCLA School of Law and at Loyola Law School, where courses that he has taught include International Finance, European Union Law, and Latin American Infrastructure Transactions. He teaches primarily non-United States lawyers in the University of California at Davis LLM program in International Commercial Law, where courses that he has taught include International Joint Ventures, International Finance, and International Arbitration.

His scholarly writings, often with co-authors, address topics such as: Mexico's expropriation law (UCLA LAW REVIEW) and its secured lending framework (UNIFORM COMMERCIAL CODE LAW JOURNAL); Italy's constitutional law relative to the emergence of its regions (AMERICAN JOURNAL OF COMPARATIVE LAW), the development of new frameworks in Italy to regulate the electric and telecommunication sectors (FORDHAM INTERNATIONAL LAW JOURNAL) and the relationship of Italian law with that of the European Community (AMERICAN JOURNAL OF INTERNATIONAL LAW); the Vienna Convention on the International Sale of Goods (various publications); and environmental law (LOYOLA OF LOS ANGELES LAW REVIEW, LOYOLA OF LOS ANGELES INTERNATIONAL & COMPARATIVE LAW REVIEW).

He is a partner of Zuber & Taillieu LLP, resident in its Los Angeles office.

ACKNOWLEDGEMENTS

I thank Walter Rodinò, retired Secretary-General of the Institute for the Unification of Private International Law ("UNIDROIT") for his suggestion that I write on the topic of harmonization of law. This work is my acceptance of his suggestion.

Another inspiration for this work is a spirited e-mail interchange between Rodney Almeida Alves and Juliana Cristina Martines, UCLA Law School LLM program classmates and each a Brazilian lawyer. Rodney was then based in Los Angeles with me, and Juliana was practicing law in São Paulo. Their interchange concerned whether to prepare in English or Portuguese a contract by which a United States citizen resident in Brazil would manage a California company's Brazilian subsidiary. They addressed Brazil's Civil Code, requirements relative to foreign-language contract documents in the event of litigation in Brazil, and a Brazilian Supreme Court decision, all discussed in this manuscript. Their common legal training in Brazil and the United States, plus fluency in English and Portuguese, afforded easy options to write the contract in either language, and so as to take into account the realities and expectations under each of the legal systems involved. Nonetheless, their interchange wrestled with what is permissible, as well as what is advisable and how the two may differ. The interchange articulated the requirements relative to use of an official language in dealings with governmental authorities, the burdens such requirements impose on party interactions, and how they condition party choices regarding use of a language in dealings with each other as well as with the governmental authorities. The interchange between these two able Brazilian lawyers also highlighted the basis for well-informed legal practitioners to formulate radically divergent strategies to confront requirements associated with language. It thus helped to spark this investigation, relative to Brazil, and also many other countries.

Thanks are due to Rodney Alves for insight into Brazilian law and assistance with other Portuguese-language legal materials; Laura Cadra, reference librarian at Loyola Law School, for assistance in locating and retrieving legal materials of many places; and John Wilson, reference librarian at UCLA Law School for assistance with quantitative materials. The author thanks Professors Maria Grazia Ascenzi, Louis Del Duca, Jennifer Moody, and Arthur Rosett for constructive feedback at various stages of the preparation of this work.

PREFACE

Parties to transnational commercial and financial deals communicate with each other in languages of their choice. Sooner or later, however, one or more of the parties, whether as part of making or of enforcing the deal, will necessarily interact with governmental authorities. Examples of such authorities include a court, a registrar of security interests in collateral to secure repayment of credit, or a regulatory body. Almost universally, such an authority mandates that an official language be used for any interactions with it. The nature and extent of the mandate for use of an official language may induce the parties to structure their deal so as to limit the mandate's infringement on their autonomy, including specifically on their choice of the language in which to advance their deal. The more burdensome are the requirements in connection with the mandated use of an official language other than that preferred by one or more of the parties, the more likely are the parties to attempt to work around such requirements. An unintended result of the language requirements associated with the governmental interaction may accordingly be to direct the parties away from both the interaction and the associated official language.

Legal systems tend broadly to favor party autonomy as to language. This tendency is illustrated in this work by the varied requirements of French-, Italian-, Portuguese- and Spanish-speaking jurisdictions relative to use of an official language, as well as by the regimes of the United States and the European Union pertaining to language and to the making and enforcement of commercial and financial business deals. Despite the tendency to favor party autonomy, requirements related to use of an official language for interactions with governmental authorities widely burden party preferences to conduct business in English or some other language. In the various systems examined, these requirements are defined principally by law relative to the constitutional status of language, contractual choice of language, civil procedure, arbitration, creation of security interests, offer of securities, and government contracting. Although the various systems examined share the requirement to use an official language for interactions with governmental authorities, the specific bodies of law that govern particular such interactions in each system result in distinctly different levels of burden. That is, for parties for whom the official language is not a preferred language, the structure of the particular governmental interaction and the associated breadth and intricacy of language use determines just how much of a burden is constituted by the need to use an official language.

Astute lawyering to structure transnational deals largely accommodates parties' desires to conduct business in the language of their choice and as they otherwise prefer, while mitigating impediments to enforcement of such transactions. However, as to topics strictly dependent on a governmental interaction, for example, registration of security interests to establish priority claims to collateral for a loan that can be defended against third parties, investment in lawyering is only partially effective to address the burden of language. In essence, initiatives to establish or exercise rights against third parties using tools of constructive notice and the coercion of administrative, regulatory and judicial authorities established under national law do not readily lend themselves to application of the lawyering tools that rely upon construction of bilateral deal terms between the parties with careful specification of governing law and forum for dispute resolution.

In view of the costs to parties of working around troublesome governmental interactions and the impracticality of completely avoiding them, governmental authorities, unilaterally and through international initiatives, have opportunities to facilitate transnational commerce and finance by coordinating legal frameworks to support cross-border transactions, including through lightening their linguistic challenges. Such coordination mitigates the motivation of transaction parties to incur the costs of working around governmental requirements and accordingly increases the likelihood of effective implementation of the requirements.

How supranational communities address language in conjunction with their efforts to harmonize relevant law, changes the landscape of language promotion. The European Union is the most notable instance, but there are also the current example of the *Organisation pour l'Harmonisation en Afrique du Droit des Affaires* ("OHADA" – Organization for the Harmonization in Africa of Business Law) and the potential of the *Comunidade dos Países de Língua Portuguesa* ("CPLP" – Community of Portuguese Language Countries)— organizations respectively of sub-Saharan Francophone states and the Lusophone countries. The promise of such supranational communities, and the reality in the cases of the European Union with its twenty-three official languages and of OHADA with its initial focus on French now being augmented to extend also to include English, Portuguese and Spanish, is to reshape parochial national approaches to language. As the European Union and OHADA pursue their development, they create new channels, defined by approach to language, for international efforts to harmonize law relevant to transnational commercial and financial deals. The experiences of the European Union and OHADA reveal that language promotion and harmonization of law, when thoughtfully channeled and linked, can yield mutually reinforcing policies, goals and tools, that are productive simultaneously of party autonomy and of government policy implementation.

Interested stakeholders—government, business, and the broad community supportive of improving the rule of law, have the opportunity to invest in initiatives working to unify and harmonize law relevant to transnational commercial and financial deals. Such initiatives, when well-founded, promote the conduct of transnational commercial and financial deals within (rather than outside) the framework of formal legal systems and their institutions.

For these initiatives to reform the legal frameworks relevant to transnational deals, the polyglot character of the global economy presents a challenge and an opportunity. The challenge derives from the conduct of transnational commercial and financial deals across the divides of the languages and the legal systems with which they are intertwined. The polyglot character of the global economy increases the challenge to the harmonization of law efforts that seek to bridge these gaps. The opportunity associated with such efforts is to harness the passion that those who speak a language tend to have, not only for their language, but also for the legal framework that they know best and with which the language is embedded. Harnessing this passion for language can greatly increase the likelihood of meaningful law reform across boundaries. Appropriately focused investment in initiatives to unify and harmonize commercial and financial law, particularly with attention to the key role of language, can support effective promotion of a language, while reinforcing the rule of law, thereby achieving a greater realization of the benefits of each.

Summary Table of Contents

Detailed Table of Contents

TABLE OF MAPS

CHOOSING THE LANGUAGE OF TRANSNATIONAL DEALS: Practicalities, Policy, and Law Reform

Patrick Del Duca

Map One - Romance Languages

Here are two anecdotes, inspired by real events, that illustrate the challenges of commercial and financial deals across borders.

(1) An American party and a French party to a contract agree to a French-language provision that the French party would accept "*la remise*" of certain documentation. The American party subsequently initiates litigation before a court in the United States on the premise that the contract provision established a consent by the French party to accept the service of process that would confirm the American court's jurisdiction over the French party. The French party consultants an American lawyer, evidently lacking familiarity with the French language. That lawyer presents the court and the plaintiff with papers seeking a dismissal of the complaint. The premise of those papers is a translation of the contract provision that incorrectly presents the term "*la remise*" as "postponement" rather than "delivery" or "consignment". The parties settle the dispute on terms favorable to the plaintiff after the American lawyer for the French party concedes the correct translation of "*la remise*" as "delivery".

(2) A Mexican company, owned by Mexicans and organized under Mexican law, with all of its assets and business in Mexico, arranges to borrow money in New York City from a group of banks and also through an issuance of bonds, all in the United States. All the lenders—banks and bondholders, seek to establish a security interest in the assets in Mexico so as to be able to seize control of them in the event of the company's default in its repayment obligations.

The lenders desire that their security interests have priority against claims of any additional creditors of the Mexican company. The agent bank for the bank group informs the company that the bank loan will be granted only if the banks receive a first priority security interest that would, in the event of a default by the company in repayment, serve as collateral to pay the claims of the banks before any claims of the bondholders are paid. The prospective purchasers of the bonds accept to receive a second priority security interest, with the consequence that the company's assets would, in the event of a default by the company in repayment of the debt, be available to pay the claims of the bondholders only after the bank lenders had received sufficient value to repay fully the amount due to the bank lenders.

The company then informs its prospective lenders that it would loose significant opportunities to expand its business if the loan amounts are not disbursed to the company by March 31. The company delivers to each of the bank and the bond lenders a written, signed declaration that it grants them each a security interest in all its assets. The written, signed declaration to the banks is delivered March 1, and dated accordingly. The written, signed declaration to the bondholders is delivered March 15, and dated accordingly. On March 20 the bank and bondholder creditors (the bank creditors through the lead bank acting as agent for the banks, and the bondholder creditors through the indenture trustee acting as their agent) sign an inter-creditor agreement that provides, "the banks have a first priority claim in any collateral in which the banks hold a security interest as of the date of the inter-creditor agreement, and the bondholders will take no action inconsistent with respecting such priority." On March 30, the bank loan agreement and the bond indenture are fully signed by the company and the various lenders, and the full loan proceeds are disbursed to the company.

The company then defaults in its repayment obligations to all the creditors. Simply put, the company ceases to make payments on the loans. In subsequent litigation among the secured creditors, it becomes clear that under the Uniform Commercial Code Article 9 as adopted in New York, a security interest in so-called personal property collateral (which would include the "moveable" assets of the Mexican borrower that are of significant value, such as accounts receivable, contract rights and governmental concessions) becomes effective against third parties after such an interest has been granted in writing, value has been given to the borrower by the secured party, and the security interest has been "perfected", meaning in the present instance by notice of the security interest having been indexed in the name of the debtor in the appropriate public registry. In contrast, Mexican law does not provide for rights in the collateral opposable against third parties until a pledge of such assets is created in a public act before a Mexican notary, which to establish the priority is then recorded in a public registry.

Accordingly, and to the surprise of the holders of the claims of the bank lenders, the holders of the bonds assert that their interests in the collateral are of equal priority (*pari passu*) with those of the holders of the bank claims. Their ground for this assertion is that no security interest under the Mexican law applicable to the collateral in Mexico had been created as of the time of the agreement to the effect that the banks would hold a first claim on any collateral in which security interests had then been created. The further premise of the bondholders' assertion is that a Mexican court evaluating competing claims of creditors to collateral in Mexico would not look to New York law to determine whether a priority security interest is constituted in such collateral.

The first anecdote illustrates the simple challenges of communication in translation, made necessary when dealing with a court that works only in an official language that is a language different from that chosen by the parties. The second anecdote illustrates the more daunting challenges of excellent New York lawyers and excellent Mexican lawyers speaking past each other, as each is most fluent not only in the predominant language of the legal system in which they work, but also in the legal concepts of that system. The anecdote presumes that the parties' respective New York lawyers did not elicit from their Mexican colleagues communication on the Mexican law pertaining to the creation of security interests sufficient to have allowed the New York lawyers to appreciate in timely fashion the differences in approach of New York and Mexican law and hence the full significance of the inter-creditor agreement. The differences in the focus of the language and associated conceptual understandings of the New York and of the Mexican lawyers led to a failure of understanding between them, notwithstanding that each may well have correctly and fully apprehended the technical substance of such lawyers' own respective legal system.

The consequence of the breakdown in understanding how the two legal systems related to each other in the instant transaction could well be an unanticipated outcome to the dispute among creditors following the borrower's default in repayment. Having an equal claim to assets versus having a first priority claim to such assets may result in a dramatically different economic outcome for the bank lenders. The potential for surprise could be all the more complete should the original lenders have sold their claims in the secondary market prior to the resolution of the claims, a development which would likely imply that none of the original lenders' counsel and other representatives would remain involved.

Throughout this work, the substance of these two anecdotes is used to explore: (i) how parties to cross-border commercial and financial transactions can assure respect of their choices concerning use of language; and (ii) the limitations associated with mandates to use "official languages" in interactions with governmental authorities. The freedom of parties to postpone interactions with courts by agreeing to arbitrate their disputes (and thereby define the language in which they prefer to interact) will be contrasted with the general necessity of using the law, procedures and official language of the place where assets are located in order to establish priority interests in such assets to assure repayment of a loan, that will be enforced by relevant courts against third party creditors. The linguistic awkwardness of the first anecdote could have been mitigated by an agreement among the contract parties to arbitrate their disputes in a language of their choosing. In contrast, the second anecdote illustrates the necessity of conforming to the procedures of the jurisdiction of the location of the assets offered as collateral for the repayment of a loan in order to establish a ranking of priorities of claims to such collateral that is clearly enforceable against such assets should the borrower default in its repayment obligation.

From this contrast will emerge the strategic value of language to efforts to harmonize law internationally. More specifically, embracing the passion that fluent speakers of a language typically have for that language is a powerful tool to advance law reform in the transnational context. In short, this work is about formulating a map, based on passion, for the harmonization of commercial and financial law across borders. This map includes practical insight as well for parties to cross-border commercial and financial transactions who need to navigate the sometimes bumpy passages of their transnational deals across legal systems and the associated languages.

Map Two

■ 56 Members

▨ 14 Observers

Map Two - *La francophonie*

I.   BENEFITS OF A CONSIDERED APPROACH TO THE LEGAL FRAMEWORK FOR TRANSACTIONAL LANGUAGE CHOICES

A.   Overview and conclusions

This investigation explores the boundaries within which transaction parties and governmental authorities navigate relative to language. It probes the governmental policies which favor the use of languages other than that preferred by the parties in connection with the establishment, performance and enforcement of significant transnational commercial and financial deals, to assess their implications and likely effects.

The analysis starts with focus on transactions and their management. The initial focus is examination of the tension between (i) party preference as to choice of language in which to conduct business and (ii) governmental strictures to use an "official" language when one or more of the parties undertakes an interaction with a governmental authority.

The analysis then moves to consideration of strategies that stakeholders in transnational business might adopt to invest constructively in the improvement of legal frameworks for transnational commercial and financial deals. Relevant stakeholders include the business community, governmental authorities, and others interested in promotion of (i) the rule of law and (ii) the language or languages of a given legal system.

This progression seeks to illuminate the burdens and limitations of what parties and governmental authorities can achieve independently, without additional initiatives to adopt frameworks that are multilaterally coordinated with attention to the issue of language. It then further outlines some strategies for collaborative and effective investment in improvement of legal frameworks reaching across borders, with specific focus on the issue of language, so as to achieve additional returns from all perspectives.

1. Languages: varied in significance and never static

Examination of how different jurisdictions that share a language treat the issue of language for purposes of transnational commercial and financial deals and the governmental interactions that are associated with them, offers insight into what may drive the adoption of particular governmental policies and how they may impact language use. Languages considered here are the romance languages of French, Italian, Portuguese and Spanish, that share common roots in Latin, as well as aspects of the use of English in dealing with governmental authorities in the United States. In each instance, particular attention is paid to the language requirements of dealings with courts generally, and with registrars of security interests in collateral to secure the repayment of loans.

The choice of languages for investigation reflects that each of these languages is spoken in multiple countries. Moreover, in various countries, these languages count as "official" languages, and they are also widely spoken as both first and second languages. The author's fluency in these languages, and hence ability to work with legal materials in them, further correspond to this choice. Moreover, although the countries that embrace romance languages as official languages share some elements of the civil law tradition, the approaches of these countries to the topic of language reflect radically different perspectives. Language is only one dimension of culture, and the set of jurisdictions addressed in respect of each of the languages considered here, displays considerable heterogeneity in many further dimensions beyond that of approach to language. Accordingly, the extremely varied approaches to language in these jurisdictions, the commonality of a shared language among groups of them notwithstanding, are argued to underline that the vitality of a language in a variety of cultural contexts can be maintained by offering frameworks to support choices to use it, at least as well as by attempting to impose its use.

Additional studies might be undertaken relative to languages such as Arabic, Chinese, Dutch, English, German, Hindi/Urdu, Turkish, and Russian, that share the attribute of being widely spoken in multiple countries with distinct legal systems, sometimes as official languages and sometimes with limited, if any, official status. With further investment of effort to address multiple languages, yet other languages, including those spoken chiefly in specific countries or places, whether of large or more modest population and global economic role, for example, Japan and Japanese in the first category of large population and global economic role, and Armenian, Basque or Hebrew in the second, could be addressed.

For any proponent of any language, no matter how modestly or widely diffused its use may be, how legal frameworks for cross-border business affect use of the language is a question of interest. English, Japanese and Armenian, for example, although they correspond to highly divergent patterns of diffusion in the world, share the characteristic of being living languages. Choices of economic and cultural actors to employ any one of them, instance by instance, determine their continued and further diffusion. Use of a language in transnational commerce and finance, and also the ability of those who speak the language to integrate the language with such commerce and finance, are clear elements contributing to the vitality of a language. Although each of the languages considered in the present investigation is widely spoken, some, notably English, emerged relatively recently, and each of them has ebbed and flowed over time as a language of transnational commerce and finance.

The use of a language for transnational commerce and finance is not the only determinant of the vitality of a language, but it significantly determines the place of a language on the global stage, and contributes to the dynamic of the evolution of that language and the population that speaks it. Arguably, for example, the historical apogee of Italian as a language of international finance occurred when renaissance Florence under Medici leadership, speaking the language of Dante Alighieri that became what is now contemporary Italian, served the role of a leading international financial center then akin in relative importance to that of current day London or New York. Italian subsequently receded in relative importance as a language of transnational finance, but the unification of Italy as a nation-state, some three and a half centuries later, established the framework within which the language of Dante has become not simply a *lingua franca* of a cultural and commercial elite, but rather a true national language, spoken as a first language by the vast preponderance of the population of a country of significant cultural, demographic, economic and political weight on a global scale.

There seems to be consensus that English is a particularly influential "world" language, because it is spoken widely as a first language and because it is widely used by non-native speakers of English.[1] French is also identified as such a language, although less people speak it in absolute than English, and relative to the total speakers of French, there are proportionately fewer speakers of French as a first language than there are of English as a first language.

Assessments of the relative status of languages in the world in this sort of qualitative fashion appear more firmly grounded than detailed counts of who speaks a language. The problematic nature of actual head counts derives from the general inaccuracy of census data, and the challenges of assessing and distinguishing those who are "native", and those who are "fluent, but non-native", speakers of a language. Questions are also raised as to the definition of a language, for example the question of whether Chinese is in fact one or several languages, including Mandarin and Cantonese, among others, or whether Arabic is one language with merely a series of strong regional variants rather than a set of distinct languages with a common root such as are the romance languages. Some languages span alphabets. Examples are Hindi/ Urdu (Hindi being written in a Sanskrit script, and Urdu in an Arabic/Persian script, a distinction which does not impede the success of Bollywood films without subtitles or dubbing in both India and Pakistan) and Serbo-Croatian (at various times and by various groups written in Arabic, Cyrillic, Greek and Latin alphabets). These instances further present the questions of what defines a language.

The practical answers to the questions of what defines a language may be analogous to the pragmatic solutions provided by the disciplines of ecology and genetics to the questions of what defines a biological species and of how a gene pool evolves. To define what constitutes and distinguishes a species, biologists through these disciplines focus on the kinds of interactions that occur among relevant populations, that allow them to reproduce and to propagate themselves in interdependence. Perhaps of even greater importance to the analytical challenge of the study of speciation is the ultimate survival of traits in the gene pool. In this perspective, for each language, its ongoing evolution and continued future vitality in human society remains a continuously open question, to be answered by the utility of the use of the language accorded by its speakers. Moreover, a language may not only evolve in time, but also borrow from and transform and meld itself with others in ways analogous to how populations and gene pools may do so as well. Recent theory on the evolution of language implies that the choices of speakers of a language as to focus of discourse affect how a language evolves, with the most stable words of a language over extended periods being those in most common use.[2]

When William the Conqueror, Duke of Normandy, invaded England in 1066, for example, English in its modern form did not yet exist.[3] However, the Norman victory not only established

French as the language of government in England for approximately the following 300 years. It also established the interplay between French and Anglo-Saxon, also known as Old English, that was a critical contribution to the emergence of modern English in the 1500's. Anglo-Saxon, a Germanic language, was the predominant language of what is now England, from the collapse of the Roman culture in Britain in the period 500 to 700 AD through the arrival of the Normans. Middle English from 1100 to 1500 was a changing mixture of Anglo-Saxon and French, with influences of Latin and the Scandinavian languages, the former a language of culture and international communication and the latter brought through Viking incursions. The morphology, pronunciation, syntax and vocabulary of English, the themes of its literature, and its emerging role in government and civic life at the expense of the French of the Norman elite, evolved continuously, drawing upon French, Latin, Germanic, and Scandinavian influences. As modern English emerged, it also drew upon the richness of the varied Anglo-Saxon regional dialects of Old and Middle English as London in particular became an increasingly dominant center for financial and political life, to which many of the most ambitious from throughout England were drawn, bringing with them their own variants of the emerging English language and its use and standardization.

Thus, in 1066 it was not pre-ordained what language would in the end be the prevalent language of what is now England, or indeed, in view of the subsequent presence in later centuries of English forces on the continental mainland, whether French or what came to be English would be the prevalent language of what is now France. Ironically, the invading Normans won their battle in 1066, and contributed significantly to the development of English. Yet, their French language did not ultimately prevail in England as such. Rather, it shaped in critical ways the birth of a new language that we know today as English. And in so doing, it contributed to the language of this manuscript and the eclecticism that continues to characterize English-language legal writing.

As a contrasting but nonetheless in some ways parallel example, Latin has been at various times a language of republican government, empire, educated society, the church, the law, and trade. Today it serves only a vestige of its former roles, although its literature survives and its progeny, including the romance languages considered here, enjoy continuing vitality. Its contributions to English and to the vocabulary and substance all of the legal systems here considered are likewise abundant and evident. Nonetheless, Latin is no longer a language of international commerce and finance, nor is it spoken as a first language by any population.

The histories of the English and French languages illustrate alternative styles to definition of what a language should be. Professor Lerer describes the history of English as:

> "a history of invention: of finding new works and new selves, or coining phrases that may gather currency in a linguistic marketplace, of singing to the cowherds or to the burlesque theater of self."[4]

The early history of English established a pattern of invention, borrowing and constant reconstruction. The emergence of English as a world language, for example, spoken as a first language by even more people in India than any other country, and spoken as a second language by more people than use it as a first language, continues to echo and replicate this pattern. However, the very attraction of French as a language of government, politics, culture and educated discourse has quite often been its standardization and continuity. Indeed, a contemporary speaker of French would find it easier to read a Norman French text from the eleventh century than would a contemporary English-speaker find the reading of the Old English *Cædmon's Hymn* or *Beowulf*, or even

Geoffrey Chaucer's *The Canterbury Tales* from the end of the 1300's. In further contrast, a contemporary American law professor can lament the inability of American law professors to identify robust English-language rules of grammar and usage to correct their students' papers.[5] Any veteran of the practice of dictation (*dictée*) as employed in a French-language grade school to teach the rules of grammar and spelling would find an analogous perplexity about the rules of French language that govern the writing of university graduate students to be quite improbable.

Of course each of English and French express the contrasting dominant styles of the other as well. That is, each language simultaneously manifests elements of creativity and standardization. And, from time to time one or the other of these styles has appeared to have greater vigor in one or the other of the two languages. For example, one of the factors contributing to the emergence of modern English was the development of "Chancery Standard" in the fourteenth century. Chancery Standard was a set of guidelines for English usage in communications and documentation generated by the growing English public administrative apparatus. In a contrary sense, dictionaries of the English language have evolved from efforts to prescribe the use of proper English to accepting a role of simply describing actual usage of English. In a similar vein of ecological ebbs and flows, one or the other of English or French has appeared from time to time more vigorous under various measures such as number of speakers, quality of literature, use in government and diplomacy, contributions to the progress of science, and relevance to the development of the law in various parts of the world.

The legal systems examined in the present work express varied policies relative to language that impinge upon the use of language in commercial and financial deals. The heterogeneity of these policies reflects the underlying diversity of concerns relative to language. These concerns include not only the obvious one of enabling parties and governmental authorities to understand what they are doing. They also include a variety of concerns that range much more broadly and which might or might not be appreciated by transaction parties directly. On occasions these concerns relate directly to promotion of the vitality of a language and its use. Broadly, the legal systems here examined present sometimes conflicting goals of construction and reinforcement of national identity, advancement of regional autochthonous languages, protection of unique cultural communities, promotion of co-existence of diverse populations, overcoming separations of social class structures, and opening of opportunities for inclusion in broader international communities.

The argument will be made that diminishing the linguistic burden of transnational commerce and finance can be accomplished in ways that empower speakers of any language of interest and hence should be consistent with whatever may appropriately be the underlying goals of effectively promoting an "official" language. As will be described, there is current reason to consider that each of English, French and the other languages here considered is flourishing in some measure as a language of cross-border commerce and finance. However, whether the ultimate fate of any of them is to continue to flourish or to wither for such purposes as has been the fate of Latin, is a question to be continuously re-determined by the choices of parties to transnational deals.

2. Party work-arounds

The exploration of governmental policies relative to language will show that the parties to transnational commercial and financial deals have substantial latitude to conduct their transactions in the language of their choosing. However, they may face potentially significant costs as the structuring and enforcement of their transactions touches governmental actors. Nonetheless, governmental leverage in such instances remains limited, in that the parties by the investment of resources may often largely circumvent governmental policies that they find troublesome.

Parties may almost entirely avoid the governmental interaction in many instances. For example, by agreement to arbitrate disputes rather than conduct them before national courts, the parties may in substantial measure avoid national civil procedure requirements relative to language in the context of litigation. In other subject matters more ineluctably linked to a governmental service, for example, the creation of security interests in collateral to support a loan transaction that is linked to the governmental service of publicity through entry in an official registry to achieve at least constructive notice of third party creditors, the governmental interaction may not be as readily or fully avoidable. Indeed, for security interests in collateral granted by a debtor to a specific creditor, the requirement of publicity to make them enforceable against third party creditors in a court where the collateral is located, mandates compliance with the rules of the jurisdiction of that court. Even in such an instance, however, the parties can in significant measure, but not entirely, isolate such interactions from the balance of their transaction.

3. Language and harmonization of law efforts

The consideration of the policies of various governmental authorities towards language and of the opportunities for parties to work around them serves as a foundation to the broader topic of the inter-relation of language and of efforts to harmonize law relevant to significant transnational commercial and financial deals. Such efforts employ techniques of unification, harmonization and reciprocal recognition of law,[6] including the implementation of:

(i)   choice of law conventions;

(ii)   uniform or harmonized substantive rules, adopted by model law, treaty, or supranational institutions;

(iii) embrace of arbitral regimes;

(iv)   creation and diffusion of non-legislated private rules, for example, the Uniform Customs and Practices for Documentary Credits and INCOTERMS, each promulgated under the auspices of the International Chamber of Commerce, a private organization, for such uses as business entities might choose to make of it; and,

(v)   formulation and diffusion of international restatements such as the PRINCIPLES OF INTERNATIONAL COMMERCIAL CONTRACTS prepared under the auspices of the International Organization for the Unification of Private International Law ("UNIDROIT") and the principles of European contract law, among others.

The argument is advanced that the goal of promotion of a language is best served by active engagement of stakeholders—government, private sector interests, and the broader "rule of law community", in the integration of the language of interest with the development and implementation of the relevant multilateral framework. Conversely, it is also argued that investment with a focus on language in multilateral harmonization of law efforts improves the likelihood of adoption of reforms and increases their effectiveness.

4.   Language and supranational organizations

The rise of supranational organizations, such as the European Union, OHADA (*Organisation pour l'Harmonisation en Afrique du Droit des Affaires*)—an organization of sub-Saharan Francophone states, and CPLP (*Comunidade dos Países de Língua Portuguesa*)—the organization of Portuguese-speaking countries, dramatically changes the dynamics of such harmonization efforts, opening new channels defined by approach to language, to carry them forward. Whereas the commercial and financial weight of the United States has assured it a leading voice throughout the post-World War II period in efforts to harmonize law relevant to transnational commercial and financial matters, the rise of the European Union as a linguistically-heterogeneous, supranational organization residing on an economic and population base comparable to that of the United States, creates a new counterpoint of significant influence. Moreover, the reality of linguistically-based supranational lawmaking and administration of justice constituted by OHADA (Francophone), and the potential of CPLP (Lusophone) for analogous achievements of law reform, together underline the importance and opportunity of linguistically-focused engagement of efforts to harmonize law relevant to transnational commerce and finance.

What remains a question for each of the two supranational entities mentioned with significant achievements as to harmonization of relevant law among its member states—the European Union and OHADA, is how far it will extend its internal harmonization of law activities into external harmonization of law activities with non-member states and other international organizations. The concluding portions of this investigation offer some thoughts about the considerations in this respect with particular regard to the European Union. Its multilingual approach to the implementation of its supranational framework in a context of significant linguistic heterogeneity, as well as its considerable diversity of Member State legal systems, augments its importance to consideration of the issue of language in the context of harmonization of law efforts generally. The European Union is a sleeping giant of global stature with respect to harmonization of law relevant to transnational commerce and finance, that is just beginning to rouse itself.

5. *Options for action*

This investigation concludes with thoughts as to how stakeholders in transnational commerce and finance, both governmental and private sector, can use the tool of language to invest effectively in frameworks to lessen the barriers to such transactions, while simultaneously increasing the engagement of such transactions with national and supranational legal systems in ways that reinforce the rule of law. Active participation in international efforts to unify or harmonize private law is not only a sound way to promote a language. Approaching such activity with consciousness of the importance of language is also a path to the increased success of such efforts. Strategies based on recognition of the significance of language offer the benefits of augmenting the promotion of each of: (i) transnational commercial and financial deals; (ii) the rule of law goals of reinforcing legal systems in the provision of foreseeable and transparent outcomes; and, (iii) use of a language in ways meaningful to its continued vitality.

This investigation focuses on tensions between party preference as to the interaction of language policies and law relevant to transnational commercial and financial deals on the one hand, and governmental policies which promote particular languages on the other. The opportunities which emerge from the present analysis relative to language are also offered as directly relevant to determinations generally by stakeholders in such transactions, particularly concerning the adoption of strategies relative to the improvement of the legal frameworks on which they rely. One important observation that emerges from the specific topic of language is the significance of the quality of institutions and the design of legal norms to whether the treatment of language facilitates or burdens the interests of stakeholders, ranging from transaction parties to governmental entities themselves. At the same time, the management of language issues emerges as an indicia of the quality of institutions and norms. Poor management of the basic element of communication, namely the use of language, immensely diminishes the likelihood that institutions and norms addressed to cross-border commerce and finance will achieve their goals. In addition, an understanding of the implications and limitations of various kinds of governmental requirements pertaining to language is not only important in its own right, but also a step towards insight into the analysis of a myriad of policies further involved with the substance of how law addresses commerce and finance across borders and the collateral social and economic implications of transnational business and its regulation.

B. Theoretical framework: Interface between party autonomy and governmental mandate

International lawyers vary in the focus of their practice, but in choosing their profession, share a fascination with the interaction of legal systems, the conduct of business across borders, and the meeting of cultures and the associated languages. This section offers the theoretical framework that the present work employs to explore these topics. Although some readers may find its conceptualization reminiscent more of micro-economic concepts than legal ones and accordingly distanced from the specifics of how various legal systems confront the issues of language use, it is the theoretical framework for the detailed romp that follows through national and supranational legal systems around the globe, the implications of their approaches to language, and how deals navigate them.

1. Context

Facilitation of the conduct of transnational business is an increasingly important challenge in general. Cross-border commercial and financial deals are growing in size and number. At the same time, the legal environment in which such deals occur is becoming increasingly complex. Sources of this complexity include the growing number of jurisdictions across which significant transactions occur and the extension of such jurisdictions to include emerging markets. These developments result in more parties of a variety of diverse language backgrounds doing business with each other, and accordingly bring to the fore the issues of language here explored. Additional sources of the increasingly complex legal environment for transnational business are the development of a variety of kinds of supranational regimes such as the European Union and the World Trade Organization that overlay and modify purely national legal systems, the rising sophistication of how legal systems seek to regulate transnational matters, and their increasing assertion of extra-territorial application of norms in subject matters ranging across antitrust policies, privacy matters, and securities law, to name a few.

These developments likewise work to increase the linguistic burden on transnational business because transaction parties need to consider the potential relevance of additional sets of norms and more governmental authorities distributed over more legal systems, each of which has its own requirements and hence demands for use of an official language as part of interactions with governmental authorities. Accordingly, containment of the cost of working around uncoordinated legal systems is one overarching reason, growing in importance, to invest in calibrating how legal systems address transnational business. In parallel to the general concern to contain costs of all types is a specific concern associated with managing the cost of the growing linguistic complexity of transnational business. The root of this complexity is not simply the number of languages involved, but rather the association of varying languages with the number of potentially relevant governmental authorities, the complexity of the interactions to be undertaken with them, and the limits of coordination of the relevant legal norms.

These factors challenge the ability of parties to cross-border transactions to achieve reliable predictability of outcomes as they conduct their business. The issue of predictability resonates throughout party conduct of their transactions, back to the first phases of such transactions. The comfort of parties in their ability reliably to enforce deals and to predict outcomes of potential disputes often turns on party understanding of legal systems and their norms that may be clearly foreign in concept, or even more treacherously, that may be apparently familiar, but in fact be false cognates. It also turns on party understanding of the outcomes that will result from plausible scenarios of party disputes. Well-advised parties will seek to structure their dealings so as to establish clearly the options of each party in the event of a falling out between them. Challenges to such predictability in transnational deals arise from the potential applicability of inconsistent norms of multiple legal systems and the likelihood of the necessity for interaction with governmental authorities of the relevant legal systems that may act in different and inconsistent ways.

2. *Key questions*

Transnational commercial and financial deals are made, implemented and enforced within linguistic environments shaped by transaction parties and governmental authorities. The parties to cross-border deals will act on their preferences as to the language or languages in which to deal. That is, they will make their own choice of the language in which to communicate with each other, largely independent of governmental strictures. However, the legal systems touched by the deal are inter-twined with the official languages in which the governmental authorities of such systems work. The governmental authorities with which the parties will inevitably interact in some way, will, as a fundamental aspect of such interactions, insist that they occur in an official language.

Consideration of these linguistic environments offers opportunities for the parties to transnational deals, for those concerned with the rule of law, and for those who seek to promote use of a language. In particular, to use language as an object of policy in order to bring transnational commercial and financial deals more squarely within frameworks sanctioned by national (and supranational) legal systems offers the potential to:

(i)   promote transnational deals by reducing the burden of working around inadequate and uncoordinated legal systems;

(ii)   advance rule of law goals by strengthening the role of legal institutions; and,

(iii) promote the languages in which such systems function.

Although language is only one component of transnational business across uncoordinated legal systems, it is a particularly important component because it is at the root of the communication required for parties to make a deal and implement it. It is likewise a foundation to the various interactions of parties with governmental authorities that are necessarily involved in making and enforcing deals, especially across borders. Any mismatch between how parties understand their direct communications on the one hand, and what is communicated to, or understood by, governmental authorities on the other, is a source of burden and uncertainty. That a governmental authority mandates use of a language that is not a party's first choice, or that in any event may not be the language in which the parties deal with each other, exacerbates the prospect of such burden and uncertainty.

The challenge of transnational commercial and financial deals examined here with reference to choice of language has two faces: how legal systems might successfully regulate the terms of transnational commercial and financial deals; and, the measure in which transaction parties are able and motivated to circumvent such regulation in order to define and apply their own agreements. A *"lex mercatoria"*, understood as a body of international customs and practices widely employed by merchants and divorced from any individual legal system, may work in substantial autonomy from governmental intervention if a community of merchants has sufficient incentive to conform to it, without the compulsion of recourse to enforcement mechanisms or other tools sanctioned by a governmental authority. However, in the absence of both a true *lex mercatoria* and also a monist global legal system that would maintain and impose a universal, pyramidal hierarchy of law, the at least occasional possibility of parties to make recourse to the mechanisms of disparate legal systems as part of establishing and enforcing their transactions, raises the following questions:

- What constrains the ability of well-advised transaction parties to circumvent legal systems and their policies?

- Are these constraints sufficient to serve as an effective foundation to a governmental policy contrary to what parties to significant transnational commercial and financial deals might agree among themselves?

- How best can interested stakeholders (governments, parties to transnational deals, and more broadly those concerned with promoting the rule of law) lessen the burden of transnational deals, while advancing sound policies?

These questions, broadly framed, pertain to much more than simply questions of choice of language. The focus here, however, is quite specifically on language. Consideration with respect to language of the first two questions posed above—focused respectively on the margins of maneuver of parties and the leverage of governmental authorities, addresses the kinds of party responses that are feasible in reaction to governmental requirements imposed in connection with interactions essential to transnational commerce and finance.

On the foundation of this consideration, the analysis will move to conclude with consideration of the third question posed, namely how due attention to the issue of language can be employed to facilitate the effectiveness of law reform efforts. Consideration of language can lead to a substantively more effective reform, that is, one that empowers more parties to undertake transnational commercial and financial deals more successfully. A further dimension of effectiveness associated with the consideration of language, is the ability of its due consideration to facilitate adoption and implementation of sound reforms that might otherwise languish. In short, the emotional involvement that people have with their languages, and indeed their passion for a language, can promote not only great literature, but also sounder, more inclusive frameworks for transnational business.

3. *Focus on arbitration and secured lending*

Among the interactions with governmental authorities that one or more parties may need to undertake in order to make, implement and enforce a transaction are:

(i) interactions with courts as a party seeks to enforce a deal; and,

(ii) interactions with governmental representatives to establish, through filings in public registries, a priority claim of a lender to collateral, based upon a non-possessory security interest in that collateral, that will be effective against third party creditors.

The present investigation explores these interactions with a focus on the issue of language. Although government has little practical ability to prevent substantial business actors from communication with each other across borders in their language of choice, party interactions with various governmental authorities are essential to the conduct of most, if not all, transnational commerce and finance. Because governmental authorities generally confine their work to the official language or languages of the legal system of which they are a part, governmental authorities do impose the choice and the role of a language in these interactions.

There are many additional potential interactions of parties with governmental authorities, including with respect to obtaining concessions, permits, authorizations and clearances of various types, in connection with securities matters, foreign investment authorizations, environmental assessments and the like, as well as responding to enforcement activity by such authorities. However, these two kinds of party interactions with governmental authorities—litigation before a court and constitution of priority claims to loan collateral, were chosen because they are so common and because they are so frequently a part of cross-border commercial and financial deals. Recourse to a court to enforce a deal is a prospect that even the most amicable of transaction parties would reasonably take into account as a possibility from the beginning of dealings and notwithstanding the absence of any actual dispute. Moreover, the dependence of economic activity on the availability and use of credit renders secured lending transactions familiar to a wide spectrum of participants in cross-border transactions. The two kinds of party interactions with governmental authorities were also chosen because of the complexity that the potential involvement of multiple legal systems creates in respect of them. As to each, the prospect of recourse to authorities and norms of more than one jurisdiction raises the specter of competing procedures and conflicting outcomes.

a. Effect of agreements between contract parties on third parties

The interactions with governmental authorities that are directed by one party to enforce deal terms against another party and the interactions that are directed to establish priority claims to collateral enforceable against third parties differ in character from each other in a way that offers insight concerning the bounds of party autonomy relative to language and the associated dynamic of party response to governmental mandates that involve use of an official language. The difference is that one involves an effort by the parties to bind only each other, while the other involves an effort to effect the rights of third parties.

In particular, the agreement between contract parties to arbitrate contract disputes can be understood as an agreement to define the scope of when and how the parties themselves initiate a potential interaction with governmental authorities, namely recourse to a court. In brief, the parties' agreement to arbitrate a dispute can largely delay interaction with courts until one party desires to enforce an eventual decision by the arbitrator. The parties' agreement is one targeted to have its effect relative to each other, not third parties.

Interactions with governmental authorities to establish a lien priority in collateral for a loan so as to obtain better terms from the lender to be accorded the priority, in contrast, are an example of consensual embrace at an early stage of a business relationship by transaction parties to governmental services critical to supporting their deal. As in the case of two parties addressing the issue of forum for dispute resolution by making an agreement to arbitrate, a borrower and a lender would collaborate in making the necessary filings with lien registrars so as to provide the legally-required constructive notice to subsequent third party creditors and thereby make the priority effective against them.

However, the borrower and the lender, if they wish the lien priority to be effective against third party creditors, have less flexibility to avoid dealing with the lien registrar than do two parties seeking to limit interaction with courts in connection with dispute resolution. The difference is that parties can more freely make agreements between each other that affect only their own rights than they can make agreements between themselves that affect the rights of third parties. The creation of a security interest that establishes a lien priority is indeed meant to limit the rights of subsequent third party creditors. It accordingly requires that the borrower and lender or lenders who wish to benefit from such a priority follow the procedures of law pursuant to which a court, in the event of a dispute, would have the foundation to uphold the priority on the ground that subsequent third party creditors had actual or at least constructive notice of the establishment of the priority claim in advance of decisions by such third parties to extend additional credit. The court of the place where the collateral is located will as a practical matter generally have the determining voice as to which creditors have the priority claims to such collateral. Agreements between borrower and lender will not deprive third party creditors of the ability to make recourse to such a court.

(1) Nonpossessory v. possessory security interests

The interactions involving the establishment of a priority claim to collateral in connection with a secured lending transaction, although of obvious import to financial parties, may be of less immediate intuitive understanding to strictly commercial parties. At least constructive notice to a third party creditor of an earlier creditor's claim to establish the priority of such a claim is required when the creditor's claim of priority in the collateral is not based on possession.

In brief, instances where a priority claim in collateral is assured by the lender's *taking possession* of the collateral raise minimal concerns of successful challenges to the priority of the lender's claim by third party creditors. Assertions by such third party creditors that they, rather than the initial lender who holds possession of the collateral, are instead entitled to the collateral are unlikely to prevail. The simple reason is that a prospective lender would widely be deemed foolish to expect to hold a priority claim in collateral of which the borrower does not have possession. The possessory creditor interest in collateral that assures the lender of a priority claim against the collateral in the event of a borrower default, however, does not work if the borrower needs possession of the collateral in order to use the collateral to generate the income to repay the loan.

What enable a lender to have confidence that its claim to particular collateral will have priority over claims of other creditors, *even if the lender has not taken possession of the collateral*, are the public registry systems that accord priority to creditor claims against particular collateral according to the time of registration of those claims. It is widely the case that courts of a legal system where collateral is located will assess the priority of claims against collateral that has remained in the possession of the debtor, that is, "non-possessory" (meaning that the creditor does not have possession of the collateral) security interest claims, only with reference to the lien registries of their own legal system. The rationale behind this approach is that creditors seeking to foreclose on such collateral can reasonably be expected only to check the lien registries of that one legal system where the collateral is located.

Another terminology to express the same thought is that creditors are deemed to have constructive notice only of lien filings in the registry of the legal system where the collateral is located. Courts of that legal system do not consider lien filings outside the registries of the particular legal system as affording prospective creditors of a debtor sufficient publicity of prior grants by the debtor of security interests in the collateral. In essence, a court of the place where the debtor holds the collateral would not impose any duty on a creditor wishing to establish a priority claim to the collateral, to the effect that such a creditor be required to verify the absence of claims against the same collateral previously registered in foreign registry systems.

b. Divergent parameters of party autonomy relative to courts and security interest registrars

The nature of governmental impositions relative to language in respect of the two interactions that are here the object of particular focus, namely recourse to courts in connection with litigation to enforce a deal and the establishment of priority claims to collateral through lien registry systems, can significantly burden transnational commerce and finance. In additional to out-of-pocket costs imposed on parties for translation and compliance with procedural steps, the burden of these impositions can elicit changes by the parties in how they structure their dealings with each other. By adjusting the structure of their transaction, the parties may in many instances minimize the impact of the governmental requirements on themselves and simultaneously frustrate the governmental policy pursuant to which the requirements were imposed. The parties' ability to do this in respect of dispute resolution and in respect of creation of non-possessory lien priorities differs because of the differences in the nature of the associated governmental interactions.

Relative to party interactions with courts in the context of litigation arising from transactions, the recourse to arbitration by parties to significant transnational commercial and financial matters is anticipated and welcomed by most jurisdictions around the world. One of the key reasons for parties to cross-border transactions to make recourse to international arbitration of their disputes is to minimize the need to cope with national requirements that an official language be used in interactions with courts. The agreement to arbitrate moves a significant part of addressing disputes among parties from national courts to the forum of arbitration, where the parties by agreement can define questions of the use of language. Most basically, the parties' agreement can of course specify the language or languages in which the arbitration proceedings will be conducted. Moreover, the parties can specify the language qualifications of the arbitrators, for example, what languages the arbitrators understand without the assistance of translation. In addition, agreement by the parties might also specify that as a qualification for service as an arbitrator, an arbitrator be familiar with the terminology of a particular subject matter in a particular language.

In contrast, establishment of priority claims in collateral offered as non-possessory security for the repayment of a loan, such that the priority can be enforced against third parties, is strictly linked to interactions with governmental authorities and hence compliance with the linguistic burdens that they impose. The reasons for this linkage, which turn on the limitations of the ability of a debtor and any particular creditors to affect the rights of third parties, will be discussed more fully in the section below on security interests and language.[7] Briefly, the linkage derives from the necessity of publicity that is the foundation of systems that permit non-possessory security interests. In general, the publicity required to alert potential future lenders that particular collateral still in the hands of the borrower has been already pledged with priority to an existing creditor must be in an official language of the jurisdiction of location of the collateral and be further accomplished in accord with the rules of that jurisdiction. Only such publicity establishes an enforceable lien priority effective against third parties. That is, only such publicity enables the debtor and the intended preferred creditor to assure that the interest of the intended preferred creditor prevails against claims of third party creditors advanced by such creditors in the jurisdiction of the location of the collateral.

In recognition of this reality of need to comply with the law and procedures of the jurisdiction of location of the collateral, parties to a transaction can and do seek to isolate from the balance of their transaction the portions of it that pertain to the constitution by particular lenders of priority claims in collateral. They do so by using the law of, and entities of, jurisdictions other than the jurisdiction of the location of the collateral in order to define matters other than the direct constitution of security interests. Nonetheless, the ability of parties to define the extent of their interaction with governmental authorities in the case of priority of security interests relative to third parties is less complete than it is in the case of choice of mechanism for dispute resolution between the parties themselves. This less complete ability of the parties gives the relevant governmental authorities, whether or not such authorities realize it, leverage over parties in respect of the linguistic burden of constitution and enforcement of non-possessory security interests that is much greater than that which such authorities hold in respect of matters pertaining to the procedure for resolution of disputes between the parties in respect of commercial and financial deal terms generally.

These two kinds of interactions, the one concerning arbitration illustrative of an agreement between parties that directly affects only their own rights, and the other concerning secured lending and therefore necessarily involving recourse to governmental authorities with the intention to effect the rights of third parties, are here a focus of exploring how the dynamic of language use resulting from interplay of the choices of parties and the impositions of governmental authorities, shapes the structure of how deals are done. These two kinds of interactions further offer a window for insight into how the interplay of party choices and governmental impositions shapes the evolution of governmental norms and institutions relevant to transnational commerce and finance.

4. Party incentives

A substantial transnational commercial or financial deal motivates transaction parties to invest resources to structure, and subsequently, if necessary, to litigate, around the impositions of governmental authorities that the parties find challenging.[8] The cross-border nature of such transactions offers the parties to them the choice of at least two legal systems in which to pursue the structuring of their relationship and the resolution of disputes that may arise. The possibility of transaction structuring and enforcement action in multiple legal systems, without coordinated norms, creates uncertainty as to whether the parties' autonomous agreements or the peremptory norms of any one of the legal systems to which a party might make recourse, or whose authorities might take action, will prevail. The uncertainty and the cost for all concerned are increased by the existence of such norms in an official language different than the language employed by the parties, and even more so to the extent that such an official language must be employed to work with and within such norms. The stricture that interaction with governmental authorities regarding the application of the norms can occur only in such an official language further increases the incidence of cost and uncertainty.

Language is at the heart of communication that achieves understanding. The greater the linguistic burdens of transnational commercial and financial deals, the greater is the opportunity for misunderstanding and commensurately the cost of achieving understanding. Indeed, the norms of a particular legal system and the governmental mandates as to the way an official language must be used in particular interactions with governmental authorities may be sufficiently burdensome to induce the parties to undertake more costly or riskier ways of pursuing their business in order to mitigate the impact. At the extreme, the burdens of a legal system, including the use of an official language in dealings with governmental authorities, might even constitute a barrier to proceeding with some transactions.

Lawyers who negotiate, document and litigate transnational commercial and financial deals generally earn a good living. Their prosperity suggests both (i) the value that they add to such transactions by advising as to the navigation of uncoordinated and often inadequate legal frameworks and (ii) the cost with which the potential and uncertain applicability of disparate norms burdens such transactions. Some lawyers are particularly gifted with the talent of coping with linguistic burdens, such talent being understood in the comprehensive sense of deep knowledge of the language, as well as of the relevant legal norms in the context of the pertinent language and its legal system. Further indication of the importance of language in the perpetuation of disparate norms, but also in bridging the disparities, is that such lawyers are among the most desired by sophisticated clients who conduct transnational business.

The benefits of investment in working around troublesome requirements of one or more legal systems, whether or not associated with issues of language, and in bridging the challenges of language, underlie the involvement of well-compensated lawyers and other advisors. What drives the degree of this investment is not typically the resources of a party, but rather the overall amount potentially at issue and the consequent prospect of realizing value by finding a suitable way to navigate the hurdles presented. Even transnational business matters potentially involving a nominally resource-poor party, for example, a start-up venture such as a new company or a green-field project financing, an insolvent debtor such as an Enron or a Parmalat, a victim of a globally-employed, but nonetheless defective heart valve, or an Italian saver left holding devalued Argentine securities, may involve significant economic value in the forms of potential gain, realization of the value of resources and aggregation of claims. Such value may be more than sufficient to justify investment of the time, the talent and the money to undertake sophisticated transactional structuring and litigation that in some combination confronts, embraces and works around the challenges of multiple legal systems and disparate languages.

5.   *Governmental interests; private law; soft power*

Language and the linguistic burdens of transnational business are appropriate priority focuses of concern for transaction parties and governmental policymakers. For governmental policymakers, assuring that governmental authorities understand communications to them and that commerce and finance are not limited by undue burdens are obvious practical reasons for this concern. The promotion of the use of an official language and the broader concern of maximizing the "soft power" influence of the culture are further reasons for governmental attention to questions of language and the linguistic burdens of transnational business.

Private law refers to law that governs interactions among private parties. Legal systems obviously differ in the substance of their private law. Parties to transnational deals may find these differences a source of confusion and lack of certainty in the definition of their deal, and hence an impediment to the conduct of their transactions.

Private international law is a term that refers to the law of each legal system on the choice of law, specifically which legal system's private law governs a matter that reaches across borders. Differences in the private international law rules of legal systems about which legal system's private law governs a matter are further sources of party confusion and uncertainty about the definition of their deal.

Private international law inherently suffers the limitation that only coordination among legal systems can assure coherent outcomes relative to disputes between transaction parties without regard to which legal system a party to a cross-border transaction might invoke.[9] Quite simply, if the respective courts of two legal systems have different views of what law applies, a party's choice of the court to which to make recourse will likely affect the outcome of a dispute. Moreover, even when legal systems agree on what law should govern a particular matter, for example, that the law of where collateral is located should govern the definition of the priority of creditor claims to the collateral, they may in fact address the topic in substantively different ways, leading to confusion or surprise on the part of those accustomed to other approaches.

Lack of private international law coordination among legal systems clouds the ability of the parties reliably to achieve the goal of predictability, as does lack of coordination of governmental authorities of various legal systems, be they courts, security interest registry officials, or others. The rise of globalization and supranational regimes pushes these fundamental challenges of harmonization of law, of the discipline of private international law, and of coordination of governmental authorities, to center stage.[10] In light of globalization and the increased complexity of legal frameworks for commerce and finance across borders, the benefits of harmonization of relevant law—both private international law and private law, and of coordination of legal systems and their governmental authorities, are as great or even greater than ever before. Attention to the issues of language that are part of these challenges is an important component of addressing them.

Like any aspect of conducting business, the costs of dealing with legal rules and governmental impositions relative to language may render transactions less profitable and create barriers to proceeding that are sufficient to deter transactions at the margins. However, it is likely that differing mastery and preferences relative to languages on the part of dealmakers and governmental authorities are rarely exclusive determinants of whether a transaction occurs or of how satisfactory a result a party obtains with respect to a deal. The more significant implication of governmental impositions that demand use of an official language is that they shape how parties conduct their transactions. To the extent that parties work to evade governmental impositions, they weaken governmental institutions by marginalizing them, even as governmental authorities may attempt to stiffen official requirements.

Harmonization of law is an instrument that can work to facilitate the exercise of "soft power" in international relations, a concept defined by Joseph Nye as the ability to reach a desired goal through attraction rather than coercion or payments.[11] Professor Nye defines soft power as arising from "the attractiveness of a country's culture, political ideals and policies" and observes that "[s]eduction is always more effective than coercion".[12] The attractiveness of attention to how issues of language and legal requirements can be managed to facilitate commerce and finance across borders derives in significant measure from the seductive quality of language. It is not only a tool for individual expression and participation, but also a means for the expression and formulation of cultural values.

To associate empowerment in the use of language with measures to improve the legal frameworks that support cross-border transactions deepens the constituency for harmonization of law. The seductive quality of language offers the promise of more fully founded support for harmonization of law initiatives that effectively harness the issue of language. In other words, the seductive quality of language can serve to motivate improvement of the interface between party autonomy and governmental mandate by transforming the interface from one of conflict to one directed to the achievement of shared goals. Such goals are likely to include the promotion of cross-border deals by lessening their cost, while simultaneously affording them governmentally-defined legal frameworks within which parties will choose to place their deals, rather than attempting to evade such frameworks.

6. Linguistic diversity – accommodation of party realities

Harmonization of law can reduce the linguistic burden and hence the cost of transnational business. It can also facilitate the exercise of soft power and thereby expand a sphere of influence. Achievements in these regards are not, however, the sole reasons to undertake harmonization of law in general or even to address specifically the linguistic burden of transnational business.

Another, parallel motivation for effort to invest in engaging legal systems in providing suitable foundation for transnational commerce and finance, is to transform linguistic diversity from a burden into a benefit. In fact, unification and harmonization of law at their best do not necessarily mean making everything the same. The limitation of monolithic approaches is precisely the lack of recognition of the value of differences and of the benefit of outlets for their expression and engagement. Language can be an enriching expression of diversity about which many kinds of constituencies can become enthusiastic when they see the approach to it as being one of empowering inclusion of speakers of a language and facilitation of communication among speakers of different languages.

The benefit of recognizing linguistic diversity is to enfranchise those who speak a different language to participate more fully in the relevant legal and economic frameworks. Encouraging transactions to occur in the language of the parties' choice by making the pertinent legal frameworks accessible with a minimum of linguistic burden, empowers each party with a stronger foundation to push forward the desired business and to do so through, rather than by working around, relevant legal institutions. Reducing the linguistic burden to a party includes obviously to make the framework accessible through the party's preferred language. It also includes to reduce the extent of essential governmental interactions required in support of the transaction that must occur in an official language other than the language preferred by one or more of the parties. Reduction in the associated intensity of use of the official language for such interactions further reduces the linguistic burden of such interactions. As anticipated, examples to be discussed in specifically dedicated sections below include: (i) respect of party choices to employ international arbitration as a way to limit the application of national civil procedural requirements for use of an official language in connection with litigation; and, (ii) the use of security interest registry systems in the style of the "notice filing" model of the Uniform Commercial Code Article 9 on secured transactions and of the recent reforms of the French Civil Code concerning priority of liens on moveable and intangible property.

A key element of the benefit of recognizing linguistic diversity derives from its facilitation of the capability of diverse legal systems, each operating in its own core language or languages, to embrace, rather than drive away, the conduct of transnational commercial and financial deals. Transaction parties who do not find, in a legal system and through the predominant language or languages associated with it, the support for the business that they seek to accomplish, will turn away from both the legal system and the relevant language. Some transactions will likely remain undone, and others may be accomplished at greater cost through party efforts to work around the deficiencies of the legal system.

Accordingly, a legal system not engaged with meeting the challenges of responding to the globalization of commercial and financial transacting, and specifically the linguistic challenges here considered, will serve poorly in multiple senses those whom it seeks to govern. It will direct transactional activity elsewhere; it will burden transactions that do occur with the costs of party work-arounds here discussed; and, it will likely disadvantage those whose primary languages are also its own by encouraging them to work predominantly in and with legal systems not tied to its core language or languages.

A fear in this sense expressed with particular vibrancy relative to French, for example, is that it not be marginalized relative to English. Such a fear was part of the motivation of the effort in France to seek to regulate choice of language in commercial dealings through the 1994 Toubon legislation to be discussed below.[13] Even today relative to transnational commercial and financial deals, concerns exist that the continuing and arguably growing market dominance of London and New York in respect of such deals diminishes the likelihood of conducting them in French. London and New York are indeed leading financial centers that are intimately linked with the evolution of legal frameworks rooted in English. Their degree of market dominance raises the concern that French language professionals and regulatory frameworks might simply be left behind in the market space of transnational commerce and finance, unless French parties accept the conduct of transactions in English and as much as possible under legal frameworks elaborated in English. That is, for French economic actors to participate freely in the global commerce and finance transacted through the centers of London and New York, it could be argued that French-language economic actors must simply work in English. Although such an acceptance of English would palliate any complete exclusion, it could in fact over time increase the insularity of the French legal system and hence further marginalize many of its actors.

Italian investment in the funds known as UCITS ("Undertakings for the Collective Investment in Transferable Securities"), variously used under European Union law as mutual, private equity and hedge funds, offers a similar example that also illustrates the complex ways in which the structure of a legal framework for transnational investment may direct activity towards or away from the use of a particular language. In this instance the technical complexity of the relevant legal frameworks that produces the impact on the use of language works to render the impact low profile, largely hidden from public or political awareness.

Italy has a sophisticated system to support the constitution and regulation of collective investment funds. The Bank of Italy and Italy's securities regulatory commission, the *Commissione Nazionale per le Società e la Borsa* ("CONSOB"), regulate collective investment funds pursuant to a framework that mandates their operation through companies organized in forms contemplated by Italian law, namely the forms of *Società di Gestione del Risparmio* (a Company for the Management of Savings) and the *Società d'Investimento a Capitale Variabile* (an Investment Company with Variable Capital). The Banca d'Italia and CONSOB regulate the operation of these entities pursuant to a series of Italian legal norms, obviously written and applied in Italian, comprised of statutes, legislative decrees and regulations.[14]

These Italian norms derive from European Union measures that seek to implement the concept of a single European market in the domain of the financial and securities markets by establishing the concept of mutual recognition by all the Member States of the investment entities organized under the laws of each.[15] The premise for the mutual recognition is the mandate of European Union legislation for implementation of the "single license" concept, namely that all the Member States conform to the imposition of minimum standards on the entities organized under their laws and that consequently an entity licensed and regulated under the law of its Member State of organization should be able to operate throughout the European Union. Thus the mandates of European Union legislative measures promoted the modernization of Italian law and also assure the ability of Italian investors and entities organized under the law of any of the Member States to conduct their collection of savings, and their investments of them, from throughout the European Union.

In principal, this framework is neutral as to whether the aggregation and investment of Italian capital occurs through the Italian regulatory framework that has been established in conformity with it, or under the norms of other Member States. However, starting in 2001 a preponderance of Italian private investment activity has in fact been accomplished through entities organized under the laws of other Member States of the European Union, notably through Luxembourg entities.[16] The preference for Luxembourg entities and the associated use of French as an official language of Luxembourg, at least as to matters other than the disclosures mandated to investors, is a banal, but highly technical difference in tax rules.[17]

Italian tax law applicable to the entities organized under Italian law passes through gains (and losses) to the investors without regard to whether the gains are realized or distributed, that is, it disregards the existence of the Italian entities for tax purposes, thereby treating them as tax transparent. The tax characterization of the Luxembourg entities under Italian tax law is such that gains are taxable to the Italian investors only when distributed to the investors, *i.e.* the entities are not tax transparent. In 2001, a provision of Italian tax law that had allowed Italian investors to pay net Italian taxes based on either of the two approaches, whether the investment vehicle was organized under Italian or foreign law, expired. Since then, Italian investors appear to have preferred to avoid the Italian entities that are treated as tax transparent, with the result that a significant slice of the legal work associated with the constitution and operation of the funds is diverted away from engagement with the Italian language, and instead as to the Luxembourg entities, conducted in French, the predominant language of business and government in Luxembourg (or in the case of entities of another preferred Member State, Ireland, in English).

The examples relative to France and Italy are both instances of insularity in respect of language, but in different ways. The example relative to France highlights the linguistic risks of insulation of a legal system from global markets. The example relative to Italy highlights the linguistic risks of an opening of a legal system to global markets without attentiveness to the implications of how that opening interacts with issues of the use of language. Most likely, the modification of the Italian tax norm that resulted in the channeling of investment activity through channels where Italian is not the predominant language happened without thought as to its implications for language use. In any instance, insularity of any kind, of any legal system relative to cross-border transactions tends to marginalize not only the relevance of that legal system for cross-border transactions, but also the relevance of those subject to it and their language. As time passes, such parties and their language may unfortunately come to have an ever less-advantageous position.

7. Shared interests of transaction parties and governmental authorities

Transaction parties and governmental authorities have complementary but distinct perspectives on the substance of transnational commercial and financial deals and the related question of what norms govern them. The parties define the substance of their agreements, including the law and procedures that they wish to govern their relationship. Moreover, the parties condition a legal system's ability to address their relationship by their choices as to the mechanisms and fora by which to establish it and to resolve disputes. However, when one or more of the parties invokes a government service, be it formalization of a security interest in connection with a loan transaction, clearance of a prospectus in connection with a securities offering, or enforcement action by a court, such a party and at least part of the transnational deal become subject to the relevant governmental authority's understanding and application of that authority's norms. The governmental authority's norms and its application of them may or may not correspond to the parties' agreements and desires as they were formulated at the time of entering into the transaction. This risk is exacerbated when the parties enter into a transnational deal that reaches across uncoordinated legal systems. This risk will motivate the parties to commit resources to address it, by investing in translation to communicate with, and comply with the requirements of, governmental authorities, and also potentially to seek ways to work around the governmental requirements so as to be less exposed to them.

The governmental requirements relative to language may fall within a range of burdensomeness. They may be peremptory requirements that a specific language be used in conjunction with at least some part of the parties' conduct of their business, for example, the requirement to use a specific language relative to the creation of priority security interests in collateral in support of loan transactions or the requirement to use a specific language in offering documentation to raise debt or equity funding, each as a condition to completion of necessary governmental interactions. More simply, they may involve the practicality of the translation necessary for a governmental authority to understand what is sought from it, for example, translation of an arbitral award as prerequisite to a court's enforcement of it. From the respective vantages of transaction parties and governmental authorities, language may be each of (i) a choice as to which the parties' autonomous agreements and peremptory governmental norms diverge; and, (ii) a burdensome filter through which parts of the parties' autonomous dealings must be translated for governmental interaction.

a. Reduced transaction costs

Governmental authorities and transaction parties share interests in the success of efforts to reduce the linguistic burdens of transnational business. Constructive engagement relative to the issue of language in law reform efforts, be they unilateral governmental efforts or multilaterally coordinated initiatives of unification and harmonization of law, offers the potential to magnify the benefits of such efforts. For governments, the premise is that governments which lower the barriers to, and indeed facilitate, transnational commercial and financial deals, are more likely not only to reap the benefits of such transactions, but also to be able more effectively to achieve the implementation of well-defined policy goals relative to language, as well as relative to other economic, legal and social issues. Parties to transnational commercial and financial deals have significant autonomy as to choice of governing law and fora for the resolution of disputes, and as to the further substance and structuring of their contractual relationships. Such autonomy notwithstanding, parties presented with unified, harmonized or otherwise coordinated governmental policies are able to undertake their transnational commercial and financial contracting at far lower cost and risk, thereby offering the prospect of increased cross-border commerce and potential associated benefits. Minimizing the hurdle of language, from both governmental and party perspectives, is one critical element of achieving the benefits of transnational business desired by stakeholders including the parties themselves, governmental authorities, and the broader constituents of the community of proponents of the rule of law.

b. Rule of law benefits

There is a further kind of benefit to transaction parties and governmental authorities from constructive engagement on the issue of language, namely the benefit of employing and exercising formal legal frameworks and their institutions. Insofar as transaction parties conduct their business within frameworks coordinated across borders, rather than working around disparate national norms, their patronage of such frameworks duly anchored in national and supranational legal systems reinforces rule of law values of foreseeability and transparency, by putting to work the relevant legal institutions. Transactions that the parties choose to shift away from legal systems that they find uncongenial, using the techniques of offshore entities, bifurcation of transactions and arbitration, among others to be discussed below,[18] leave the legal institutions of such systems idle and unchallenged to cope with the demands of parties who desire to conduct transactions effectively.

In addition to depriving those institutions of activity, the shift reduces the pressure of party expectations that such institutions be made to work well. The consequence may be court systems, security interest registries, capital markets regulators, and substantive law, among other features of a legal system, that remain outmoded and ill-adapted for the challenge of supporting transnational commercial and financial activity. The diminution or loss of transnational activity involving such institutions of a legal system is a particular concern. By virtue of its international dimension, such activity may present an impetus for the achievement of quality and reform not fully provided by strictly domestic matters. Precisely because parties to transnational deals include actors from outside a domestic reality, they may constitute a constructively destabilizing force in respect of consolidated local equilibria that are otherwise less likely to accept reform.

Notes to Chapter I

1. See George Weber, *Top Languages: the World's 10 Most Influential Languages,* Language Today 12-18 (Dec. 1997).

2. Mark Pagel, *Human language as a culturally transmitted replicator,* 10 Nature Reviews Genetics 405 (June 2009).

3. The discussion of English language history draws on Seth Lerer, Inventing English, a portable history of the language (2007), plus the author's notes from Humanities 9b, *Folklore and Mythology,* Prof. Alfred Lord, Harvard College, Spring 1976.

4. Lerer at 266, *supra* note 3.

5. Eugene Volokh, *Correcting Students' Usage Errors without Making Errors of Our Own,* 58 J. Legal Education 533 (2008).

6. *See* Author Rosett, *UNIDROIT Principles and Harmonization of International Commercial Law,* 1996, *available at* www.unidroit.org, and Louis Del Duca, *The Accelerating Pace of Common Law and Civil Law Convergence in A Global Society—Harmonization and Subsidiarity in the Twenty-First Century,* 42 U. Texas Int'l. L.J. 625 (2007).

7. *See* text *infra* at Section IV.C.

8. As Arthur Rosett, *supra* note 6, observed,

   "If the law is permitted to stand still and fail to respond to the needs of the business people who engage in trade transactions, these business 'consumers' of the law will certainly find other, non-legal, ways to structure their commercial lives and the law as administered in the national courts will become increasingly irrelevant to their concerns."

9. *See* Friedrich K. Juenger, *The Problem with Private International Law,* 37 Saggi Conferenze e Seminari (Centro di studi e ricerche di diritto comparato e straniero, Rome, 1999).

10. *See* Mathias Reimann, *Comparative Law and Private International Law* in Mathias Reimann and Reinhard Zimmermann, eds., The Oxford Handbook of Comparative Law 1363 (2007).

11. Joseph S. Nye, Jr., Soft Power: The Means to Success in World Politics x (2004).

12. *Id.*

13. *See* text *infra* at note 63.

14. *See, e.g.,* Legislative Decree no. 58 of Feb. 24, 1998 (*Testo unico delle disposizioni in materia di intermediazione finanziaria*-"TUF"), Gazz. Uff., supp. ord. no. 71 of March 26, 1998, as amended; Bank of Italy Regulation of April 14, 2005 on collective management of saving, Gazz. Uff. no. 109 of May 12, 2005, supp. ord., as amended; CONSOB Regulation no. 16190 of Oct. 29, 2007, Gazz. Uff. no. 255 of Nov. 2, 2007, supp. ord. no. 222, as amended; and Joint Regulation of the Bank of Italy and CONSOB of Oct. 29, 2007, Gazz. Uff. no. 255 of Nov. 2, 2007.

15. *See* Paulina Dejmek, *The EU Internal Market for Financial Services–a Look at the First Regulatory Responses to the Financial Crisis and a View to the Future*, 15 COLUM. J. EUR. L. 455, 472-474 (2008-2009).

16. Marcello Messori, *I problemi del settore italiano del risparmio gestito*, ASSOGESTIONI WORKING PAPER 2008/4, 22 (July 2008), *available at* www.assogestioni.it.

17. *Id.*

18. *See* text *infra* at Section V.

Map Three - English

II. ENGLISH AND TRANSLATION IN TRANSNATIONAL BUSINESS AND FINANCE

A. English

Languages are neither equal nor fungible. Some are much more widely-spoken than others, and some languages from time to time are more pivotal than others to the cutting-edge of literary, scientific, technical, economic and other human endeavors. English, like some other European languages, including French, Portuguese and Spanish—languages here considered, spread in the colonial era through large parts of the world. That these languages were widely diffused rather than others, for example, Italian whose association with a nation-state came only after the end of the principal era of European colonial expansion, arises from their association with the creation of expansionist states. Their use as official languages of these states reinforced the construction of the relevant state itself, and the colonial expansion of the state further diffused the language.

The linguistic legacy of the diffusion of languages during the European colonial era varies. In some places the colonial language remains as a *lingua franca* that binds together populations of diverse language. In other places, for example, Brazil (for Portuguese), Congo (for French), India (for English), Mexico (for Spanish) and the United States (for English), the former colonial language is at the core of a society that is much more numerous than that of the contemporary ex-colonial power, and its role, notably in the cases of Brazil, India, Mexico and the United States, is far more than that of a mere *lingua franca* bridging a number of local languages. Rather, it is the principal language of the dominant culture.

In recent decades, the economic and cultural dynamism of the English-speaking world has further diffused the English language. This world includes such English-speaking jurisdictions as

England and its former colonies. The United States with its global cultural and media reach is of course a leading example of such jurisdictions. However, the dynamism of English also includes the increasingly global diffusion of English as a second language and the diaspora of English-speakers from such countries as India, Pakistan and the Philippines. Moreover, English, spoken even as a second language by less than 10% of the world's population, is often embraced as the language of transnational commercial and financial deals, even ones that may involve a party from a jurisdiction where English does not predominate and where public policy may promote use of languages other than English.

When the parties to a transaction are not all from English-speaking jurisdictions, the conduct of a transnational commercial or financial transaction in English has potentially both favorable and unfavorable implications, for the parties themselves and for their countries of origin. At one time, English might likely in many instances have been a language imposed on a party whose first language was not English simply by virtue of greater economic leverage of the English-speaking party. The use of English in significant transnational commercial and financial deals now appears more likely to result from a mutual choice of the parties, for reasons including the wide and growing diffusion of English, the high volume of transacting in English, and the globalized character of the world economy.

English may well be the common language of parties whose first language is not English, as increasingly occurs within the European Union. Indeed, in 2005 almost half the population of the European Union was reported able to have a conversation in English—13% of its population being native English speakers and 34% otherwise knowing enough English to do so.[19]

However, a choice by the parties to conduct a transaction in English may derive not from purely linguistic considerations, but rather from substantive business reasons. For example, the parties might be doing business with each other in English in order to access markets for debt or equity financing, goods, and services in such English-speaking business centers around the globe as Hong Kong, Johannesburg, London, Mumbai, New York or Sydney. In addition, locating a commercial or financial transaction, for example, an issuance of securities, in an English-speaking jurisdiction outside of a party's home jurisdiction may offer market, tax and other regulatory benefits. For example, it may give the recipient funds not otherwise accessible in shallow local financial markets, or simply distance aspects of the transaction from unfavorable tax exactions and other regulatory impositions. Conducting a transaction in English in an English-speaking marketplace such as New York or London may achieve reputational benefits of economic significance to transaction parties because of some combination of the reality and perception of higher standards pertaining to accounting, disclosure, corporate governance and the like.[20] Moving parts of a transaction across borders is not however without its unique burdens. For example, conducting a securities transaction in an English-speaking marketplace such as New York or London might have the consequence of maintaining the distance of assets in a non-English-speaking jurisdiction that are supportive of the transaction from potential claimants in the English-speaking jurisdiction.

Alternatively, the parties may believe that use of English enables a more precise, effective or reliable formulation of their deal. Reasons behind such a belief might include the high volume of transnational commercial and financial dealing in English, as well as the association of English with the law and institutions of such global commercial and financial centers as New York and London. Such centers may be perceived as offering sophisticated law, abundant jurisprudence clearly understandable based on precedent, courts that are reliable, efficient and neutral, readily available arbitration, and seasoned practitioners, employed by dealmakers of all sorts from around the world.[21]

On the other hand, when English is not a party's first language or when the law of a non English-speaking jurisdiction may be relevant, conducting a deal in English presents risks of misunderstanding. Notably, entering into English-language contractual documentation presents the risk that a party whose first language is not English may have a different understanding of the substance of such documentation than the counter-party. Such a risk is exacerbated by the dissonant combination of an English-language contract text and the choice of a governing body of law not rooted in English. An English-language contract, governed by the law of an English-language legal system, as to which disputes are to be resolved by institutions and procedures of that legal system, likely enjoys a coherency of legal terminology and conceptual foundation as understood by the relevant legal system. Specifically, the parties, their lawyers, and the courts, arbitrators and others to be involved in any dispute resolution process are likely to employ a coordinated set of language and legal concepts as they work through the dispute. They may vigorously debate and dispute facts, application of norms to facts, and the identity and substance of the relevant norms, but they are likely to do so from the common, coordinated reference of language and legal system. More plainly, a legal system not working in English may be challenged in its ability to grasp the true meaning (or at least the meaning intended by one or more of the parties), and apply the text, of contracts and other deal documentation written in English. The same is of course true for an individual venturing outside of the comfort zones of that individual's first language and the associated, familiar legal system. These observations apply with equal force to an English-language legal system and to an English-language speaker, confronted with materials in some other language.

Further, to the extent that the practice of drafting contracts in English diminishes the use of a jurisdiction's favored language other than English, concerns might be raised that its legal system and the language are marginalized and subject to atrophy. For example, the choice by a French company to borrow money by having a Luxembourg subsidiary issue bonds under an English-language, New York law indenture, might be argued to constitute a release of pressure that would otherwise promote effort to confront and rectify the issues of French law and policy that lead the French company to push its financial transaction abroad, as well as direct the provision of legal services away from French lawyers and governmental actors. Recent reforms of French law appear motivated to address precisely these kinds of challenges. French law was perceived not to offer, for example, a legal structure equivalent to a common law trust such as is routinely employed in the issuance of bonds, or to offer a clear foundation for one lender to represent multiple co-lenders to the same borrower in dealings after the initial extension of credit. As a result of recent reforms, French law now contemplates the institution of a *fiducie*, analogous to a trust, and offers a clear legal basis for the role of a collateral agent, a role critical to multi-lender transactions.[22]

The necessity of using a language for specific governmental interactions may, along with other factors such as concern about becoming subject to specific provisions of law, shape the structuring of a transaction. Certainly when any party to a transaction conducted in English interacts with a non-English speaking governmental authority as part of structuring or enforcing a transaction, it faces the burden of using the relevant language, and perhaps also of translation of relevant documentation from English. This linguistic burden is in addition to the burden of understanding whatever law may be pertinent to the interaction. For example, to create an effective first priority security interest in collateral located in a given country, it is generally necessary to follow procedures of that country, in a language of that country. Likewise, to conduct a securities transaction in a given country, for example, to issue new securities or to trade existing securities, may require compliance with norms that include the mandate to use a particular language for disclosure and other purposes. And of course, enforcement of a transaction in a given jurisdiction's courts will require some level of translation into the working language of such courts. Although the parties' agreement on arbitration may avoid most national requirements of civil procedure to use a particular language before that country's courts, at a minimum the enforcement of an arbitral award through the country's courts would require some use of the language of those courts.

Transaction parties confronted with government requirements that impose use of a language, as well as other governmental mandates, have the option to structure their dealings so as to limit, or even avoid altogether the exposure of their transaction to such requirements. By way of example, transnational loans are often accomplished with English-language loan documentation prepared under New York law, while the collateral package against which a lender would foreclose in the event of a borrower default in loan repayment, is established under the law and language of the borrower's jurisdiction where the collateral is located. Also, transactions such as joint ventures, securities issuances, and project financings are routinely accomplished through special-purpose entities. The parties establish such entities in jurisdictions that mitigate exposure to corporate law, tax, disclosure and other requirements of the jurisdictions of organization or presence of the real parties and of the operational entities through which business is conducted. And, as mentioned, agreements to arbitrate limit the need to interact with national courts in national languages should litigation arise, by seeking to postpone and restrict interaction with such courts to the moment of enforcement of an arbitral award.

The risk to any legal system of not engaging in the process of confronting its impositions and inadequacies that direct transaction parties elsewhere, is to remain at the margins of an increasingly globalized world. The same is true of a language that aspires to serve those who speak it as a tool for participation in globalizing commercial and financial markets. Participants in French markets worry that London is more a global financial center than Paris in part because it is an English-speaking center. As Mexico further opens its economy through trade agreements with its North American neighbors and Europe, its economic and legal actors worry that what transpires in New York may matter as much or more than what happens in Mexico City, in part because New York is an English-speaking center. As the European Union has expanded to its twenty-seven Member States, its outlying members worry about being left out of the core of the further development of the Union's commercial and financial law, also because they may feel more remote from English-speaking commercial and financial centers. For example, it has been observed by leaders of efforts to map the commercial and financial laws of European countries that:

> "There is today in Europe a dramatic lack of communication between the legal cultures of north-western countries, which are highly integrated and communicating among themselves, and the rest. Both Latin countries and former socialist countries live today at the margins of legal Europe, with a consequent dualism that is neither legitimate politically nor justified from a scholarly perspective."[23]

Governments and parties who prefer to work in English might be forgiven for assuming some measure of complacency about the continuing importance of English in international efforts to harmonize law relevant to transnational commercial and financial deals. Any such complacency, however, would be misplaced. OHADA, the supranational organization of sub-Saharan francophone countries, is one potent example of creation of a non-English language framework to support transnational commerce and finance.

Likewise, as will be discussed, the emerging rise of the European Union as a premier laboratory for the harmonization of law across national borders, has the potential to constitute a tectonic shift in the dynamic of international efforts to reform and harmonize law. The extent to which the evolution of its law pertaining to commercial and financial matters will turn on English-language and common law concepts remains to be seen. To the extent that the other widely-spoken languages of the European Union assume a central role in its development, the European Union may constitute a force which directs momentum away from such English-speaking legal and financial centers as London and New York. To the extent that the commercial and financial law of the European Union develops with stronger roots in English, it may accentuate the momentum towards such centers. Regardless of the role that English plays in the evolution of European union commercial and financial law, it is clear for the reasons to be discussed in the concluding portions of this investigation that the European Union is likely to be an increasing counterbalance to the weight of the United States in international harmonization of law efforts. Engagement of the United States and the European Union in such efforts, if coordinated, may offer the prospect of driving them forward significantly further.

A proponent of any language has strong incentive to participate in international efforts to develop improved frameworks in support of transnational business. The evolving global marketplace leaves no room for complacency about the continued role of any language.

B.   Translation

The challenge for parties of different languages, cultures and legal systems who desire to undertake a cross-border transaction, particularly one that involves an ongoing relationship, is to understand each other well enough to conduct the desired business. This necessitates that they bridge the gaps in their respective points of departure as to both language and legal system so as to each be able to participate collaboratively in the articulation of the terms of their transaction.

What the parties seek to achieve is not simply the comparative law challenge of establishing comparable terminology across legal systems to enable their comparison.[24] Rather, the challenge of communication and collaboration pertains to the construction of the parties' relationship. This is more akin to the challenge of translating constitutional concepts between the national context and the domain of international and supranational organizations such as the United Nations, the European Union and the World Trade Organization.[25] In that context:

> "Institutional design, even in the most venerable and venerated constitutional settlements, must always be viewed as a derivative and contingent exercise, always at the service of the core values and the changing detail of material and cultural conditions and of diversely located solutions which influence the articulation and optimal balance of these core values."[26]

Although parties to transnational commercial and financial deals seek simply to accomplish their business and certainly do not seek in the context of specific transactions to design frameworks of public constitutional law, the point of the quoted observation about the public law definition of how legal systems and their institutions inter-relate, to the effect that the structure of their relationship must always serve their purpose, is highly pertinent. The framework that transaction parties create to conduct their business relationship is in this sense indeed analogous to the framework that legal systems create for interaction among themselves. Governmental institutions of different languages and legal systems working out how their legal systems will relate, share a common challenge with transaction parties of varying cultural frames of reference, core values and languages.

The challenge is to establish a "constitutional framework" for their interaction, albeit with the difference that the interests of transaction parties are ultimately associated with profit in some form. The interests of transaction parties may, however, extend from a one-time deal to the establishment of structures for a sustained relationship. Indeed, the costs of establishing a significant transnational business deal incentivize the creation of longer term relationships to support continued deal flow. The incentive to establish structures of agreements to support extension of the parties' dealings with each other reinforces the "constitutional" parallelism. Effective use of language, and as needed, translation across languages, are obvious critical elements of the constitutional exercise in pushing forward a deal.

The parallelism in the challenges faced by (i) private parties seeking to establish the framework of a deal between them and (ii) public actors working through the interaction of legal systems, extends beyond the merit of continuous evaluation of whether the definition of a relationship serves its ends. It also extends to the maintenance and tolerance of elements of lack of full understanding, and even of conflicting views as to the foundation of common positions. The exercise of translation across languages may often promote such instances.

A range of interactions of legal systems illustrates the phenomena of establishing common positions based on divergent reasoning. An illustration could be provided by a conventional challenge of private international law, that is, for example, that the legal systems of France and the United States may provide common outcomes to a particular dispute among private parties that stretches across borders, while maintaining quite different norms of private and private international law. Further illustrations are afforded by the emerging challenge of interaction between Member States and supranational organizations, for example, the interaction of European Union law with that of its Member States or Mexico's acceptance of jurisprudence of the Inter-American Court for Human Rights.[27] Legal systems, as has occurred in the referenced instances, may, for extended and indefinite periods, maintain uncoordinated and indeed outright inconsistent views about their interaction. The differing views about the supremacy of European Union law over Member State law held by various national courts and the European Court of Justice through much of the European Union's history, are yet further examples.[28] Transaction parties routinely do likewise, that is, they conduct their business while maintaining inconsistent understandings of their relationship. What may distinguish transaction parties from public law actors in respect of the differences in their positions is that divergent understandings of transaction parties may perhaps become apparent only in the phase of dispute resolution, when one or more of the parties seeks to enforce its understanding of the deal.

Nonetheless, transaction parties are well-motivated (and well-advised) to agree on their deal and the framework in which they desire to consummate it. This motivation may be deeper than that of governmental authorities to resolve constitutional issues of inter-action among legal systems. For transaction parties, avoiding the risk and expense of disputes may translate in obvious ways to better economic returns. Moreover, transaction parties may have the further increased motivation that fuller agreement on the terms of their transaction increases the likelihood of respect of the autonomy of their agreements by reducing the probability of a successful challenge to the agreements by one of the parties. Indeed, minimization of the prospect of disputes also decreases the likelihood of interaction with governmental authorities, be they courts or regulators, because there is diminished likelihood of a disgruntled party to trigger such interaction. Moreover, precision and thoughtfulness by the parties in their agreements not only make a dispute less likely to arise, but also increase the likelihood that a complaining party in the event of a dispute will prevail in efforts to enforce the bargain that it achieved. Precision and thoughtfulness do so by offering courts and arbitrators a clearer map as a basis for resolving any dispute about what the parties agreed.

As the parties work to achieve the desired meeting of the minds to structure their bargain, translation in the conventional sense may become a useful tool. Among themselves, the parties have the incentive to communicate fully and effectively with each other to establish a good transaction. Conventional translation is clearly a second best solution to meeting this challenge of communication. The parties will much prefer to choose a language in which each can communicate. Should they not adequately master a common language, they are likely, for a substantial transaction, to engage lawyers and other advisors for whom the relevant language or languages present less of a barrier to communication.

The incentive of the parties relative to communication with governmental authorities with whom some interaction may be necessary differs from the nature of the incentive to achieve clear communication among themselves. Governmental authorities are less open to use of non-official languages, and each of the parties will want to limit its investment in such communication to what is necessary to achieve the desired result. Accordingly, the role of conventional translation is likely to be greater in interactions of one or more parties with governmental authorities than in dealings among the parties. Given the lesser flexibility of governmental authorities on the choice of language, conventional translation, when one or more parties is conducting its business in a non-official language, more likely becomes a necessity as the primary means of communication, rather than simply an adjunct to the dealings among parties.

In any event, even merely conventional translation from one language to another, as it pertains to significant transnational commercial and financial deals, is nonetheless frequently a difficult exercise. In addition to the general need for precision in the translation of legal documentation, the familiarity of each transaction party with its own language, that further corresponds to a specific legal system, renders challenging the precise translation of legal concepts. As one author has observed,

"The language of law is bound to the inner grammar of legal systems, cultures and mentalities, which in turn impede communication in words that are borrowed from another legal system, culture and mentality."[29]

Indeed, the association of a legal system with a corresponding language may demand invention of appropriate legal vocabulary in the target language of translation.[30] The law of the counterparty's legal system may employ not only different vocabulary, but also different legal concepts, or even similar vocabulary, but with different meaning in view of differences in the legal systems, arising, for example, from divergent procedural rules. The issue of translation may even arise when the relevant legal systems share a language. For example, the legal terminology of England and Wales, India, the United States, and other English-speaking jurisdictions differs, as does the legal terminology among various Francophone jurisdictions such as Belgium, France, Québec, Switzerland, and the OHADA member states, among others. Differences in culture even among jurisdictions that share a language will likewise complicate the process of translation and interaction in general.

Even conceptual differences in the approaches to contract drafting may pose translation issues. For example, conceptual differences between common law systems, which are overwhelmingly English-language, and civil law systems, which are typically not, complicate the drafting of a document in two languages. While a common law approach to contract drafting may focus on articulating at length the desires of the parties in the face of various possible scenarios, a civil law contract drafting approach might rely to a far greater extent on implicit principles and standard terms, some of them peremptory, established by a code framework.

Translation of a contract at the time of its making is an often-used device to promote mutual understanding by the parties of their agreement.[31] However, the parties always face a temptation to delay and limit translation in view of its cost in time and money. Translation may be delayed until it becomes an essential prerequisite to enforcement action before a national court, or be limited, for example, to the documentation necessary to create a security interest in collateral within a jurisdiction that mandates use of an official language not otherwise employed by the parties for their transaction.

Moreover, translation of a document into two languages, even at the time of its making, is at best a partial solution to the challenges of assuring that the parties to a transaction share a common understanding of its meaning and that the document is accessible to courts and others to be engaged in dispute resolution and enforcement. In addition to the general challenges of quality translation and to achieving a common substantive understanding among the parties, translation leaves open the prospect of argument based on divergent translation. Typically, well-advised transaction parties will specify in the text of any such dual language document that the text in one language is the governing text in the event of any disparity of meaning between the two versions. Even so, the prospect of the text in one language being used to support argument as to the meaning of the text in the other language remains.

Notes to Chapter II

19. Commission of the European Communities, *Communication from the Commission to the Council, the European Parliament, the European Economic and Social Committee and the Committee of the Regions: A New Framework Strategy for Multilingualism*, COM(2005) 596 final, Nov. 22, 2005. *See also* Richard L. Creech, Law and Language in the European Union: The Paradox of a Babel "United in Diversity" 39-44 (2005).

20. *See* Jordan Siegel, *Can Foreign Firms Bond Themselves Effectively by Renting US Securities Laws?*, 75 J. Financial Economics 319 (2005) (analyzing motivations of foreign issuers to access US capital markets).

21. For an extended advertisement of the merits of English law relative to transnational business, see *Introducing the Bar of England and Wales*, American Lawyer Media and the Bar Council of England and Wales (Oct. 2007).

22. Law no. 211 of Feb. 19, 2007, J.O.R.F. no. 44 of Feb. 21, 2007, at 3052 (institution of *fiducie*); new Civil Code art. 2328-1 (collateral agent).

23. Mauro Bussani and Ugo Mattei, *Preface* in Mauro Bussani and Ugo Mattei, eds., Opening Up European Law: The Common Core Project towards Eastern and South Eastern Europe xv (2007).

24. *See* David J. Gerber, *Reading the Map of European Private Law: Language and Knowledge in Contemporary Comparative Law*, in Mauro Bussani and Ugo Mattei, eds., Opening Up European Law: The Common Core Project towards Eastern and South Eastern Europe 49, 60-62 (2007) (sketching the challenge of developing terminology to facilitate comparison of private law across the legal systems of European countries).

25. *See* Neil Walker, *Postnational constitutionalism and the problem of translation*, in J.H.H. Weiler and Marlene Wind, eds., European Constitutionalism Beyond the State 27, 37 (2003).

26. *Id.* at 54.

27. *See* Patrick Del Duca, *The Rule of Law: Mexico's Approach to Expropriation Disputes in the Face of Investment Globalization*, 51 UCLA Law Rev. 35, at 113 and 125-128 (2003).

28. *See, e.g.*, Antonio La Pergola and Patrick Del Duca, *Community Law, International Law, and the Italian Constitution*, 79 Am. J. Int'l L. 598 (1985).

29. Vivian G. Curran, *Comparative Law and Language*, in Mathias Reimann and Reinhard Zimmermann, eds., The Oxford Handbook of Comparative Law 675, 678 (2007).

30. On the challenges of translation of legislation in bilingual systems, specifically Louisiana and Canada, see George A. Bermann, 54 *Bilingualism and Translation in the U.S. Legal System: a Study of the Louisiana Experience*, Am. J. Comp. L. 89 (supp. 2006).

31. Translators and translation do not guarantee that transaction parties understand each other. *See, e.g.* MCC-Marble Ceramic Center, Inc. v. Ceramica Nuova D'Agostino, S.P.A., 144 F.3d 1384 (11th Cir. 1998), *cert. denied*, 526 U.S. 1087 (1999).

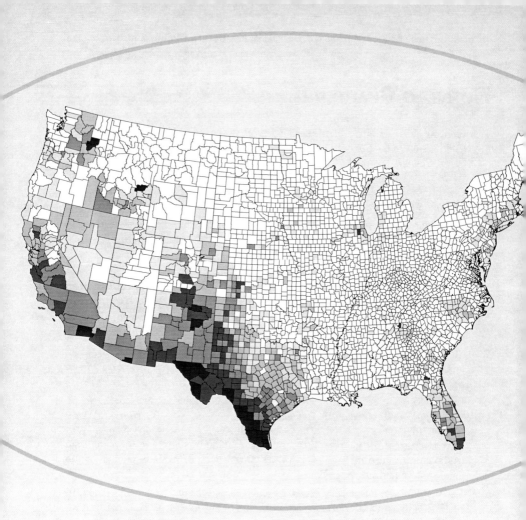

Map Four - Spanish in the United States

III. *LAISSEZ-FAIRE* APPROACH OF ONE ENGLISH-SPEAKING JURISDICTION: UNITED STATES

The approach of United States law to the question of language for transnational commercial and financial deals is broadly one of *laissez-faire*, an attitude consonant with the indulgence of taking for granted the size and depth of the United States economy and hence its leading global role, as well as the domestic prevalence of the English language. For purposes of United States law and practice generally, the conduct of transnational commercial and financial deals in a language other than English, as between parties who do not benefit from consumer protection measures, raises principally the issue of what must be provided to governmental authorities to make disclosures and to obtain services or clearances from them.

Elements of the legal framework of the United States generally supportive of commercial and financial transactions include: (i) its national common market founded on the implementation of its constitution's Commerce Clause giving the federal government the power to regulate commerce with foreign nations and among the states: (ii) its path-breaking implementation of a Uniform Commercial Code ("UCC") as a model law adopted in each of its states to provide a common commercial law, notably for sales of goods and for secured lending and the constitution of lien priorities through the "notice-filing" approach of the Uniform Commercial Code's Article 9; (iii) its elaborations of restatements of various subject matters of the law and the affirmation in general of their content by state and federal courts throughout its federal system; and (iv) its national securities markets founded on New Deal principles of transparency and expert agency regulation.

The development of this framework is a source of the significant prominence that the United States and its law have held in the marketplace of transnational commercial and financial deals and accordingly in discussions of how to harmonize law relevant to them. Both the size of the marketplace in the United States and the quality of its norms have contributed to the broader role of the United States in initiatives pertaining to harmonization of law. The subsequent discussion of supranational organizations, specifically the European Union, will suggest the benefit for the United States, as well as for other countries generally, of active engagement in international harmonization of law efforts, particularly if the United States wishes that such efforts establish frameworks consistent with relevant United States law and practice.

To facilitate comparison with the various legal systems to be addressed below, this section reviews the approach of United States law to issues relative to language that are also raised in such systems, namely requirements: (i) that a particular language be used as a condition to the validity and enforceability of a contract; (ii) of translation as a predicate to enforcement of a deal not conducted in an "official" language; and (iii) pertaining to use of an "official" language and associated formalities in respect to the creation of a priority claim to collateral offered by a borrower, without the borrower's surrender of possession of the collateral, to secure repayment of a loan.

These three issues span a range of concerns that parties to a transaction may have. The first pertains to the basic choice of the parties as to what language to use in regard to their dealings with each other. The second concerns the language to be used in a governmental interaction, namely civil litigation before national courts, that can be substantially truncated by the parties at the time of contracting through the simple expedient of an agreement to arbitrate any dispute that may arise. The final issue concerns a transaction element that, like enforcement of an arbitral award, unavoidably requires governmental interaction. However, the establishment of a priority claim to collateral by registration of a security interest is an interaction with government that cannot be as completely removed from governmental intervention as dispute resolution, because of the essential role of the governmentally-sanctioned registrar of security interests in establishing the publicity of non-possessory security interests necessary to trump competing claims of other creditors. Accordingly, registration of a security interest involves a governmental service that in matters of language and associated burdens may impinge to a greater degree on party choices about how they wish to conduct their relationship.

A. Official language for transactions

Although naturalization as a citizen requires a minimal knowledge of English, the United States Constitution contains no express declaration of a national language, perhaps because for those who participated in its adoption in 1789 there was little question that English was their common language. However, under current federal law, there are requirements of outreach to those who do not speak English.

For example, federal statutory law pertaining to civil rights prohibits discrimination on the basis of national origin in connection with the administration of programs receiving federal financial assistance.[32] Accordingly, the executive branch of the federal government, in line with a 1974 Supreme Court decision to the effect that a school district with a significant number of non-English speaking students of Chinese origin was required to take reasonable steps to provide them with a meaningful opportunity to participate in federally funded educational programs,[33] has interpreted this prohibition of Title VI of the Civil Rights Act of 1964 as mandating that federal agencies and the recipients of federal funding take steps to assure that persons of limited proficiency in English be able to "meaningfully" participate in their programs and services.[34] Recipients of federal funding include not only schools, but also police departments and courts, among many other state and local government functions. The Department of Justice guidance on what constitute reasonable steps to take considers the roles of oral interpretation and written translation in light of factors such as the population to be served, the nature of the services rendered and the availability of resources. The tools to be considered for purposes of assuring the "meaningful" participation of persons of limited English proficiency range from engaging bilingual personnel to using outsource telephone interpreter services.[35]

At various times in the history of the United States, various of its states have taken action to promote or to suppress, *e.g.* German during World War I, the use of a language associated with particular ethnic groups.[36] In recent years a number of states have conferred on English, by constitutional amendment or legislation, some degree of official status for purposes of state law.[37]

In contrast to the provisions in some states for an exclusive official status for English for state law purposes, Puerto Rico, pursuant to its Official Languages Act of 1993, is one territorial entity of the United States for which English and Spanish are each official languages. For purposes of dealings with Puerto Rico's government, both languages may be used "indistinctively."[38] Further,

> "When necessary, written translations and oral interpreta-
> tions shall be made from one language to the other so that
> the interested parties can understand any proceeding or
> communication in said languages."[39]

Also, Hawaii's constitution proclaims English and Hawaiian as its official languages, although adding "except that Hawaiian shall be required for public acts and transactions only as provided by law."[40] Hawaii, however, differs from Puerto Rico in that almost all of Puerto Rico's population speaks Spanish as a first language, while only a small fraction of Hawaii's population speaks Hawaiian.

The focus of federal and state authorities on issues associated with the use of language corresponds to an increase in the proportion of the population in the United States that reports speaking a language other than English at home. This proportion rose from 11% in the 1980 census to 18% in the 2000 census. Almost 11% of the population reported the language spoken at home as Spanish, with Chinese, French, German, Tagalog, Vietnamese, Italian, Korean, Russian, Polish, Arabic, Portuguese, Japanese, French Creole, Greek, Hindi, Persian, Urdu, Gujarati, and Armenian, in that order, rounding out the top twenty languages other than English spoken as the primary language at home in the United States.[41]

The impact to transnational commercial and financial deals, and particularly litigation that may arise in connection with them, of any movement at the level of states within the United States to declare English to be an "official" language, is likely of limited relevance. Reasons include the constitutional definition of federalism in the United States, the inter-relation of state and federal courts, and the availability of arbitration under state and federal law. A further reason in connection with secured lending for business purposes is the notice-filing approach of Article 9 of the Uniform Commercial Code to the establishment of priority creditor claims to collateral held by a debtor.

In the competitive national market established under United States federalism, each one of the fifty states has an incentive not to divert economic activity to other states, including by burdening the enforcement of transnational commercial and financial contracts with language rules. Moreover, any such effort would face the challenge of preemption under the Commerce Clause of the federal constitution.[42] Such preemption could be declared by any court, federal or state, in the United States exercising its power of constitutional review of laws and other governmental actions. Moreover, each one of the fifty states has an affirmative incentive to capture the benefits of as much transactional activity as possible. The Full Faith and Credit Clause of the United States Constitution reinforces each state in its efforts in this sense.[43] It affords each state a basis for expecting that other states of the union will respect what transpires pursuant to the law of that state and what is established by its courts. Thus for example, the state of Delaware has succeed in establishing itself as a favored jurisdiction of incorporation for businesses operating throughout the United States, particularly publicly-traded companies, based on the quality of its law and legal institutions relative to the formation and governance of corporations.[44] Any state that would attempt to burden commercial and financial transactions, including those with a cross-border dimension, with requirements that intruded on the autonomy of the parties to such transactions, including in matters of language, would likely see such parties move the governance of as much as possible of such transactions to the law and institutions of another state.

In addition, so-called diversity jurisdiction of the federal courts regarding disputes involving more than US$75,000 between "citizens of a State and citizens or subjects of a foreign state"[45] limits the practical ability of states to achieve language policy goals by burdening litigation in their courts with language and translation requirements that go beyond those of the federal courts. If the requirements of state courts are excessively burdensome, a plaintiff that meets the diversity requirement will simply avail itself of the opportunity to bring the action in federal court, where it is not subject to the state procedural requirements. In addition, defendants have a similar opportunity. As to controversies involving more than US$75,000, so-called federal removal jurisdiction enables a foreign party, understood as a party from outside the relevant state, to remove state court actions brought against it to a federal court.[46]

Moreover, not only is the United States a party to the New York Convention on the Enforcement and Recognition of Arbitral Awards, as discussed below, to facilitate the enforcement of international arbitral awards, it is also a jurisdiction receptive to arbitration in general. It thereby affords parties to transnational commercial and financial deals who agree to arbitration, the ability to conduct dispute resolution with whatever use of language they might agree.[47]

Notwithstanding state measures declaring English to be an official language or the unique exceptions of the official bilingualism of Hawaii and Puerto Rico, transnational commercial and financial deals are not generally burdened in the United States by language requirements, other than the general need to interact with governmental authorities in English. Conversely, given the proportion of the population of the United States that reports speaking a language other than English at home, there would appear to be no shortage of business people in the United States willing and able to conduct commercial and financial transactions across borders in many languages other than English.

B. Language and litigation

In dealing with a court in the United States from which enforcement of a deal might be sought, the challenge of a transaction conducted in a language other than English is to provide English-language materials to enable the court adequately to understand the content of a relevant contract. Indeed, as to contract disputes addressed in the United States federal courts that arise even from Puerto Rico, where Spanish is not only the prevalent language but also recognized as an official language by the law of Puerto Rico, the practice is for such federal courts to insist on access to materials in English. For example, the United States Court of Appeals for the First Circuit, whose territory is comprised of New England and Puerto Rico, faces Spanish language materials with frequency in disputes involving parties active in Puerto Rico. The First

Circuit's so-called "local" Rule 30(d) provides that the "court will not receive documents not in the English-language unless translations are furnished."[48]

However, neither the federal rules of civil procedure nor of evidence directly themselves speak to the question of non-English-language commercial and financial contracts. They simply leave to those who desire their application the burden of translation to the extent necessary to persuade a court that such application should be granted. For example, a federal district court in a patent litigation matter, faced with the issue of how to understand words in the patent filings, analogized the interpretive challenge as akin to that of a foreign language contract. In a footnote, the court laid out a mechanistic view of the challenge of translation as similar to the challenge of confronting any other issue of expert knowledge:

> "When a judge interprets the meaning of a term in a run-of-the-mill contract, she is determining how an ordinary speaker of English would understand the term, in context, and she cannot look to extrinsic evidence unless there is some ambiguity. A dictionary constitutes extrinsic evidence of the "plain and customary" meanings that members of the relevant language community ascribe to various words, but it also serves as a tool to enhance the judge's cognitive capacities, which capacities are then applied to the task of interpretation. In theory, at least, a judge interpreting a contract written in a foreign language would follow the same process, though she might want to gain some background understanding of the language from experts."[49]

A professional translator would likely quarrel with the court's apparent presumption that effective translation is largely achieved by rote consultation of dictionaries. However, the point for present purposes is that the court would consider foreign language materials as presenting simply the obstacle of translation, which is capable of being surmounted by expert assistance.

Moreover, contract law in the United States in general leaves each of the parties the burden of understanding their agreements.[50] In its decision of the *Gaskin* case[51] for example, a federal district court upheld a German employer's effort to enforce a forum selection clause. The forum selection clause established Germany as the place for resolution of disputes between the German employer and its employee resident in the United States. That employee did not speak German. Although the employee argued that his signature of a German-language contract that he could not read ought not to bind him, the court determined that it was his responsibility as a well-paid manager, with a prestigious Park Avenue office, for a German trading company, to know what he was signing.

C.   Language and security interests

The judicial role in the enforcement of deal terms established by contract is one way that government touches transnational commercial and financial deals. The governmental role in conjunction with establishing the priority to be accorded to competing claims of security interests in collateral is another.

The approach employed in the United States relative to the establishment of security interests and their priority relative to other creditor claims is largely to allocate the burden of effective documentation to the relevant economic actors. That is, the responsibility to complete the steps to establish a priority claim of a particular creditor in collateral that is effective also against third parties is the burden primarily of that creditor and its debtor. Governmental representatives have little affirmative role to play in assuring the proper constitution of the priority of the claim of the creditor against the collateral offered by its debtor. Instead, the role reserved to government is simply to maintain a registry of security interests. This role of governmental authorities is essentially to receive forms for filing, to which transaction parties, at their own risk, may insert and append such content as they choose, and then to index the filing in a registry by name of the debtor. Relative to transnational commercial and financial deals that in some way rely on this system in the United States, this approach burdens the parties' choice of language in which to conduct their transaction in only a limited way.

The limited need for a creditor and a debtor to use English in connection with establishing a priority claim of the creditor to collateral held by a debtor derives from several factors. The overarching factor is the modest nature of the governmental requirements relative to what documentation needs to be filed in the public registry of security interests, essentially the name of the debtor and a description of the collateral. Reinforcing the limited need to use English is the extremely limited nature of formalities for the creation of security interests in collateral in general. Unlike many other systems, including those to be discussed below, there are no requirements for the preparation of relevant agreements before governmental authorities and no need to obtain the advance approval of governmental authorities as to the form of such agreements.

The perfection of security interests and the establishment of priority of creditor claims are accomplished in the United States primarily by filing in two sets of registries. For real property collateral, local real property registries are typically maintained by county governments and governed by state law. For other kinds of collateral, secretaries of state of each of the fifty states maintain registries in conformity with the relevant state's adoption of the Uniform Commercial Code.

In the case of the real property registries, filings are indexed by grantor and grantee so as to create a chain of title. In some parts of the United States, the oldest filings in the real property registries are in languages such as French, Hawaiian, or Spanish, reflecting the history of those areas prior to their becoming part of the United States. There is a well-developed title insurance industry which assumes the burden of reviewing the contents of the filings so as to determine whether it is commercially feasible to insure a given interest in the relevant real property.

Although a requirement to file a deed in a real property registry may be notarization of the signature of the grantor, such "notarization" is no more than verification of the identity of the signer to the satisfaction of the notary public. In the United States, becoming a notary public is a straightforward licensing matter akin to acquiring a license to be a real estate broker or indeed not that much more difficult than acquiring a license to operate a passenger car. California, for example, requires a six-hour course of study as a condition to sitting for the examination to become a notary public.[52] The cost of notarization of a signature by a notary public in the United States is nominal. For example, California generally caps such fees at US$10.[53]

The concepts of Article 9 of the Uniform Commercial Code, as adopted in the fifty states of the United States, for security interests in personal property are that the security interest "attaches" for the benefit of a lender when three conditions are satisfied: (i) the lender extends credit; (ii) the debtor has valid rights to transfer the lender; and, (iii) the debtor grants those rights to a lender through a "security agreement." Priority of the security interest relative to claims of other creditors who have not previously perfected a security interest in the relevant collateral is achieved by "perfecting" it, which typically is done by filing in a central registry, but as to some kinds of collateral may be achieved by possession.

The conceptual approach of civil law jurisdictions is generally different. The creation of a security interest generally is intimately bound with its public registration. That is, a "private writing", a writing simply between two parties, may not be adequate to create or grant the security interest. Instead, the writing would need to be transcribed before a notary and then registered in the appropriate registry to establish its priority. As will be discussed, Mexico is an example of a civil law country that imposes this heavy burden, and France, in respect of its recent reform of the system for establishment of non-possessory security interests in moveable and intangible property, is an example of a civil law country that does not impose such a burden.

The Uniform Commercial Code registry in each state is indexed by name of debtor, and although some title insurance is available,[54] the task of understanding what liens burden a debtor's property is primarily assumed by prospective further creditors who conduct searches of the registry to verify whether collateral newly offered to them is free of liens associated with prior lending. In either case, the government employees who handle the filings have little or no need to understand their content, and accordingly beyond the requirement to use basic forms in English to accomplish the filings, there is typically no "official" control on the language or substance of the document filed. A creditor is entitled to make a filing in the registry once it has obtained a writing—the security agreement, signed by the debtor in which the debtor grants the security interest. The registry officials do not request to see this writing, and there is no formality required in connection with its signature.

Moreover, Article 9 of the Uniform Commercial Code puts the burden on the filing party, typically the creditor, to provide adequate notice of what collateral is covered by the filing. For example, California Commercial Code Section 9502 defines a "financing statement" to be filed in the appropriate registry as "sufficient" if it provides (i) the name of the debtor; (ii) the name of the secured party or a representative of the secured party; and, (iii) "indicates the collateral covered by the financing statement". The criterion for what constitutes adequate description is straightforward:

"a description of personal or real property is sufficient, whether or not it is specific, if it reasonably identifies what is described."[55]

It is not the registrar who determines whether a collateral description is adequate. Indeed, the personnel of the registrar typically would not even read it. The adequacy of a collateral description is left to be tested in litigation over priority of creditor claims, if not previously resolved as a condition to defining the terms of a refinancing or other further extension of credit. Further, there is no requirement to file in the registry the underlying instrument which grants the security interest or any of the documentation establishing the extension of credit. The "lightness" of the UCC Article 9 system's imposition relative to language resides principally in three elements: (i) the limited formalities for the constitution of the security interest, *i.e.* for a security interest to attach to the collateral; (ii) the limited requirement as to the nature of the information to be publicly filed; and (iii) the lack of formalities associated with the filing process.

Although the limited information as to collateral, *i.e.* identity of debtor and creditor, together with "adequate" description of collateral, could be filed in a language other than English, it is unlikely that a lender would attempt to do so, as such a description would raise an issue of the adequacy of the description, that is, of whether adequate public notice of the identify of the collateral is provided. However, there is nothing that outright prevents a description that incorporates foreign language material. Thus, for example, a statement in English that the collateral includes all inventory of a corporation, which inventory happens to be in, for instance, Québec, with a further French language description of that collateral is not prohibited.

For purposes of jurisdictions where the current version of the Uniform Commercial Code is in force, the Uniform Commercial Code resolves the challenge of conflicting private international law rules, that is, of conflicting rules on choice of law, by establishing common, coordinated substantive rules. Thus, for example, the proper place to file for organizations such as corporations and limited liability companies whose organization requires registration under the law of a state of the United States, is the Secretary of State of that state.[56] Accordingly, to establish what filings have been registered against the assets of, for example, a Delaware corporation, it suffices to check the registry maintained by the Delaware Secretary of State. The current version of the Uniform Commercial Code designates the District of Columbia as the proper place of filing relative to other entities whose organization requires registration pursuant to United States federal law or pursuant to law of another country, for example, an Italian *Società per Azioni*.[57] The place of filing relative to entities not subject to registration in connection with their creation is established by the broader rules of the Uniform Commercial Code.[58]

Of course, notwithstanding the Uniform Commercial Code rules that establish the appropriate place of filing as the place of organization of a corporate debtor and that point to the District of Columbia as the proper place of filing for corporations organized outside the United States, a lender would be ill-advised not to also follow the procedures established under the law of relevant jurisdictions outside the Uniform Commercial Code system, to confirm its priority in the collateral in the event of any contest among creditors there. Continuing with the example of Québec law, the reference to Québec serves to make the point that as one changes country, any presumption that the applicable law remains the same is simply naïve and that the laws of one jurisdiction are unlikely to be recognized by the jurisdiction of the location of collateral against claims of third parties in that jurisdiction, unless as is the case with the relatively uniform adoption of the Uniform Commercial Code within the United States by all of the relevant jurisdictions, multiple jurisdictions have established a coordinated framework.

1. Detour to Québec

Québec's procedures relative to secured lending involving collateral classified as "movables", *i.e.* in a general sense, personal property in terminology of the Uniform Commercial Code, include provision for establishing the priority of a claim by filing a notice in a central provincial registry analogous to the procedures of Article 9 of the Uniform Commercial Code and the Personal Property Security Acts in the same vein adopted by Canada's other nine provinces. However, Québec's civil law tradition and its attachment to the French language maintain a distinction from the rest of Canada and the United States in its handling of security interests. In particular, Québec's Civil Code maintains a focus on formal conceptions of property, pursuant to which it defines a concept of "hypothec" that is narrower than the notion of security interest as defined under the Uniform Commercial Code. The consequence for a lender desiring to confirm the priority of its claim is that the lender must also consider further Civil Code provisions contemplating additional procedures associated with retention of title as the basis for the security interest, so as to be fully aware of potential claims on the same collateral by third parties.[59]

By way of example, Canada's Supreme Court, on hearing a group of appeals of Québec court decisions arising from competing creditor claims to automobiles claimed as collateral for outstanding extensions of credit and a seller's reservation of ownership in an installment sale contract, chose to recognize and affirm the formalities of recognition of title under Québec law rather than to apply the overriding concepts of security interest that privilege substance rather than form, as expressed in the Personal Property Security Acts of Canada's other provinces, as well as Article 9 of the Uniform Commercial Code. In those cases, the Supreme Court of Canada held that failure to comply with the provisions of Québec's legislation providing for public notice of automobile leases through filing in the Québec Register of

Personal and Movable Real Rights was not ground to preclude consideration of the lessor's claim that its ownership interest prevailed over assignment of the lessee's interest in bankruptcy proceedings.[60]

Not entirely surprisingly, the Québec Court of Appeal rulings were protective of the unsecured creditors, while the Supreme Court of Canada's holding vindicated the rights of the parties who purported to retain title, but nonetheless failed to comply in timely filing with the requisites of registration of their interests to put third parties on notice of them. Paradoxically, the Québec Court of Appeal rulings that were appealed to the Supreme Court would have served to move Québec law toward the mainstream of emphasis on the importance of providing at least constructive notice to third parties by timely filing in the relevant registry. Although in the short run the Court of Appeal rulings would have favored the unsecured creditors in the instant cases, in the longer run their rulings would have facilitated the efficient functioning of registry systems to promote secured lending. The overriding result of the rulings of the national Supreme Court and the Québec Court of Appeals, plus the Québec Civil Code, however, is to affirm Québec's law on security interests as presenting a nuance relative to that of the law of the rest of Canada and the United States. The French language and Québec's civil law tradition by no means ineluctably dictate this particular result, but they are clearly associated with the persistence of a difference from the relatively uniform substantive law with respect to security interests in the English-speaking parts of North America that bound it.

NOTES TO CHAPTER III

32. §601, Title VI, Civil Rights Act of 1964, 42 U.S.C. §2000d.

33. *Lau v. Nichols*, 414 U.S. 563 (1974).

34. Department of Justice, *Guidance to Federal Financial Assistance Recipients regarding Title VI Prohibition against National Origin Discrimination Affecting Limited English Proficient Persons*, 67 Fed. Reg. 41455 (June 18, 2002).

35. *Id.*

36. *See, e.g. Meyer v. Nebraska*, 262 U.S. 390 (1923) (state prohibition of teaching in languages other than English invalidated); Heinz Kloss, THE AMERICAN BILINGUAL TRADITION (Center for Applied Linguistics, 2nd ed., 1998); James R. Maxeiner, *Uniform Law and its Impact on National Laws—Limits and Possibilities: Uniform Law and its Impact on National Laws Limits and Possibilities*, MEMOIRS OF THE INTERNATIONAL ACADEMY OF COMPARATIVE LAW, GENERAL AND NATIONAL REPORTS OF THE FIRST INTERMEDIATE CONGRESS, THE IMPACT OF UNIFORM LAW ON NATIONAL LAW: LIMITS AND POSSIBILITIES, 2009, *available at* www.ssrn.com.

37. *See, e.g.* Jenning Kohlberger, *Using Principles of International Law to Reshape American Legislation of State Official English Laws*, 29 J. OF LEGISLATION 253 (2003).

38. 1 LAWS OF PUERTO RICO §59.

39. 1 LAWS OF PUERTO RICO §59a.

40. Constitution of the State of Hawaii, art. XV(4).

41. Hyon B. Shin with Rosalind Bruno, *Language Use and English-Speaking Ability: 2000*, CENSUS 2000 BRIEF (Oct. 2003).

42. Article 1, Section 8, Clause 3.

43. Article IV, Section 1.

44. *See* Oren Bar-Gill, Michal Barzuza, and Lucian Bebchuk, *The Market for Corporate Law*, 162 J. INSTITUTIONAL AND THEORETICAL ECONOMICS 134 (2006).

45. 28 U.S.C. §1332.

46. 28 U.S.C. §1441.

47. On the state of arbitration law in the United States, see Edward Brunet, Richard E. Speidel, Jean E. Sternlight, and Stephen H. Ware, ARBITRATION LAW IN AMERICA: A CRITICAL ASSESSMENT (2006).

48. In *Ramos-Baez v. Bossolo-Lopez*, 240 F.3d 92, 94 (1st Cir. 2001), the court declined to waive the rule's application, but specified that plaintiff would have lost even with the excluded Spanish-language documents.

49. *Amgen, Inc. v. Hoechst Marion Roussel, Inc.*, 339 F.Supp. 2d 202, 227 (D.Mass. 2004).

50. *But see* Julian S. Lim, *Tongue-Tied in the Market: The Relevance of Contract Law to Racial-Language Minorities*, 91 Cal. L.R. 579 (2003) (examining contract law doctrines pursuant to which members of non-English speaking groups in the United States might claim more equitable treatment in commercial transactions).

51. *Gaskin v. Stumm Handel GmbH*, 390 F.Supp. 361, 366 (D.N.Y. 1975), applying Justice Burger's reasoning in the *Bremen* decision discussed *infra* at note 281.

52. California Government Code §8201.

53. California Government Code §8211.

54. *See, e.g.* James D. Prendergast, *Secured Real Estate Mezzanine Lending (with Form)*, The Practical Real Estate Lawyer 35 (March 2007) (expounding the relevance of insurance of UCC Article 9 perfection of security interests in intangible property, *e.g.* contract rights and governmental entitlements, with reference to early stage financing of real estate development).

55. California Commercial Code §9108. *See also* California Commercial Code §9504.

56. *See, e.g.*, California Commercial Code §9307(e).

57. *See, e.g.*, California Commercial Code §9307.

58. *See, e.g.*, Chapter 3 of Article 9 of the Uniform Commercial Code as implemented in California.

59. *See* Aline Grenon, *Major Differences between PPSA Legislation and Security over Moveables in Quebec under the New Civil Code*, 26 Canadian Bus. L.J. 391 (1996).

60. *Lefebvre (Syndic de); Tremblay (Syndic de)*, [2004] 3 S.C.R. 326, 2004 SCC 63; *Ouellet (Syndic de)*, [2004] 3 S.C.R. 348, 2004 SCC 64.

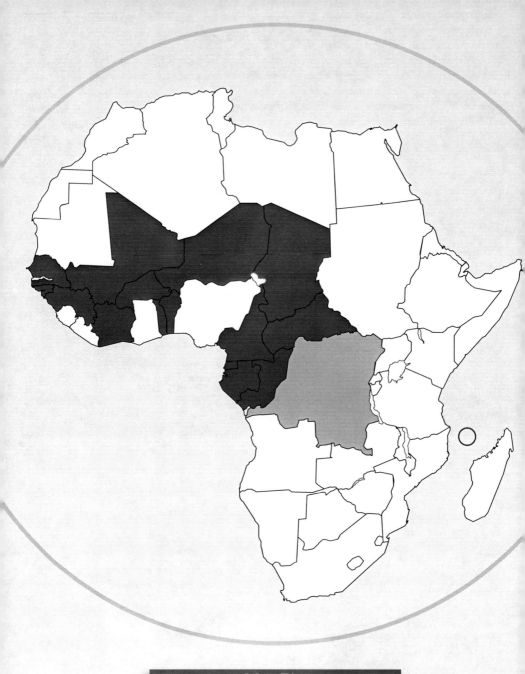

Map Five - OHADA Members

IV. GOVERNMENTAL TREND TOWARDS CHOICE

How the legal systems of the various jurisdictions here examined address the issue of language with relevance to transnational commercial and financial deals is profoundly conditioned by the differing realities and history of the diffusion of languages within them. Communities confront language and the challenge of communication through many models, the simplest being that everyone speaks, or at least should speak, one language. For example, the historical development of states such as France (the *Académie Française* having been founded in 1635) and Italy (following creation of the Italian state in the 1860's) was associated with sustained effort to define and diffuse one language as the unifying national language, even though other languages predominated in large parts of the relevant population. Other models of linguistic community include: (i) for a common language to be shared across populations speaking other languages (the situation in many of the countries here considered where French or Portuguese serves as a *lingua franca, i.e.* the common language among populations who speak other languages); (ii) for the language of one part of a community to dominate the languages of others (something which Québec has been concerned to resist in Canada); (iii) for the bulk of the community to be multilingual (Luxembourg being an example of one such jurisdiction); (iv) for various regions or populations to enjoy specific rights of linguistic autonomy (for example, the autonomous communities of Spain and the cantons of Switzerland); and, (v) for governmental services to be provided in the language of choice of the citizen (for example, the autonomous community of Catalonia in Spain as between *Catalán* and Spanish). These models and permutations and gradations of them are illustrated in the various jurisdictions examined below.

The general contemporary tendency throughout the various jurisdictions, particularly in reference to commercial and financial transactional dealings, is to allow parties to conduct business in whatever language they mutually prefer. From the perspective of the parties to a specific transaction, only when a transaction requires some recourse to governmental authority does the issue of conformity to governmental strictures as to language become germane. And, as a practical matter, the leverage of governmental authorities to regulate the language in which parties to commercial and financial transactions conduct their business derives principally from the instances in which one or more of the parties must interact with governmental authorities as part of making and enforcing the deal.

The various jurisdictions considered diverge in their approach as to "official" language, that is, the language to be employed in communications with governmental authorities. As will be described, some recognize just one official language, for example, Argentina (Spanish), Brazil (Portuguese) and France (French). Others, in recognition of some form of federalism and of heterogeneous linguistic realities of their populations, accept in some degree multiple languages. Examples are the francophone jurisdictions other than France (Belgium, where French, Flemish and German are recognized; Canada, where French and English are recognized), the Portuguese-speaking jurisdictions other than Brazil and Portugal (in all of which the first language of a majority of the population is a language other than Portuguese), and Spanish-speaking countries such as Mexico (according limited recognition of its autochthonous languages other than Spanish) and Spain (according recognition to the "other languages of Spain" in its autonomous communities, for example, *Catalán*).

Within the jurisdictions here considered, the promotion, and more specifically the imposition in dealings with governmental authorities, of "official" languages for use in transnational commercial and financial deals occurs across a spectrum of intensity. Representative of the extreme end of the spectrum is the current of French politics which fought, ultimately without success, to mandate that contracts not concluded in French, be unenforceable in France. Less extreme approaches that are broadly adopted, including in France itself as to transnational commercial and financial contracts, include mandating that: (i) contracts be translated as a condition to their enforcement through national court proceedings; (ii) governmental entities will only contract in an official language; and, (iii) governmental services relevant to a transnational commercial or financial contract must be rendered in an official language. An example of the latter kind of stricture to be discussed is the extent of requirements for use of an official language in connection with satisfaction of the formalities of registration of a security interest as a necessary prerequisite, in connection with a loan, for a creditor to establish a priority claim to collateral that remains in the possession of the debtor.

In practice, as to the use of language in transnational commercial and financial deals, the various jurisdictions considered have reached a common result, albeit from conceptual frameworks which diverge significantly in the general approach to language. In general, they allow transnational commercial and financial business to be conducted and documented in the language of the parties' choice. However, they impose burdens of translation of varying rigor as a condition of the enforcement of such deals. Further, to benefit from governmental services often essential to transnational commercial and financial deals, for example, the registrations that may be necessary in some jurisdictions to create security interests as well as the registrations to assure priority of such interests over the claims of other creditors, they impose requirements of varying scope and stringency that involve the use of an officially-sanctioned language.

A. Status of language

1. French

The approach to the status of French in (i) France, (ii) Canada, (iii) Luxembourg, (iv) Belgium and Switzerland, and (v) Francophone sub-Saharan Africa, presents distinct models. The present investigation does not consider other countries where French has status as an official language, such as Burundi, Djibouti, Haiti, Lebanon, Madagascar, Rwanda, Seychelles and Vanuatu, and yet other countries where French is widely-used, but not recognized as an official language, for example, the North African countries of Algeria, Morocco, and Tunisia.

Although a century ago French was hailed by some as a potentially universal language of public international law and diplomacy,[61] some French-speaking jurisdictions in recent decades have at times been motivated to adopt legislation not only to encourage, but also to mandate use of French in specified contexts even outside of interactions with governmental authorities. These efforts have gone beyond mandating use of a language to ensure that monolingual consumers understand the content of the agreements they make, or that public officials with knowledge only of an official language, who are working with a contract or other deal-related document for procurement, registration or other purposes, are able to know its content. Rather, in France (where French is the sole national official language), Québec (where French is the primary language of about 90% the province's population but spoken as a primary language by just over a fourth of Canadians overall, most of whom are in Québec[62]), and the French-speaking south of Belgium—Wallonia, the political concern underlying governmental requirements relative to language has at times been expressly to promote the use of the French language to the exclusion of other languages. Such concern is distinguished from the less strident approaches of Luxembourg, where French is a second language of most of the population; Switzerland, where the French-speaking cantons have not perceived any threat of a national challenge to the status of their language; and, Francophone sub-Saharan Africa, where the status of French as an official language is premised on its role as the *lingua franca* of heterogeneous populations speaking varied languages, for none of which is French the traditional first language.

a. France

French legislation of 1975 mandated the use of French for transactions and advertising related to provision of goods and services addressed to consumers, employment matters, public signs and services, contracts with public entities, and radio and television programming other than such programming directed to foreigners.[63] It was not vigorously applied. In 1994 as a replacement, France's parliament adopted the so-called Toubon legislation, referred to as the "all-good" legislation in English, as a play on the translation of the phonetic pronunciation of the surname of Jacques Toubon, the French minister of culture and *"francophonie"*, who sponsored it.[64] The 1994 text, as initially adopted by the French parliament, sought broadly to impose the use of French in private dealings. Arguably, it would have conditioned the validity of transnational commercial and financial contracts on use of French.

The 1994 law was founded on Article 2 of the French constitution which proclaims: "The Language of the Republic is French." This text of Article 2 was added to the constitution in 1992 in conjunction with a further constitutional amendment to implement a then new European Community requirement that immigrants from elsewhere in the European Community were to be allowed to vote in a Member State's local elections. For France, this meant that citizens of other Community Member States resident in France were required to be allowed to vote in local French elections.[65] To achieve this result, the constitution was accordingly amended. The purpose of introducing specification of the national language in the constitution, at the same time as the modification to allow citizens of other Member States resident in France to vote in French local elections, appears to have been to underline the continued French character of France, notwithstanding the limited electoral rights extended to immigrants from other Community Member States, for almost all of whom French is not the first language.

The adoption of the 1994 statute created a renewed opportunity for constitutional challenge to the validity of language regulation under the French constitution. France's system for judicial review of the constitutionality of laws has been limited in comparison to the systems of such countries as the United States, Germany, Italy and Spain. France has had no provision for decentralized judicial review of the constitutionality of laws on the United States' model, nor has it had a constitutional court on the model of such courts elsewhere. Unlike France, the United States allows any judge at any time in the context of a dispute to determine the constitutionality of a law. Unlike France, countries such as Germany, Italy and Spain, as part of their transition from authoritarian to democratic governance, allow any judge, at any time in the context of a dispute, the power to refer a question of the constitutionality of a law to a central national constitutional court for a binding determination that has general effect.

The only entity in the French system with the power to review the constitutionality of acts of parliament is the *Conseil Constitutionnel* (Constitutional Council). The limitation of the French system of judicial review of the constitutionality of laws has been that it afforded the possibility of constitutional review only within a brief time following Parliament's adoption of a law. Absent invocation of review by the *Conseil Constitutionnel* within a limited window of time following adoption of legislation, there has been no mechanism provided for any court, including the *Conseil Constitutionnel* itself, to set aside the legislation on constitutional grounds. Only following the pending implementation of a 2008 amendment of the French Constitution in the sense that any court can, through the filter of the *Cour de Cassation* if such a court is an ordinary court, and through the filter of the *Conseil d'Etat* if the court is an administrative court, pose a question for consideration by the *Conseil Constitutionnel*, will this limitation be surpassed.[66]

In essence, the 1958 Constitution allowed prior to this amendment only any of the President, the Prime Minister, the president of either house of parliament, or sixty members of either house, to have an opportunity at the end of the legislative process to ask the *Conseil Constitutionnel* to block all or part of a law from taking effect on grounds of unconstitutionality.[67] If none of such actors chose to invoke the *Conseil Constitutionnel*'s review, there was no mechanism for judicial review of the measure on constitutional grounds. Even as the *Conseil Constitutionnel* becomes accessible to address constitutional issues even well after conclusion of the legislative process, the French diffidence to judicial resolution of constitutional disputes will continue to be reflected in the screening role assigned to its supreme ordinary and administrative courts, a filter not present in the many countries that have adopted the system of constitutional review through a centralized court.

Prior to the 1994 Toubon statute taking definitive effect, a dissatisfied minority of the French parliament, meeting the constitutionally-defined threshold of sixty members to undertake such action, challenged the then new legislation within the brief period allowed following its adoption. The *Conseil Constitutionnel* declared various parts of the law unconstitutional, including as they might have pertained to transnational commercial and financial contracting.[68] It reasoned that human rights relative to freedom of personal and political expression, as recited and recognized in the 1789 French-revolutionary Declaration of the Rights of Man and Citizen incorporated into the French constitution, prohibited the general imposition of a requirement that French be used in private dealings. In a subsequent decision of 1999,[69] the *Conseil Constitutionnel* reasoned on similar grounds that provision for the usage of "regional" languages, for example, Basque, Breton, Corse, and Tahitian, for teaching and administrative formalities, would be constitutionally valid on condition that French remain the official language of the Republic and that, in respect of services provided as public functions, the use of French remain consistently available. However, on other grounds related to the "indivisibility" of the Republic under the constitution as then written, it upheld the constitutional challenge to France's ratification of the European Charter for Regional or Minority Languages. In the continued absence of such ratification, the rights pursuant to the treaty relative to use of "regional" languages do not apply in France.

Although the *Conseil Constitutionnel* found the 1994 legislation, as initially adopted, to impose unconstitutionally on private rights of expression, the *Conseil Constitutionnel's* reasoning permits the requirement that French be employed: (i) for protection of employees and consumers; (ii) by the government in connection with its work; and, (iii) in connection with the provision of public services. Hence, the law may require that governmental entities employ French for the commercial and financial contracts to which they are party. The law as now in force accordingly mandates that contracts with governmental entities be in French, with the proviso that if foreigners are among the contracting parties, one or more versions of the contract may be established with equal validity in a foreign language. It also exempts from the French-language requirement contracts by French governmental entities that are to be performed entirely outside France.

Various civil and criminal actions, by public prosecutors and by associations for the defense of the French language officially granted standing for such purpose, have been brought in application of the parts of the law not invalidated by the *Conseil Constitutionnel*.[70] Such actions have occasionally been clamorous. An example is the consumer protection action by an association "for the defense of the French language" against the American university program

(Georgia Tech Lorraine), which posted information on the internet only in English about its study-abroad program in France. The action was ultimately dismissed on procedural grounds.

However, the European Union provision that governmental measures having an effect equivalent to a quantitative restriction on trade are void, unless justified by a public policy which is not "a means of arbitrary discrimination or a disguised restriction on trade", constrains the vitality of actions seeking application of the French law favoring use of French in commercial transactions.[71] In a case arising from a question raised by a French court of first instance considering an enforcement action against a retailer for selling Coca-Cola without French-language labeling, the European Court of Justice clarified in 2000 that European law required that the French legislation on use of language be set aside in favor of the pertinent European treaty provision prohibiting measures having an effective equivalent to quantitative restrictions on trade. The European Court of Justice held that:

> "Article 30 of the [European Community] Treaty and Article 14 of Directive 79/112 preclude a national provision from requiring the use of a specific language for the labelling of foodstuffs, without allowing for the possibility for another language easily understood by purchasers to be used or for the purchaser to be informed by other means."[72]

b. Belgium

Belgium, since joining the direct predecessors of the European Union in the 1950's as a founding Member State, has followed a path of transition from a unitary state to a federal state organized along the lines of the distribution of language use. Belgium's official languages are Flemish, French and German. Flemish is a variant of Dutch. About 60 percent of Belgium's population is in its Flemish area, 10 percent in the bilingual capital of Brussels, and most of the balance in the French-speaking Wallonia area, with a small German-speaking community near the German border.[73] Belgium may continue even further on the path of devolution away from a unitary state, splitting into independent Flemish- and French-speaking entities that remain within the umbrella of the European Union.[74]

At the moment, Belgium's constitution defines it as a federal state, in contrast to a unitary state like France. The Belgian constitution defines Flemish, French and German communities as distinct entities, and paralleled by the definition of the Flemish, Walloon and Brussels regions, corresponding respectively to predominantly Flemish- and French-speaking regions, with Brussels being officially bilingual. Municipalities are assigned to one of four linguistic regions: Dutch, French, German, or the bilingual Dutch and French region of Brussels.

Article 30 of the Belgian constitution provides:

> "The usage of languages used in Belgium is optional; it can only be regulated by law, and only for acts of the public authority and for judicial matters."

Thus, the Belgian constitution offers express basis for the result that transnational commercial and financial contracts, at least those not with Belgian governmental entities, are not subject to regulation as to language.

Flemish is currently the primary language of more Belgians than is French. As French is not the dominant, and certainly not in any current sense the "unifying" language of Belgium as it might be asserted to be relative to France, the *laissez-faire* approach of the Belgian constitution varies considerably from the French constitutional declaration of French as part of the French Republican identity. To be clear, in each of France and Belgium, the language of commercial and financial dealing with governmental entities is regulated, and the language of transnational commercial and financial contracts is otherwise unregulated, except to the extent that translation is necessary in connection with judicial enforcement or that some other interaction with governmental authority, such as the conveyance of an interest in real property through a notary, is required. The difference is that Belgium's constitution expressly adopts an open approach to languages, which includes the freedom to undertake transnational commercial and financial contracts in any language; whereas, France reached this outcome through judicial interpretation by the *Conseil Constitutionnel* of the French Constitution and its roots in the 1789 Declaration of the Rights of Man and Citizen. The foundation of the French outcome on an express consideration of human rights, as opposed to a specifically worded constitutional provision, may contribute to the resonance of the French outcome in other legal systems, including the evolving law of the European Union and pursuant to the European Convention on Human Rights, to be discussed.

c. *Switzerland*

The Swiss approach to language has similarities to that of Belgium. The Swiss constitution, effective in 2000, recognizes four national languages—French, German, Italian, and Romansh. It further guarantees a personal freedom of language that is not limited by reference to the four national languages,[75] although there is no right provided to interact with governmental authorities in other than official languages. Switzerland is comprised of twenty-six cantons, the states which form its confederation. In some cantons one of German or French is the official language. There are other cantons where both German and French are official languages, plus one Italian-speaking canton, and another where German, Italian and Romansh are official languages. Switzerland has undertaken to nurture Romansh and Italian as "less widely used official languages" entitled to support in conformity with Switzerland's ratification of the European Charter for Regional or Minority Languages.

d. Luxembourg

Luxembourg is one of Europe's smallest countries, and with a population under 500,000, much smaller than either Belgium (population slightly over 10,000,000) or Switzerland (under 8,000,000). It presents another linguistic reality, that of multi-lingualism of essentially the entire population. A law of February 24, 1984 defines the national language as Luxembourgeois (*Letzeburgesch*), a Germanic language, in recognition of the fact that it is the first language of virtually the entire population.[76] However, it provides that French is the language of legislation, reflecting the historical reality of how its administration and governance were handled. Consistent with the foundation of its economy on financial services and with its linguistic mélange of Luxembourgeois, French and German, Luxembourg does not attempt to regulate the language of commercial and financial contracts, and accepts each of Luxembourgeois, French and German for administrative and judicial matters.

e. Canada

Canada has been labeled a laboratory for legislative drafting across civil and common law legal systems for several reasons.[77] Most obviously, it is a country that includes significant populations of English-speakers and of French-speakers. Accordingly, from the inception of Canadian federal legislation, there has been a concern that such federal legislation be understood by all Canadians, regardless of whether English or French is the primary language. However, what makes Canada such an interesting laboratory is not just the presence of two predominant languages, but also Canada's division into its civil law province of Québec and its English-speaking common law provinces. The province of Québec, with almost a quarter of Canada's population, is ninety percent French-speaking, although it contains an English-speaking minority that traces its roots back to the origins of Canada. Québec's law is based on civil law traditions distinct from the

English common law roots of the law in the predominantly English-speaking parts of Canada. In addition, Canada contains the unique province of New Brunswick, with a common law legal system, but constitutionally-guaranteed a bilingual English and French society.

English and French are co-equal languages of the Canadian federal government, and the status of French varies by province. The Canadian Charter of Rights and Freedoms,[78] adopted in 1982 in connection with the definitive devolution of constitutional authority for Canada from the United Kingdom to Canada itself, declares English and French the official languages of Canada, and generally promotes bilingualism and multilingualism. The Interpretation Act, a federal statute as amended effective 2001, mandates that federal law be interpreted in light of a province's common or civil law system when the federal law's application depends upon elements of provincial law, such as provincial law relating to property and civil matters.[79] Moreover, from Canada's 1867 constitution,[80] federal legislation and the provincial legislation of Québec have been required to be prepared in equally authoritative English and French texts. In addition to the particular treatment of Québec, there are constitutional guarantees of the equal status of the English- and French-speaking communities in the province of New Brunswick[81] and of the right to use English and French in the parliament and the courts of the province of Manitoba.[82] Although less than 5% of Manitoba's population speaks French as a first language, and unsurprisingly most of its statutes were enacted only in English, Canada's Supreme Court declared them unconstitutional in a 1985 decision, but stayed the effectiveness of its ruling for enough time to allow them to be re-enacted in French as well as in English.[83]

In 1977 Québec adopted the "Charter of the French Language", which declares French to be the province's official language.[84] Although touching such topics as the use of French in commercial signs, the language of instruction in public schools and the right of employees to work in French, it does not directly address the language of transnational commercial and financial contracts. Notwithstanding the historical divisions in Canadian society between French and English speakers, it imposes no restriction on the language of transnational commercial and financial contracts. More recently, in 1991 Québec adopted a new Civil Code, effective 1994, to replace its 1865 civil code.[85] Although the new Civil Code was adopted in English and French as mandated by the Canadian Constitution, part of the intent in its adoption was to renew the civil law character of Québec contract and property law. Over time, such content was felt to have been eroded through its interpretation on appeal, by first the Privy Council in London and later Canada's Supreme Court, under common law techniques.[86] The new Civil Code does not impose restrictions as to use of language. However, by re-invigorating civil law concepts of contract and property law, it offers a firmer ground for the conduct of business, including transnational business, in French.

Nonetheless, Québec law and in particular the decisions of its courts remain subject to appeal to the Supreme Court of Canada.[87] The tradition concerning that Court is that three of its nine judges hail from Québec, and accordingly they can be expected to bring a civil law perspective to all of its work. Nonetheless, they are outnumbered by the six judges of the court traditionally chosen from the provinces that work in the common law tradition.[88] Moreover, given the general correspondence of those judges to English-speaking Canada, the fact of their constitution of the majority of the Court tilts its language orientation in the direction of English.

Since the British victory over the French forces on the Plains of Abraham just outside of the city of Québec in 1759, Québec has been a predominantly French-speaking island of population immersed in otherwise largely English-speaking Canada. The desire for interaction with the neighboring United States, for commercial reasons and as a lever against any perceived domination by

English-speaking Canada, may have encouraged that efforts to promote the use of French be focused on local matters and away from transnational commercial and financial contracts. As an example of Québec's openness to use of English in such dealings, the provincially-owned electric utility, HydroQuébec, exports significant quantities of electricity to the northeastern United States, working in English, including through its wholly-owned subsidiary HQ Energy Services (U.S.), licensed as a power marketer in the U.S. wholesale market.

f. Sub-Saharan francophone countries/Organisation pour l'Harmonisation en Afrique du Droit des Affaires (OHADA – Organization for the Harmonization in Africa of Business Law)

The sub-Saharan francophone countries share the reality of populations divided among multiple autochthonous languages, for whom French is the common language. By treaty among themselves, sixteen predominantly francophone sub-Saharan states have created the *Organisation pour l'Harmonisation en Afrique du Droit des Affaires* ("OHADA" – Organization for the Harmonization in Africa of Business Law).[89] Its constituent states have delegated legislative power as to commercial and financial law to a treaty-established international process. They have further established an international judicial mechanism to promote the application of such law.

Current members of OHADA are: Benin, Burkina Faso, Cameroon, Central African Republic, Comoros, Congo, Ivory Coast, Gabon, Guinea, Guinea-Bissau,[90] Equatorial Guinea, Mali, Niger, Senegal, Chad, and Togo, with membership of the Democratic Republic of the Congo pending. The Democratic Republic of the Congo's accession to OHADA would be a significant expansion. It is the second most populous country where French is an official language, with a population just under that of France itself.

OHADA's institutions include a Council of Ministers comprised of the finance and justice ministers of each participating state, and the "Common Court of Justice and Arbitration," located in Abidjan, Ivory Coast. The approval of both institutions, unanimous in the case of the Council of Ministers, is required prior to the adoption of a "Uniform Act." Uniform Acts are "directly applicable and obligatory . . . notwithstanding any contrary provision of internal law, prior or subsequent".[91] National courts may refer questions arising in the context of litigation before them to the Common Court of Justice for binding answers, and the Common Court of Justice is a court of last instance for resolution of disputes turning on "Uniform Acts."[92] The association for the *Unification du droit en Afrique* (UNIDA), an association of 100 plus enterprises, supports OHADA's work.

OHADA's official language was initially French.[93] An amendment and restatement of the OHADA Treaty, signed by the heads of state and government of the OHADA member states on October 17, 2008 in Québec, would amend the original status of French as the official language to establish that the working languages of OHADA are French, English, Spanish (the one African country for which Spanish is an official language being Equatorial Guinea) and Portuguese. The proposed restated treaty provision that designates these working languages would continue to privilege French, providing:

> "Before translation into the other languages, the documents already published in French produce their effects. In case of divergence among the different translations, the French version controls."[94]

Although there is no prohibition against contracting and conducting business in other languages, the OHADA framework of French-language legislation and of institutions that work in French, notably its court, creates a strong incentive to conduct business in French. The designation of additional working languages does not fundamentally change these incentives. Any significant expansion of OHADA beyond its current membership of francophone, civil law countries to Africa's common law, English-speaking states and further to states with official languages that are neither English nor French, would likely require its investment of the resources to operate at least in some measure in the style of the European Union, that is, with more than one official language and an infrastructure of qualified translation. The proposed treaty amendments establish a potential legal basis for movement in this direction, but by no means assure it.

The OHADA membership of each of Cameroon and of Guinea-Bissau has presented an issue relative to language that the proposed treaty amendment is meant in part to palliate. As to Cameroon, there is a conflict between Cameroon's constitution and the OHADA treaty provision of French as OHADA's sole official language. Cameroon's constitution includes assurances of the status of English and French as official languages of equal status. The incompatibility of OHADA's use of French as its sole official language with protection of those in Cameroon who rely upon the national Constitutional guarantee of the status of English is a conundrum whose resolution is rendered more difficult by Cameroon's lack of an applicable mechanism of judicial constitutional review. That is, there is no provision in Cameroon law by which a court could declare Cameroon's ratification of the OHADA treaty unconstitutional or mandate some mechanism of translation at the national level. Were either instance a prospect, it would provide a basis to provoke a negotiated resolution of the issue with OHADA's other member states.[95] Guinea-Bissau presents an altogether different issue, namely that its legal system and governmental institutions nominally function in Portuguese, notwithstanding the presence of a significant immigration of French-speakers. The desires of each of Cameroon and Guinea-Bissau to participate in OHADA suggest that their courts will confront the issue of translation as a practical matter, rather than seek a conceptual solution of constitutional magnitude at the national level. The proposed treaty revision's designation of English and Portuguese as working languages of OHADA would appear to lessen the concerns of constitutional compatibility on linguistic grounds relative to each of Cameroon and of Guinea-Bissau.

Part of the measure of the success of OHADA is its adoption of a series of Uniform Acts spanning a significant range of subject matter pertinent to transnational commercial and financial deals. Its Uniform Acts now in force, together with the year of their adoption, concern: (i) general commercial law (1997); (ii) commercial companies (1997); (iii) surety law (1997); (iv) simplified collection procedures (1998); (v) insolvency (1998); (vi) arbitration (2000); (vii) corporate accounting standards (2000); and (viii) contracts for the carriage of goods by road (2003).[96]

OHADA is considering promulgation of a Uniform Act on contract law, based on the International Organization for the Unification of Private International Law ("UNIDROIT") PRINCIPLES OF INTERNATIONAL COMMERCIAL CONTRACTS.[97] At OHADA's request, UNIDROIT has prepared a draft Uniform Act on contract law, available on UNIDROIT's web site, together with explanatory commentary, under the leadership of Marcel Fontaine, a Belgian law professor.[98] At the November 2007 colloquium to consider the proposed Uniform Act on contract law, held in Ouagadougou, capital of OHADA member state Burkina Faso, the experts present were by no means limited to those from French-speaking jurisdictions. Notably, they included experts from common law jurisdictions and from China, a commercial partner of growing importance in Africa. However, financial support for the colloquium came from Luxembourg and Switzerland, and partnering organizations included Belgian, Canadian and Swiss-based institutions.[99] The association of francophone experts from leading commercial jurisdictions is an obvious wise investment of each of OHADA and UNIDROIT. The association of such experts also illustrates the incidental benefit of OHADA to *la francophonie* in a broader sense, namely the sophisticated use of French through its application to the establishment of a state-of-the-art framework for contract law in multiple countries. Such application contributes to the further consolidation and evolution of French as a living language in the space of cross-border commerce.

OHADA's first decade of operation receives generally positive reviews. OHADA's limitations are identified as: (i) lack of provision for how OHADA relates to membership of its constituent states in other supranational organizations; (ii) absence of a mechanism for its constituent states to give full faith and credit to judgments of the courts of other constituent states; and, (iii) the provision for a national Court of Cassation only to defer a matter entirely to the OHADA Common Court of Justice rather than enjoy the option to refer a question of OHADA law to the Common Court of Justice for a preliminary ruling, in the style of the preliminary reference procedure contemplated in connection with the European Union's Court of Justice. These limitations, however, are tied mainly to the recognition by the drafters of the OHADA treaty of institutional and normative challenges beyond the bounds of commercial and financial law. Accordingly, they reflect the deliberately measured ambition of the design of the OHADA framework; namely, so as not to delay its launch, that it work within, and with recognition of, those continuing challenges.[100]

2. *Italian*

Although Italy's predominant language is now Italian, its first parliamentary debates when it emerged as a unified country in the 1860's were conducted in French, as the fraction of the population that spoke the variant of Tuscan that emerged as modern Italian was then extremely limited. At Italy's unification, 10 to 12 percent of the population is estimated to have been Italian-speaking, with 75 percent illiteracy, accentuated in the south.[101] Through World War II, an important dimension of construction of the Italian state was the promotion and diffusion of standard Italian. The Italian constitution of 1948, adopted in reaction to the debacle of fascism and its association with authoritarianism and centralization, introduces a different emphasis, by providing that the Italian Republic is to protect linguistic minorities.[102] The charters of the special statute regions created in conjunction with the 1948 constitution provide specific rights in respect of language, for example, for German speakers in Trentino-Alto Adige/Südtirol and for French in Valle d'Aosta.[103] Relatively recent national legislation in implementation of the constitutional provision for protection of linguistic minorities focuses on education and interactions with the public administration. It provides for protection of the language and culture of members of Italy's linguistic minorities who speak Albanian, *Catalán*, Croatian, French, Friulian, German, Greek, Ladino, Occitan, *Provençal*, Sardinian and Slovenian.[104] Notwithstanding protections relative to these languages and the lack of any express restrictions on the parties' choice of languages in transnational commercial and financial matters, interactions with Italian governmental authorities and services relative to such matters generally require use of Italian.

3. *Portuguese—Comunidade dos Países de Língua Portuguesa (CPLP – Community of Portuguese Language Countries)*

Portuguese is the world's sixth most-spoken language, and the language of just over half of South America's population. Portuguese-speaking countries promote solidarity among themselves through such measures as preferential paths to citizenship for immigrants from Portuguese-speaking countries and communities[105] and the institution of the *Comunidade dos Países de Língua Portuguesa* ("CPLP" – Community of Portuguese Language Countries).[106]

Founded in 1996, the CPLP is comprised of: (i) Brazil and Portugal, for which Portuguese is the first language of virtually everyone; (ii) five African states (Angola, Cape Verde, Guinea-

Bissau, Mozambique, and São Tomé and Príncipe), for each of which Portuguese is the first language of a minority of the population and the national *lingua franca*; and, (iii) East Timor, recently independent of Indonesia and for which *Tétum* is the lingua franca.[107] East Timor's constitution declares *Tétum* and Portuguese to be official languages of the country, while mandating that the other "national languages" be recognized and developed by the State.[108] Its constitution further provides that "Indonesian and English are working languages in use in the public administration with parity to the official languages, in so far as necessary."[109] Macao, a special administrative region of China, retains recognition of the use of Portuguese as an official language, together with Chinese.[110] It is not a formal member of the CPLP, on the premise that such membership is so far limited to states, and Macao is not a state.

The Portuguese-speaking jurisdictions other than Brazil and Portugal were generally colonies of Portugal at least through Portugal's stepping away from all of its overseas territories following the 1974 overthrow in Portugal of the remnants of the Salazar dictatorship regime. The largest of the former Portuguese colonies—Angola, Mozambique and East Timor, each suffered conflict which until recently prevented focus on law reform and development of vibrant legal institutions.[111] Angola in particular is emerging as a significant oil exporter, a development which increases the opportunities and potential benefits of engagement in law reform relative to cross-border investments.

Unlike the case of its francophone African counterpart of OHADA, the CPLP's constitutive documents do not contemplate a direct role for it in adopting supranational legislation and contributing to judicial resolution of disputes.[112] CPLP was created by a Declaration of the Heads of State and Government of its member states of July 17, 1996, subsequently ratified by each state.[113] CPLP's institutions are a Conference of Heads of State and Government, a Council of Ministers comprised of the member states' foreign ministers, a Committee of Permanent Coordination, and an Executive Secretariat, headquartered in Lisbon. Its institutions include neither a formal legislative body nor a court. CPLP's purposes include: (i) political and diplomatic coordination of its member states, (ii) cooperation in economic, social, cultural, legal and scientific and technological matters, and (iii) promotion and diffusion of the Portuguese language. In 2002 the CPLP created the *Instituto Internacional de Língua Portuguesa* ("IILP", International Institute of Portuguese Language), with headquarters in Cabo Verde, to further its language goals.[114]

The CPLP is a vessel, as yet largely unfilled, through which dual goals of law reform and promotion of Portuguese language might be pursued. There does not appear to be any imminent likelihood of reforms to endow it with legislative and judicial institutions on the models of those of the European Union and of OHADA. Language promotion through law reform could, however, easily be considered within the CPLP's purposes, including those of also promoting coordination and cooperation among its participating states. In the absence of its being fortified with legislative tools and law-making institutions like those of the European Union and of OHADA, the approaches of restatements, expert association working groups and model laws to be discussed below in the concluding portion of this investigation,[115] appear to offer the best opportunity of aligning the CPLP's goal of language promotion with law reform to support transnational commerce and finance.

a. Macao

Of all the Portuguese-speaking jurisdictions, Macao distinguishes itself for its commercial and financial law. This is so notwithstanding its population of only about 500,000—of whom only a tiny fraction are Portuguese-speakers. Moreover, even that fraction is outweighed by the number of English speakers. Macao's 2006 census reports total population of 492,291, of whom 2,838 are fluent in Portuguese, and 29,135 in English, with the predominant language spoken being Cantonese.[116]

Macao stands out for its recent adoption of modern commercial law drafted in Portuguese and the intensity of inbound investment, supported by sophisticated secured finance, all associated with the development of casino and resort infrastructure.[117] The key collateral in support of the secured lending in course during recent years consists of rights to use of land (a scarce resource given Macao's limited territory) and concessions to operate casinos. With a "two systems—one country" status parallel to that of Hong Kong, Macao, shortly following its 1987 confirmation as a special administrative region of China, adopted, in Chinese and Portuguese texts, modern legislation drafted with the support of leading Portuguese jurists.[118] To further facilitate the investment activity, the recently crafted Commercial Code has been "unofficially" translated into English at the initiative of the Macao government.[119] Although Macao is not a part of the CPLP, its contemporary Portuguese-language commercial and financial law is a valuable resource for law reform efforts within the framework of the CPLP. It is an example of rapid adoption of a new legal framework to support international commercial and financial deals in the face of a significant influx of investments, as well as of support by Portugal for the maintenance of Macao's Portuguese heritage through its assistance in the drafting of Macao's modern Portuguese-language Commercial Code.

b. *Brazil and Portugal*

Both Brazil—the most populous Portuguese-speaking country,[120] and Portugal,[121] constitutionally declare Portuguese to be their national language, and they each mandate that Portuguese be used for consumer transactions.[122] Nonetheless, consistent with the independent development of their legal systems following Brazil's 1822 succession from Portugal and Portugal's present-day membership in the European Union, their approaches to the primacy of use of Portuguese differ.

Three provisions of Portugal's law, adopted in decidedly different historical moments, and in response to different considerations, express a policy of openness to language. Adopted after the 1974 *coup d'état* which ended the prolonged authoritarian regime in Portugal, Portugal's constitution provides:

> "Everyone shall possess the right to freely express and publicize his thoughts in words, images or by any other means, as well as the right to inform others, inform himself and be informed without hindrance or discrimination."[123]

Anticipating the permissive approach of the present Portuguese constitution with respect to freedom of expression generally, Portugal's *Código Comercial* of 1888, that governs dealings between merchants and commercial acts, took a similarly expansive approach in the commercial sphere. Consonant with Portugal's legacy of international trade on a global scale, it provides that commercial documents are valid without regard to the language in which they are prepared.[124] Further in the spirit of liberality as to language, and subsequent to Portugal's membership in the European Community, Portugal's *Código Civil*, as revised in 2003, provides that documents authenticated or concluded in a foreign country in conformity with the law of such a country have the same probative value in Portugal as in such country.[125]

Brazil burdens those who would use a language other than Portuguese for a transnational commercial or financial deal to a greater degree than Portugal. This may arise from Brazil's size and consequent insularity relative to Portugal, which also is propelled to linguistic openness by its membership in the European Union.

Brazil's Civil Code, as federal legislation applicable throughout Brazil, requires translation into Portuguese of foreign language documents as a condition of their enforcement in Brazil.[126] Likewise, for foreign documents to have effects relative to third parties, including both private documents, for example a contract between two companies, and public documents, for example a governmental concession, they must be filed in the *Registro de Títulos e Documentos*, together with a due translation.[127] Moreover public writings, which Brazilian Civil Code article 215 defines as endowed with "public trust, making full proof", must be prepared in the "national language", namely Portuguese.[128] Further Brazilian legislation on registration of documents requires that the translation of foreign language contracts be registered with a notary as a prerequisite to their enforcement in the courts.[129] Because these requirements express a public policy of enabling the legal system to function in Portuguese, contract parties have no ability, as a matter of Brazilian law, to waive them.

However, none of these provisions of Brazilian law prohibits enforcement of a choice of governing language as other than Portuguese or of an associated choice of governing law from a non-Portuguese-speaking jurisdiction. By their literal terms, they simply mandate that a document written in a language other than Portuguese be translated into Portuguese as a condition of enforcement. In so doing, they recognize the existence and validity of documents written in a foreign language. Indeed, the Brazilian Civil Code's express affirmation of parties' freedom to contract anything that is licit,[130] includes by implication the freedom to make an agreement written in a foreign language. The Civil Code further supports such freedom by providing that the substance of a party's declaration of intent weighs more than "literal sense of the language."[131]

A panel of Brazil's Supreme Court addressed the issue of enforceability of a foreign language contract in a 2004 judgment, to resolve fifteen years of contention between two shipping companies over a contract to move containers from Montreal to Rotterdam and then to Brazil's port of Santos, which contract was not written in Portuguese. The court pragmatically addressed the case so as not to allow the issue of language used for the contract to impede disposition of the dispute. That the goods entrusted to the defendant shipper were a total loss, was not contested. Minister Barros Monteiro, the Brazilian Supreme Court justice whose view prevailed, had little sympathy for the defendant's claim that the contract should be unenforceable against it through a Brazilian court because the contract was not written in Portuguese.

Echoing the view of the United States federal judge as to the burden of contract knowledge to be imposed on the sophisticated English-speaking manager in the *Gaskin* case, who claimed ignorance of the content of the German language contract that he had signed,[132] the Brazilian justice wrote: "Once one is party in the contract, it is to be presumed that it has broad and total knowledge of its clauses," and found no basis in Brazilian federal law for the proposition that a non-Portuguese language contract was unenforceable.[133] The decision went even further, saying that there was no need to translate the documents since the parties had complete knowledge of their meaning and had no reason to question or negate their validity. The decision applied the maxim *"pas de nullité sans grief"*, in essence meaning "no nullity without injury", to conclude that the failure to provide the Brazilian courts the original contract and the relevant translation was of no consequence to the resolution of the dispute.

The outcome of the case illustrates the capacity of the Brazilian court system to resolve a case without ultimately tripping over the procedural requirements relative to enforcement of a contract not written in Portuguese. Nonetheless, a party considering the length of the instant dispute until its final resolution in the Brazilian judicial system by the Supreme Court, might well choose, if it believes that enforcement of the contract will be sought in

Brazil, simply to contract in Portuguese or to avail itself of the arbitration option to be discussed below.

4. Spanish

Countries where Spanish is an official language include Spain in Europe, eighteen countries in Latin America, and Equatorial Guinea in Africa. Spanish is also spoken by significant portions of the population in various parts of the United States, including Puerto Rico where it is the first language of almost everyone and has official status, and states such as Arizona, California, New Mexico and Texas which were once part of Mexico, as well as Florida, Illinois, New Jersey and New York, all of which include Spanish-speaking communities of diverse origins in Cuba, the Dominican Republic, El Salvador, Mexico, Puerto Rico and elsewhere in Latin America.

The Real Academia Española of Spain publishes a dictionary of the Spanish language with the stated purpose of maintaining the unity of the Spanish language.[134] It does so in collaboration with members of the Association of Academies of Spanish, comprised of correspondent associations in various jurisdictions in which Spanish is an official language as well in the United States and the Philippines. The internet version of the dictionary is in fact regularly consulted by lawyers of Spanish-speaking jurisdictions as an authoritative source of guidance on Spanish usage.

Argentina, Mexico and Spain are here considered as specific examples of the varying roles of Spanish as an official language. These three countries share the requirements of translation of foreign language documents into Spanish as a condition of their consideration by courts, but treat the topic of "national language" differently. The differences as to national language arise from the presence in Mexico and in Spain, unlike in Argentina, of recognized autochthonous communities for whom Spanish is not the primary language. Thus, each of Mexico and Spain recognize, although in quite distinct ways, some languages other than Spanish as languages that can be used in interactions with courts and other governmental authorities.

Spain's approach to language more fully integrates all concerned into an economic mainstream than does Mexico's, in that Mexico's accommodation of autochthonous languages relative to business matters is limited to civil procedure, without, for example, extension to the creation of priority of security interests in collateral, that under Mexican law to be discussed, is restricted to occurring through dealings before notaries. A key point is that Spain's constitution accepts speakers of "the other Spanish languages", namely the languages other than Spanish that are indigenous to Spain's territory, as equals to those who speak Castilian Spanish, while imposing a duty on all Spaniards to know Castilian Spanish. In contrast, Mexico's constitution addresses speakers of autochthonous languages as members of disadvantaged communities who require special protection. Further, in apparent deference to the maintenance of the cultural autonomy of such communities, it recites no specific expectation that the members of such communities know the national language of Spanish.

a. Argentina

Argentina's constitution does not specify a national language. However, as will be discussed in the analyses below relative to civil procedure and creation of security interests, its legislation clearly recognizes Spanish as its national language and requires or presupposes its use in dealings with governmental authorities.[135]

b. Mexico

Mexico's constitution includes relatively recent provisions, added in 2001, that address the indigenous communities which comprise about ten percent of its population.[136] The fraction of

Mexico's population that maintains autochthonous languages and cultures has declined in the centuries following the arrival of Cortés. However, throughout Mexico's history under Spanish rule and as an independent country, the questions of what rights and what law pertains to that population have been given diverse answers predominantly as a function of the waxing and waning of conflicting premises of either assimilation of that population or the need to protect its autonomous functioning.[137] The current constitutional provisions introduce an express prohibition of discrimination based on ethnic origin,[138] and recognize the "multicultural composition" of the Nation based on its indigenous peoples at the time of colonization by the Spanish.[139] The scope of application of the provisions addressed to indigenous communities is determined by self-awareness as follows:

"Consciousness of their indigenous identity shall be fundamental criterion to determine to whom are applied the provisions on indigenous peoples."[140]

The focus of the current constitutional provisions for indigenous communities is to preserve them, and within the constraint of national unity, to grant them autonomy. Although the constitutional mandate includes "to preserve and enrich their languages, knowledges, and all the elements that may constitute their culture and identity,"[141] and notwithstanding its provision for initiatives to promote the economic welfare of such communities,[142] Mexico's constitution makes no provision for the use of such languages outside the community of reference, except in regard to judicial proceedings, where the effort is to assure that those members of an indigenous community who do not speak Spanish are not harmed as a consequence.[143] The implementation of this constitutional mandate as to civil procedure is discussed below.[144]

Oaxaca is a state in southern Mexico with a concentration of indigenous communities. Indigenous communities comprise over a third of its population of about 3,500,000.[145] Its constitution is a leading example of the development of state constitutions in Mexico to nurture the cultural identity of diverse communities. The Oaxaca constitution recognizes the indigenous communities comprised of the Amuzgos, Cuicatecos, Chatinos, Chinantecos, Chocholtecos, Chontales, Huaves, Ixcatecos, Mazatecos, Mixes, Mixtecos, Nahuas, Triquis, Zapotecos and Zoques.[146] Its approach is not to integrate such communities, but rather to protect their autonomy. In particular, the Oaxaca constitution provides that:

> "the State recognizes to indigenous towns and communities their forms of social, political and governmental organization, their internal normative systems, the jurisdiction that they have in their territories, the access to the natural resources of their lands and territories, their participation in the educational effort and in the plans and programs of development, their forms of religious and artistic expression, the protection of the same and of their cultural expression and in general for all the elements that comprise their identity."[147]

The state constitution leaves to further implementing norms specification of how such protection is to be assured through a general prohibition of discrimination, as well as the availability of judges and prosecutors in judicial proceedings who speak such languages as their first language, provision of translation when such speakers are unavailable, and in such proceedings provision for "taking into consideration within the framework of the prevailing Law, their [indigenous peoples'] condition, practices and customs."

c. Spain

The post-Franco constitution of Spain proclaims:

> "Castilian is the official Spanish language of the State. All Spaniards have the duty to know it and the right to use it."

It then further provides that "the other Spanish languages", for example, *Catalán, Euskera* (Basque), *Gallego,* and *Valenciano* (closely related to *Catalán*), shall also be official in their respective autonomous communities, the units into which Spain's territory is divided, in accord with their charters.[148]

The reference to "the other Spanish languages" is to other languages rooted in the territory of Spain, not to other variants of Spanish. Although *Catalán, Gallego* and *Valenciano* are romance languages that share common roots with Spanish, they are distinct from it. Basque is not only not a romance language nor even an Indo-European language, but rather a language classified within its own linguistic family, that is, as an "isolate".

A number of the autonomous communities have adopted "linguistic normalization laws" to promote their autochthonous language. The denomination of such laws derives from their adoption in reaction to the suppression during the Franco era of languages other than Castilian Spanish. The most aggressive of the linguistic normalization laws with respect to business transactions is Catalonia's *Ley de Política Lingüística*.[149] It provides that:

(i)   *Catalán* is the preferential language in which to deal with the public, not only by the public administration, but also by businesses offering services to the public;

(ii)   civil and commercial documents are valid for all purposes in either of *Catalán* or Spanish without further translation, meaning, among other implications, that public registries are to work in both languages; and,

(iii)   government-owned companies, as well as companies operating pursuant to a governmental concession or subsidy, are "normally to use *Catalán*", although without detriment to a citizen's right to receive communications in Spanish.[150]

A milestone in establishing the validity of these requirements was the Spanish Constitutional Court's resolution of a challenge to the constitutionality of the predecessor legislation on linguistic normalization adopted by the Catalan autonomous community. That legislation, as does the current legislation, required new civil servants to demonstrate competence in both *Catalán* and Spanish. The Court found the requirement to demonstrate competence in *Catalán* to be reasonably associated with the obligation to demonstrate the necessary capacity to perform the duties involved and therefore constitutionally permissible.[151]

5. *European Union and language rights relative to commercial and financial deals*

The recently adopted Lisbon Treaty[152] amends and updates the constitutive treaties of the European Union, namely the Treaty on European Union and the Treaty establishing the European Community, the latter the direct successor of the 1957 Treaty of Rome that created the precursor European Economic Community. The update provides for a European Union with stronger executive institutions and with legislative processes that include greater roles for the European Parliament as well as greater use of qualified majority voting by the representatives of the Member States in the Council. The Lisbon Treaty's innovations relative to qualified majority voting of the Member States include the definition of new criteria for such qualified majority voting that combine thresholds of numbers of Member States plus voting weights based on their populations. The Lisbon Treaty reforms seek to adapt the European Union's governance procedures to its expansion to its current twenty-seven Member States covering most of Europe, a significant increase beyond its 1950's founding members of France, German and Italy, plus the Benelux countries of Belgium, Luxembourg and the Netherlands.

The Lisbon Treaty reforms, but builds upon, the prior provision of the Treaty on European Union that the European Union was comprised of three distinct so-called pillars. Two of these pillars, devoted to common foreign and security policy, and to police and judicial cooperation in criminal matters, were spheres directly of European Union action. When the European Union took action in these spheres, such action was generally to be premised on consensus of the heads of state and government of the European Union Member States. The European Community was the third pillar of the European Union. The European Community was the oldest of the three pillars, with its roots in the European Economic Community created by the 1957 Treaty of Rome, as well as in the European Coal and Steel Community established by the 1951 Treaty of Paris. In the European Union as updated by the Lisbon Treaty, the three pillars are fused into an undivided European Union, but what was the European Community, with its well-developed institutions and decision-making processes relative to legislative and judicial matters, remains for the present the aspect of the European Union most directly relevant to the topics of transnational commerce and finance and the related role of language.

The European Community long distinguished itself from conventional public international organizations (and what were the other two pillars of the European Union) by the participation of its Member States in its legislative activity on the basis of qualified majority voting of such states, by the applicability of its legislation not only to its Member States, but also to their citizens, and by its European Court of Justice. The European Court of Justice has been noteworthy not only for the key role in the evolution of European Community law played by its jurisprudence proclaiming the supremacy of European Community law over national law. It has also made a significant contribution to the evolution of the law of the European Community (and now the European Union) by enlisting all the judges of Member State courts as its partners in assuring the effective implementation of European Community law. The European Union as updated by the Lisbon Treaty retains these features of the European Community in full vigor.

Within the supranational framework of the European Union, the role of its Member States relative to language and to transnational commercial and financial deals remains far more incisive than the analogous role of states of the United States within their federal union. The diversity in language and in legal systems of the European Union's Member States, far greater than that of the states of the United States, presents challenges to unification and to harmonization of law not faced within the United States.

Differences between the European Union and the United States in the structure of court systems and in the scope of harmonized law highlight the differences in environment. To take just one example relative to structure of courts, notwithstanding the importance of European Community law (now European Union law) as articulated by the two European courts established under the European Union's constitutional treaties—the General Court (prior to the amendments of the Lisbon Treaty known as the European Court of First Instance) and the European Court of Justice, and the deputization of national courts by the European Court of Justice to assure the application of European law, there continues to be no European Union equivalent to the federal courts of the United States. Proceedings before a national court cannot be removed to a federal court system in the same way that diversity jurisdiction allows disputes to be resolved by federal rather than state courts in the United States. Likewise, the two European Union courts established under the European Union's constitutional treaties are not courts of appeal from Member State courts. The jurisdiction of the two European Union courts established specifically as institutions of the Union by its constitutional treaties remains limited to a defined sphere of original jurisdiction matters, advisory opinions and the reference of questions from national courts. Indeed, answering questions posed by national courts as to the meaning and application of

European Union law has been and remains the preponderance of the volume of the European Court of Justice's work.

Hence, within the European Union, there is not the same check on the ability of state courts to impose procedural burdens as there is in the United States, where the federal court system offers foreign litigants a respite from potentially-burdensome state procedural requirements. The European Court of Justice's ability to address procedural burdens of national court systems is substantially its enunciation, in response to questions referred to it by national courts, of principles of European Union law. In the European Union system, the European Court of Justice relies on national courts as its partners to assure the application of these principles. The application through this mechanism of partnership, of the principles of European Union law in national court systems, including as to matters of procedure, has profoundly affected national legal systems, including for example as to the ability of courts to issue injunctions against the state so as to assure the application of European law even when national law did not contemplate such a power[153] or the ability of courts to "disapply" national legislation that conflicts with European norms.[154] However, the operation of courts in Europe remains far less unified in substance and in practice than in the United States. In the same vein, European commercial and financial law, notwithstanding the significant progress achieved through European Union legislation and the development of European Union institutions, remains similarly less integrated than the analogous body of law in the United States.

Nonetheless, as the European Union has grown and consolidated itself, the notion of limiting transnational commercial and financial dealings to any particular language appears to continue to recede in prominence as discouraged, or even prohibited, by European law. Before addressing the elements of European Union law that discourage, and in some circumstances prohibit, governmental impositions on party autonomy with respect to language in such dealings, it is helpful to consider the nuances of the European Union's general approaches to official languages.

a. European Union institutions and language

In the European Union, any governmental policy to promote exclusive use of specific languages confronts the policy articulated by the European Union's Commission in favor of multilingualism[155] and tacitly encouraged by the European treaty provisions establishing that the Union has twenty-three official languages, each constituting an official language of one or more Member States, and that the treaty text in each of them is equally authentic.[156] Further, the Treaty on the functioning of the European Union encourages the use of these twenty-three official languages by citizens in dealing with the European institutions, by entitling each citizen of the Union to a written response to a query made to any one of the principal European institutions in such a language.[157]

Each of English, French, Italian, Portuguese and Spanish, the languages here considered, is an official language of one or more Member States of the European Union. English is an official language of Ireland, the United Kingdom, and Malta. France is the official language of France, as well as an official language of Belgium and Luxembourg. Italian, Portuguese and Spanish each serve as an official language of one Member State of the European Union. Even though each is an official language of the European Union that is widely spoken by substantial populations, even these languages are not in all instances treated equally.

Notwithstanding the European Union's promotion of multilingualism and its considerable investment of resources in translation of its normative materials into and among each of its official languages, its approach to language is not necessarily to treat all official languages equally or to mandate that all such languages always be employed on equal terms.[158] Indeed, the institutions of the European Union themselves give preference to the widely-spoken languages, and especially English and French, in their daily work. The Commission works internally almost exclusively in English and French, and the Court of Justice conducts its deliberations in French.[159]

Moreover, the European Union makes no provision for languages that are not among its "official" languages, even though some of them are more widely spoken within the European Union than official languages. For example, there are more citizens of the European Union who speak either *Catalán* or Russian as a first language than there are speakers of either Danish or Maltese. The treaties that established the European Union do not speak directly to the languages spoken within the European Union that do not have official status, whether they are autochthonous languages spoken essentially only within the European Union such as *Catalán*, or languages that are official languages of states outside the European Union but that are spoken by significant populations comprised either of citizens of the European Union who have historically resided in what is now the territory of the European Union, for example, Russian (spoken for example as a first language by many citizens of Baltic Member States of the European Union), or of immigrants from non-Member States who may have become citizens of the European Union, for example, Arabic or Turkish.[160]

Further, European Union law in many instances restricts governmental authorities from promoting a language that has official status by mandating its use. As for example mentioned below in connection with the language of securities offering documentation,[161] European Union law mandates that an issuer of securities offering them to residents of a Member State have the option to prepare its offering documentation principally in "a language customary in the sphere of international finance," which may well not be an official language of the targeted Member State. A further example is the prohibition of mandates to employ a language that are found to be simply disguised restrictions on trade, discussed in the immediately following section.

Article 342 of the Treaty on the functioning of the European Union (*ex* Article 290 of the European Community Treaty and previously *ex* Article 217 of the Treaty of Rome) enables the Council (comprised of the Heads of State or Government of the Member States), acting unanimously, to establish rules governing use of languages by European Union institutions other than the Union's judicial branch. In a 2003 ruling,[162] the European Court of Justice rejected challenges to one such set of rules which narrowed in a specific instance the availability for use of the Union's officially recognized languages.

The challenge concerned the language regime of the European Trademark Office, adopted pursuant to a European Community Regulation. Pursuant to the Regulation, applicants for registration of a mark may apply in any one of the Union's official languages, but must indicate one of only the five languages of English, French, German, Italian or Spanish (to the exclusion of any of the seventeen other official languages) as a second language for use in contestation proceedings should someone challenge the registration of the mark and the disputing parties then be unable to agree on a language for such proceedings. The Court, responding to a challenge by a Dutch lawyer, found the system to be a proportionate response to the challenge of "the legitimate aim of seeking an appropriate linguistic solution to the difficulties" arising from the litigating parties' failure to agree on which language to use.[163]

In any event, European Union law is likely to override any Member State policy mandating use of a specific language for transnational commercial and financial contracts, on the grounds that such a policy constitutes an impermissible restriction on commerce, or perhaps as an infringement of fundamental rights. For these reasons, a governmental policy to promote use of a language in respect of transnational commercial and financial contracts is most likely to be sustainable if focused on a governmental need, either the need of governmental entities themselves to contract in a national language or the need of governmental representatives, such as judges deciding disputes or notaries assisting with the recordation of security interest documents, to understand what they are doing.

b. Language impositions as measures equivalent to quantitative restrictions on trade

Articles 34 and 35 (ex articles 28 and 29 of the Treaty establishing the European Community) of the Consolidated Version of the Treaty on the Functioning of the European Union prohibit quantitative restrictions on respectively imports and exports between Member States, as well as "measures having equivalent effect" to such restrictions. Article 36 of the same Treaty (ex article 30 of the Treaty establishing the European Community) permits exceptions to these prohibitions based on "public policy," but not if they "constitute a means of arbitrary discrimination or a disguised restriction on trade." Any governmental effort to impose generally a specific language for transnational commercial and financial contracts would run afoul of the European Court of Justice's broad construction of these provisions, starting with the well-known *Cassis de Dijon* case,[164] in favor of striking down barriers to an effective internal market. In that case the European Court of Justice declined to recognize a German standards scheme that would have precluded the sale of a traditional French liqueur in Germany on the ground that it failed to meet the higher alcohol content set by the German standard for labeling as a liqueur. The Court did not accept the argument that German consumers required protection from the potential experience of misjudging the potency of properly labeled German liqueurs of high alcohol content following habituation to the softer, less alcoholic French product. Instead, the Court considered the scheme as a measure equivalent to a quantitative restriction on trade that was not redeemed, as an exception to the prohibition of such restrictions, by any plausible public health, consumer protection or other public policy ground.

Bruno de Witte characterizes this line of jurisprudence as a "negative language policy" because it strikes down national measures that interfere with assuring equal treatment of European Union citizens, as well as in some measure thirdcountry nationals.[165] Broadly, the purpose of this "negative language policy" is to prevent restrictions on trade from arising through the mechanism of imposing language requirements on commercial and financial deals.

Other decisions of the European Court of Justice in a parallel vein have articulated the criterion of proportionality as the metric to assess the permissibility of (i) mandating knowledge of Gaelic for a teaching job in Ireland and (ii) a mandate for exclusively local certification of Italian and German fluency to meet customer relations needs at a bank in the bilingual (Italian/German) Italian province of Bolzano.[166] In application of this criterion, Ireland, as part of its promotion of the continued vitality of Gaelic as a national language, is allowed to mandate on the part of any job candidate for a public teaching position some knowledge of Gaelic, but not full fluency. Such a mandate is permissible even if the teaching position at issue involves no use of Gaelic. Likewise, in application of the criterion of proportionality, it is not acceptable to restrict employment opportunities only to those who hold locally-issued certifications of German and Italian fluency; rather, other certifications of bilingual ability in German and Italy must also be accepted as satisfactory.

The full content of what constitutes a prohibited "measure having equivalent effect" to a quantitative restriction on trade remains open to further specification by the European Court of Justice. In particular, the European Court of Justice may well face further instances of questions about how language rules may be subject to the prohibition.

For example, the linguistic burden of requiring a notary in a civil law system to understand the content of documents to be registered for security interest purposes, together with the requirement of notarization as a public writing of the underlying financing agreement and pertinent deal documentation, all translated into an official national language, could perhaps be argued to be a measure having an effect equivalent to a quantitative restriction on trade.[167] By comparison with the newly-implemented French system for the constitution of security interests in moveable and intangible property, inspired by the notice-filing model of Uniform Commercial Code Article 9, the costs of any system requiring recourse to notarization could well attract such an argument. However, any such identification of a requirement for notarial involvement as a measure equivalent to a prohibited quantitative restriction on trade would need to overcome counter-arguments related to the purposes of consumer protection served by notarial involvement and even the cultural significance associated with the well-embedded tradition of notaries in the European Union's founding Member States and in the preponderance of those states which joined in the European Union's initial expansions. In particular, the burdens of the notarial system would likely be argued as justified in connection with assuring the functioning of the broader systems of which they are a part, including in order to ensure appropriate judicial enforcement of obligations and protection of contracting parties from assuming unintended obligations.

c. Language impositions as human rights violations

In due course, human rights law may afford an additional ground for restriction of national impositions relative to language in connection with cross-border commercial and financial transactions. These restrictions could emerge in part through some combination of the operation of the Treaty of Lisbon, as of November 2009 ratified by all the Member States of the European Union, or by judicial decision on a variety of grounds of any of the European Court of Justice, one or more Member State courts, or the European Court for Human Rights.

The Treaty of Lisbon significantly enhances the basis for protection of language-related rights in the European Union. It does so by elevating a November 2007 text of the Charter of Fundamental Rights of the European Union, "solemnly proclaimed" by the principal European Community institutions, specifically the Parliament, the Council and the Commission,[168] to "have the same legal value" as the European Union treaties.[169] The Charter's Article 22 mandates that the Union respect linguistic diversity, and its Article 21 prohibits discrimination based on a number of grounds, including language. The significance of giving the Charter, including these two articles, the same legal value as the European Union treaties is that they become binding on, and available to, the courts of the Member States, as well as the two courts established by the European Union treaties, for use in the review of, and application of, European Union and national law. Three Member States, namely, the Czech Republic, Poland and the United Kingdom, obtained that a protocol to the Lisbon Treaty will exempt them from application of the Charter, whether by their own national courts or the European Court of Justice.[170] Nonetheless, all of the Member States have joined in the Treaty of Lisbon's modification of the Treaty on European Union to provide that the Union itself:

> "shall respect its rich cultural and linguistic diversity, and shall ensure that Europe's cultural heritage is safeguarded and enhanced."[171]

The Treaty of Lisbon through its recognition of the Charter's legal value and its mandate that the European Union respect its "linguistic diversity" affords the European Court of Justice further basis for articulating the principles of European law relevant to issues of language.

Article 6(3) (*ex* article 6(2)) of the Treaty on European Union, in force from 1993, expressly mandates that the Union itself respect fundamental rights,

> "as guaranteed by the European Convention for the Protection of Human Rights and Fundamental Freedoms signed in Rome on 4 November 1950 and as they result from the constitutional traditions common to the Member States, . . . as general principles of Community law."

Both branches of this provision potentially speak to language rights and transnational deals.

The European Convention on Human Rights is a treaty of the Council of Europe, separate from the system of the European Union. Many states that are part of the Council of Europe, but not part of the European Union, have ratified it and recognize the jurisdiction that it establishes of the European Court for Human Rights. All the Member States of the European Union are parties to the European Convention on Human Rights, and the Convention and its construction by the European Court of Human Rights, headquartered in Strasbourg, are an influential part of the human rights law within the European Union and its Member States. Indeed, the Lisbon Treaty provides that the European Union will itself also become a party to the European Convention on Human Rights,[172] so that the Convention applies fully to European Union law and the actions of the institutions of the European Union. The Treaty on the functioning of the European Union underlines the importance attached to the European Convention on Human Rights through its specification of how the Union will ratify the Convention. Specifically, the Council is to adopt the Convention unanimously after having obtained the consent of the European Parliament, and the Convention's ratification by the Council will have effect only after such Council decision is unanimously ratified by each of the Member States in accord with the corresponding national constitutional requirements.[173] As the European Union becomes a party to the European Convention on Human Rights, not only will the European Union's own institutions be responsible for their compliance with the Convention, but also the Convention's institutions, and notably its Court of Human Rights, will be available to address the compliance of the European Union institutions with the Convention.

The European Convention on Human Rights includes provisions on freedom of expression and prohibitions of discrimination including on grounds of language, such as its Article 10 on freedom of expression, and the prohibitions of discrimination on grounds of language pursuant to its Article 14 and its Protocol no. 12, Article 1.[174] However, the case law of the European Court for Human Rights has yet to develop these provisions with reference to the specific topic of language rights and transnational business. Indeed, the Council of Europe's supplementation of the European Convention on Human Rights with the European Charter for Regional or Minority Languages, can be understood as a reaction to the limited jurisprudence of the European Court for Human Rights generally on the topic of language. The European Charter for Regional or Minority Languages first took effect in 1998 and as discussed below is now in force for the fourteen European Union Member States and nine European states not members of the European Union that have ratified it as a further human rights treaty.[175]

Likewise, the constitutional traditions common to the Member States, particularly as articulated in European Union documentation relative to human rights, may well speak to the issue of language rights and transnational deals. Prior to the ratification of the Lisbon Treaty, the potential significance of the Charter of Fundamental Rights of the European Union, proclaimed by European Union leaders in 2000,[176] was to be understood as a restatement of such principles to be given application through this channel. This channel maintained the viability of the Charter notwithstanding abandonment of efforts to adopt the proposed Treaty establishing a Constitution for Europe that like the Lisbon Treaty would have accorded it binding status. Those efforts ended following the rejection of that Treaty by Dutch and French voters in national referenda in 2005.

However, prior to the effectiveness of the Lisbon Treaty, the European Court of Justice did not extend to the Union's Member States the applicability of the mandate that the Union itself respect fundamental rights. A basis for this reticence was that the preamble of the Treaty on European Union, by reciting that the Member States "create the Union", identified the Union as distinct from Member States. In that vision, the compatibility relative to human rights norms of national requirements as to use of language was left to the constitutional law of each Member State and to the over-arching system presided by the European Court of Human Rights pursuant to the European Convention on Human Rights. Nonetheless, just as the French *Conseil Constitutionnel*, through an examination of French constitutional law, found on human rights grounds rooted in the Declaration of the Rights of Man and Citizen that the Toubon legislation overreached in its mandates for the use of French, any of (i) a national court, (ii) the European Court for Human Rights, or (iii) the European Court of Justice, could be the source of a decision founded on human rights grounds that would establish further limits on legal requirements that would limit or burden the use of language, including in respect of cross-border commercial and financial transactions. The full ratification of the Lisbon Treaty with its promotion of the status of the Charter of Fundamental Rights of the European Union, as well as its provision for accession of the European Union to the European Convention on Human Rights, increases the basis for such a ruling by any of these courts.

A decision in this vein from a national court would be in the context of exercise of a power of judicial review of the constitutionality of laws pursuant to a national constitution. Such an exercise, which would be limited to a constitutional court in those countries, like Germany, Italy and Spain, that employ a system of centralized judicial review of the constitutionality of laws, would likely include reference to the norms of the European Convention on Human Rights. Such norms are binding on the states which have ratified the Convention and accordingly as a matter of national law may be afforded a superior or constitutional rank relative to ordinary law.

The Italian Constitutional Court, by way of example, recently responded to queries from the Italian Court of Cassation about the constitutionality of Italian law relative to expropriation. The queries concerned such law's conflict with principles of the European Convention on Human Rights, as articulated by the European Court of Human Rights.[177] The Italian Constitutional Court concluded that the European Convention on Human Rights does not constitute a supranational legal system like that of the European Community (now European Union) with direct applicability to individuals. Accordingly, the Court further concluded that the Convention does not mandate under the Italian Constitution's Article 11 that ordinary judges directly apply its norms to the exclusion of conflicting provisions of Italian law. Rather, the Constitutional Court reasoned that the European Convention on Human Rights imposed its obligations on the states that ratified it. On this premise, the Italian Constitutional Court recognized its own power and duty, pursuant to Italy's ratification of the European Convention on Human Rights and relevant associated protocols, to invalidate Italian legislation on compensation for expropriation that the Constitutional Court would find, and in the specific instance did find, inconsistent with such norms. Just as the Italian Constitutional Court invalidated provisions of national statutory law in this case relative to compensation for expropriation, it could exercise its power to invalidate Italian legal measures relative to language that the Court would find incompatible with Italy's obligations under the European Convention on Human Rights.

The European Court for Human Rights, presented with an appropriate case, could likewise declare the incompatibility with the European Convention of burdens on the use of language in connection with cross-border commercial and financial transactions. It would thereby confirm the obligation on the state, under the law of which such burdens were imposed, to remove them. In addition, the European Court of Justice extending Article 6 of the Treaty on European Union to the Member States or relying on Article 6 of the Lisbon Treaty following its adoption, might well determine that requirements associated with the use of an official language in interactions with governmental authorities relative to cross-border transactions constitute an impermissible burden on analogous human rights grounds.

In summary, any one of these three kinds of courts, namely, a national court with the power of constitutional review of laws, the European Court for Human Rights, or the European Court of Justice, as a matter of, respectively national constitutional, European human rights, or European Union law, could in the coming years be the source of further restrictions on the imposition of legal burdens on the use of language for transnational business.

d. European Charter for Regional or Minority Languages

For European states, the European Charter for Regional or Minority Languages, a treaty of the Council of Europe, provides some incentive that governmental authorities broaden the scope of the languages in which they accept to work to include relevant "regional or minority languages".[178] The focus of the European Charter for Regional or Minority Languages is not to accord individual or collective rights to use of a language, but rather that a ratifying state undertake to protect and promote "regional or minority languages".[179] The Charter identifies the opening of administrative and court proceedings to use of relevant "regional or minority languages" as among the measures that a ratifying state may elect to take as part of fulfilling its commitment.[180] In addition to nurturing a language through opening judicial and administrative proceedings to its use, the Charter provides for each ratifying state to identify from a menu of policy goals, pertaining to education, the operation of administrative authorities and public services, media, cultural activities and facilities, economic and social life, and transfrontier exchanges, a set of measures that will constitute the steps that it will undertake in pursuit of protecting each of the relevant languages.[181] Accordingly, the Charter can work to reinforce the opening of governmental authorities to the use of more than one language. An incidental result of the Charter's implementation by a ratifying state may thus be to lighten the language burden imposed on parties to a cross-border commercial and financial deal when recourse is made to its governmental authorities in connection with making or enforcing the deal.

The impact of the Charter is limited by a number of factors. First, its focus is directed to "regional or minority languages" that it defines as languages that are:

> "(i) traditionally used within a given territory of a State by nationals of that State who form a group numerically smaller than the rest of the State's population; and

> (ii) different from the official language(s) of that State . . ."[182]

These languages may be relatively little used in cross-border deals. Moreover, languages such as Arabic in France, Turkish in Germany and Russian in the Baltic states fall outside the Charter's definition of "regional or minority languages". In fact, France and the Baltic states are not party to the Charter, and Turkish is not one of the languages that Germany has designated for protection in connection with its ratification of the Charter. In addition, the Charter expressly states that it does not override pre-existing rights as to language, whether derived directly from national law or through the European Convention on Human Rights.[183] Thus for example, it is doubtful that the Charter adds much of substance to, for example, Spain's existing regime relative to language, although as treaty obligation, it may serve to further consolidate the legal foundation of that regime. Lastly, the Charter is not presently ratified as a treaty by many large states.

The Charter is now in force among twenty-three of the forty-seven states that comprise the Council of Europe.[184] Of the states in which the Charter is in force, fourteen are Member States of the European Union. Of the states here examined, it is in force for Luxembourg, Spain and Switzerland, and as to those states does not fundamentally alter the pre-existing approach to language, particularly in respect of the languages available for use in interactions with governmental authorities and cross-border transactions. Luxembourg's population as discussed below is substantially trilingual, and accordingly Luxembourg has made no declaration in which it identifies regional or minority languages within its territory; Spain's declaration of regional or minority languages mirrors those identified in its constitution; and, Switzerland's declaration declares the official languages, constitutionally-identified as discussed above, of Romansh and Italian as "less widely used official languages" to be the object of nurturing measures as contemplated by the Charter.[185]

B. Civil procedure and language: the arbitration escape hatch

1. National requirements

A court can only grasp what is at issue in the disputes brought before it if its judges and their support staff are enabled to understand what the parties wish to communicate. Accordingly, national legal systems have some mechanism for addressing the issue of translation from languages other than the ones or ones in which the legal system typically functions. Indeed, the American Law Institute/UNIDROIT PRINCIPLES OF TRANSNATIONAL PROCEDURE, a current international effort to restate principles of civil procedure applicable to transnational matters, contemplate that a court should work in the language in which it is fluent and that translation should be provided as necessary, whether by the court or the parties.[186] Unlike the federal civil procedure rules of the United States, many of the civil law jurisdictions here considered have express civil procedure code mandates for translation of documentation into an official language in which the courts work. They likewise feature express provisions relative to assisting parties or witnesses unable to communicate in, or adequately to understand, the language in which the legal system works, for example, France[187] and Portugal.[188]

Some jurisdictions are more trusting of their judges and court personnel to use their personal discretion and language capabilities to deal with multiple languages than others. This is more likely the case in the presence of some degree of multilingualism in the relevant legal system, but may also reflect trust in the sophistication of the judicial personnel and the bar that practices with them. France, for example, is a sophisticated jurisdiction, with but one official language, that allows a judge to dispense with an interpreter, if unnecessary for the judge to understand the language employed by a party or witness.[189] This in particular might be understood as a manifestation of the French system's tradition of entrusting elite civil servants with responsibility for making significant decisions based on personal skills and training.[190]

Argentina, Brazil, France and Portugal are instances of legal systems which recognize only one language for procedural purposes. Other systems such as Canada, Mexico, Spain and Switzerland confront the reality of populations comprised of groups that do not all speak the same primary language. These systems display a spectrum of arrangements to accomplish the goal of enabling courts to understand the matters brought before them.

Canada's federal courts and Québec's provincial courts illustrate a bilingual approach. The right to use each of English and French in them dates back to Canada's 1862 constitution.[191] More recently, the Canada Constitution Act (1982), affords an express right to an interpreter for any party or witness in a legal proceeding.[192] Although the Québec provincial courts work predominantly in French, English and French are equally acceptable for use before them, and any judgment in English or French must be translated into the other language on the request of a party.[193]

Mexico also places a linguistic responsibility on its courts, but in a different way. Unlike Spain, which respects the use of recognized autochthonous languages on a substantially co-equal basis with Spanish, and unlike Switzerland where the dominant language varies by canton, Mexico requires its federal courts to exercise particular solicitude for its indigenous communities, as the courts otherwise routinely conduct their work in Spanish. Mexico's Federal Code of Civil Procedure makes special provision, in conformity with the 2001 amendments to Mexico's constitution, for such indigenous communities. For such communities, an interpreter with "knowledge of the witnesses' language and culture" is required, if the witness is not literate in Spanish.[194] There is an exception to the general rule that court filings are to be made in Spanish, with translation into "castellano" of any communication in a foreign language. The exception is that filings made by indigenous communities or individuals may be made in their own language, with translation to be provided by the court.[195] Likewise, decisions rendered in cases involving an indigenous party must be translated by the court into that party's language.[196]

Spain is an example of a jurisdiction that allows its courts and litigants to assume significant freedom in respect of multilingualism. The Spanish civil procedure code conforms to the Spanish constitutional provision recognizing Spanish and "the other Spanish languages".[197] The civil procedure code provides that proceedings are to occur in *"el castellano, lengua oficial del Estado"* (Castilian, official language of the State), but that court personnel including the judges can use the official language of the relevant autonomous community, if no party complains that lack of understanding prevents its comprehension.[198] The parties and their lawyers, as well as witnesses and experts, can freely use the official language of the relevant autonomous community in both written and oral submissions.[199] Documents produced in an official language of the relevant autonomous community need only be translated if to be given effect outside the relevant autonomous community.[200] In oral proceedings, the court can appoint any person knowledgeable of the language as a translator, subject to an oath to faithfully translate.[201]

Switzerland presents an example of greater complexity because it has four national languages, corresponding to its cantons in a complicated way. Most cantons have one official language, but a few have more than one. As in the case of Canada, federal law mandates translation. The Swiss constitution makes civil law and the law of civil procedure a federal competence, but leaves the general administration of justice and of the courts that address civil matters to the cantons.[202] That is, the civil law and procedure that the courts apply is federal law, but the cantons are responsible for the organization and functioning of their courts that apply such law. The Law of Federal Civil Procedure of December 4, 1947 provides that the judge and the parties must avail themselves of one of the four national languages of the Confederation and that the judge must order translation where necessary.[203]

Argentina, Brazil, Italy, Mexico, Portugal and Spain illustrate various procedural mechanisms to allocate the burden of translation and to address the issue of its adequacy. In some systems, for example, Brazil, there is an express civil procedure code requirement of "sworn translation" or of translation by a certified translator.[204] Often, as is the case in Brazil and Portugal, documents presented without translation may be the object, at the instance of the parties or the judge, of a judicial order for translation, with the option of further expert translation in case of question as to the quality of the translation.[205]

Other systems combine the provision for translation with a statement that the system's dominant language be employed. For example, Argentina's "Civil and Commercial Procedural Code for the Nation" provides that the "national language", implicitly understood to be Spanish, is to be used in all acts of a proceeding.[206] It further provides that documents presented in a foreign language must be accompanied by a translation accomplished by a registered public translator.[207]

The Italian civil procedure code on its face imposes a specific mandate for use of Italian before the Italian courts, but this mandate is modified in part by subsequent constitutional law. The Italian Code of Civil Procedure, adopted in 1940 as the culmination of an extended expert drafting process, provides that the use of Italian is required throughout a civil proceeding.[208] The judge may appoint a sworn translator for persons who must be heard in the process, should such persons not know Italian.[209] The judge may also name a sworn translator when documents not written in Italian must be considered.[210] Italy's special statute regions are associated with exceptions of constitutional status to the Code of Civil Procedure requirement for use of Italian. For example, citizens of the province of Bolzano in the Special Statute Region of Trentino-Alto Adige/Südtirol may use German in dealing with judicial authorities, the public administration within the region, and the holders of public concessions in their province.[211] Likewise, in the Special Statute Region of Val d'Aosta,

French has equal status with Italian, although judicial decisions are prepared in Italian.[212]

Mexico and Spain afford parties an adversarial procedure to assure acceptable translation. In Spain, documents that are written in neither Spanish nor the official language of the relevant autonomous community must be translated.[213] Such translation can be done privately, but the court can order an official translation at the expense of the party presenting the translation, if another party challenges the translation within five days of its presentation. The risk to the challenging party is that it will be ordered to pay the cost of the official translation if it results substantially identical to the translation challenged.[214] Mexico's Federal Code of Civil Procedure is also the model of its thirty-one states' codes of civil procedure. It provides that foreign language documents to be submitted to a court, are to be sent with translation to the adversary party. The adversary then has three days within which to confirm that it concurs with the translation. Absent such concurrence, the court is to name a translator.[215] Witnesses who do not speak *"castellano"* (Castilian Spanish) may present testimony through a translator, named by the court.[216] Argentina, in contrast, provides that anyone who must make a declaration, but does not know the language, is to receive assistance from a public translator designated by the court by lottery.[217]

2. *Arbitration – conventions and national law*

For parties to transnational commercial and financial deals, the escape valve to language burdens associated with litigation before national courts is international arbitration, widely available due to the nearly universal adoption of the New York and similar conventions.[218] In the relevant arbitration clause, the parties have the latitude to express their choice of language for the conduct of the arbitration proceedings.

National law provisions in addition to the ratification of the relevant arbitration convention may confirm this inherent liberty of international arbitration and thereby offer further basis for party choice of language in which to conduct business and through which to resolve disputes. Argentina, Brazil and Mexico offer examples. What national provisions may add to the national ratification of a treaty that provides for recognition of international arbitration is the extension to purely domestic matters of the freedom of choice of language in which to conduct the arbitration.

Argentina's civil procedure code allows transaction parties to provide for arbitration of their disputes without limitation of their choice of language for the conduct of the arbitration.[219] In implementation, the rules of the arbitral tribunal of the Buenos Aires Chamber of Commerce establish Spanish as the default language for arbitration, but allow parties, at their cost, to agree to conduct proceedings in another language.[220]

Brazil's arbitration law, adopted in 1996, represents a significant break from the prior diffidence of the Brazilian legal system to arbitration. It likewise allows the parties freedom to select the language of arbitration, but requires translation of any arbitral award into Portuguese, as a prerequisite to its recognition and enforcement by Brazilian courts.[221]

In recent years, Mexico has softened its insistence that foreigners accept its courts and law for resolution of disputes. Mexico's 1917 Constitution continues to embrace the Calvo doctrine of prohibiting foreigners' recourse to their home governments for assistance when faced with expropriation actions,[222] with particular regard to real property ownership.[223] However, Mexico updated its 1890 Federal Code of Commerce as to arbitration in 1989,[224] with a further amendment in 1993 to incorporate partially the UNCITRAL model law on commercial arbitration.[225] Pursuant to those updates, parties to transactions may agree that arbitration, rather than recourse to Mexico's courts, will be used to resolve their disputes. In addition, parties to transactions may decide freely the language, as well as the place, of arbitration.[226] Should the parties fail to address the question of language for the conduct of the arbitral proceedings, the arbitrator may resolve the question. The arbitrator may also mandate that documents to be considered in the arbitration be translated into the language or languages agreed by the parties or otherwise determined by the arbitrator for use in the conduct of the arbitration.[227] As a federal law, the Federal Code of Commerce applies throughout Mexico, and accordingly its rules apply to all Mexican commercial arbitrations, including both purely domestic arbitrations and international arbitrations held in Mexico, except as otherwise provided by treaty.[228]

Mexico is similarly open relative to language in respect of the transnational activities of its two leading state-held monopolies. Mexico's federal constitution contains provisions that reserve the conduct of oil and electric sector activities to state-held monopolies.[229] The provisions concerning hydrocarbons spring from the nationalization of the oil industry by President Cárdenas in the late 1930s. Although the nationalization expropriated the interests of British and United States oil companies, the exuberance of the assertion of national authority did not result in any constitutional mandate as to the use of language by such entities in their business dealings or any constitutional restriction that such entities confine their choice of dispute resolution mechanisms to proceedings before Mexican courts. Currently, legislation permits each of CFE and PEMEX, respectively the state-controlled electricity and oil monopolies, to agree, as to "international" matters, to choice of non-Mexican law to govern their agreements, as well as foreign court or arbitral jurisdiction for resolution of commercial disputes.[230]

The adoption of the arbitration conventions and the consequent respect of party autonomy associated with them, dramatically exemplify the trend toward allowing and respecting party choice relative to language. By agreeing to arbitration, the parties drastically reduce their exposure to national procedural requirements, including as to language.

In light of this trend, the key factor in evaluating the significance of burdens imposed by civil procedure rules relative to use of language, for instance, requirements of "certified translation" or of registration of notarized translations, is perhaps not how they may burden significant transnational deals. Because of the parties' ability to dodge them by agreement to arbitrate disputes, the more salient question may be the extent to which such requirements are useful to making the national legal system function, when the parties fail to agree to an arbitral forum for resolution of their disputes. The question is whether such requirements are necessary to facilitate the work of the courts, the bar, and litigants, or at least whether the costs of such requirements are commensurate with their benefits.

Because parties to substantial transnational matters are able to agree on arbitration and thus have substantial freedom to choose the language in which to deal with each other and any dispute, such parties may have little interest in the question of the need for reform of national procedural rules relative to language. For transaction parties, agreement on arbitration and language renders national requirements of civil procedure that pertain to language in most instances largely irrelevant for their cross-border deals. A corollary of this irrelevance is that cross-border deals and the stakeholders in them are likely the source of little if any impetus for reform of otherwise burdensome national requirements pertaining to civil procedure and use of language.

C. Security interests and language; differences in roles of civil law notaries and UCC-style filing officers

The link of language to creation of priority security interests in collateral, of which the debtor (not the creditor) retains possession, that are binding against third parties is a much greater issue for parties to transnational commercial and financial deals than national civil procedure requirements as to language and translation. For the creation of priority claims in property intended to remain in the possession of the debtor while serving as collateral for the repayment of a loan, there is no escape hatch equivalent to that of agreement on arbitration, in order to sidestep burdensome national requirements concerning use of an official language.

The importance of language to the creation of non-possessory security interests of creditors in transactions among sophisticated parties and the associated lack of ability to work around relevant governmental requirements as to language arises from two factors: (i) the inability to avoid the jurisdiction of courts of the place of location of the collateral to resolve contests involving third party creditors; and, (ii) the related requirement of some form of publicity so that one creditor's security interest might be accorded priority against claims of third party creditors.

As to the first point, foreclosing creditors, perhaps even in the context of involuntary bankruptcy proceedings of the debtor that they might trigger, will make recourse to national courts of the place where the collateral that they seek to seize is located. Actions in other courts, and collection and enforcement efforts based on them, are likely to be untimely and in any event disregarded by national courts of the place of location of collateral. The essence of theories by which courts of the jurisdiction where collateral is located will deny effect to rulings about claims to such collateral by other courts, is that any agreement, as to choice of law and forum for dispute resolution, cannot prejudice the rights of third party creditors under the law of the place where the collateral is located.

As to the second point, which is closely related to the first point, public registries are a widely-diffused and effective tool to accomplish the publicity required to make one creditor's lien have priority against potential claims of third party creditors to the same collateral. This is particularly so as legal systems open themselves to non-possessory liens, that is liens over collateral of which the debtor retains possession, likely so as to be able to use the collateral as part of generating the revenue stream intended to repay the extension of credit. In respect of a possessory lien, the transfer of possession of collateral from debtor to creditor constitutes the publicity to other potential creditors that the debtor has granted a preferred interest to one creditor. Implementation of the more sophisticated non-possessory lien is dependent on publicity through the relevant registry, and this makes language an inherent component of its use. As the intensity of requirements imposed to satisfy the requisite of publicity increases, the linguistic burden of meeting that requisite likewise increases.

When the lien is non-possessory, there must be some mechanism to verify its existence in order that it can be enforced against third party creditors. Another way to state this, is that third party creditors must be put on notice, at least constructive if not actual notice, that particular assets of the debtor still in the possession of the debtor have been previously pledged on a priority basis to a particular creditor of the debtor as security for the repayment of credit. The need for a mechanism of verification that property in the possession of the debtor has been designated by the debtor and a particular creditor as collateral securing the repayment of obligations to that particular creditor implies the use of a writing and some degree of interaction with a governmental authority in respect of the writing to assure the necessary publicity.

Within these parameters, there are two broad approaches to the issue of language in respect of the establishment of creditor priorities in collateral offered as non-possessory security for the repayment of a loan. One approach is to impose the responsibility for proper creation of the lien on the parties, while leaving the verification of their work to a court should litigation arise. The other approach is to involve an impartial professional in the creation of the lien, with the responsibility and power to prepare effective documentation on which a court at the time of eventual litigation can rely as binding proof of the act of the parties so documented.

The legal systems that adopt, or that are inspired along the lines of, the Uniform Commercial Code Article 9, accomplish the publicity relative to security interests in property, generally personal or moveable property, as distinguished from real or immoveable property, by the simple expedient of filing in a central registry, indexed by name of debtor. The adequacy of filings to establish the desired priority are entirely the responsibility of the creditor.

The other approach to the constitution of priorities in collateral offered for the purpose of establishing a non-possessory security interest is to involve a neutral professional. Such a professional is a civil law notary. The notary's purpose is to verify that the appropriate formalities are observed and that each of the parties understands the significance of what it is undertaking. To a common law lawyer, imbued with the concepts of adversarial representation and the loyalty of a lawyer to the lawyer's client, the concept of accomplishing a transaction with the services of a neutral professional, who owes the same duty of impartiality to each party, is a novel concept.

The approach in the United States to secured transactions, as to both personal (moveable and intangible) property pursuant to the Uniform Commercial Code ("UCC") and real property, contrasts with that of other jurisdictions that may involve a civil law notary in the creation of the security interest and its registration to assure that the public act creating the security interest is properly drawn in substance and that the parties to it understand its import. The notarial system, which evolved historically in a time of limited literacy both as to the law specifically and also as to the ability to read and write generally, involves a neutral professional—the notary, to verify the correct legal form of the instrument and the intelligibility of its description of the collateral. In the "Latin" variant of the notarial system, the notary is an independent professional benefiting from a territorial monopoly. In the "Germanic" variant, the notary is a State civil servant. In either instance, the notary is present as a representative of the State.

The notarial system is employed in some form in nearly all of the European Union's twenty-seven Member States (with the notable exceptions of its common law jurisdictions in three countries—Cyprus, Ireland and United Kingdom) and broadly in Latin America as well as elsewhere in the world. The extent to which notarial involvement is required to establish a security interest varies across these jurisdictions. Notarial involvement is widely required in respect of interests pertaining to real property; however, jurisdictions vary in respect of its requirement with respect to other kinds of property. The requirement of notarization as a condition of being able to register documentation to constitute a security interest and establish its priority is a step that requires confronting the issue of language and its conformity to specific State norms as to choice of language because the notary, as a representative of the State, may be affirmatively required to verify the proper form of the substance of the transaction. This step of verification does not arise under the UCC Article 9 model. As laid out below, notarial involvement is, for example, required with respect to significant transactions involving moveable property as collateral in Mexico, but not in France.

Accordingly, the question arises, particularly with respect to transnational commercial and financial deals among sophisticated parties, as to what value the requirement of "notarization" adds in addition to the recordation in the registry. It might be argued that omitting the role of the "notary" relative to creation and establishment of the priority of security interests would diminish the role of a national language, as well as remove an important creditor and consumer protection mechanism. In particular, it could burden national economic actors with a need to read an unfamiliar language in order to understand the extent of prior liens on a potential borrower's assets. It could also be argued to increase the risk that recipients of credit might grant liens and assume obligations that they do not fully appreciate, with the consequence that that they might unexpectedly lose property through foreclosure in unanticipated circumstances. Further, it could be argued that the requirement of notarization must be evaluated together with its implications for the burdens on courts and parties at the time of litigation were it to be omitted.

In addition to the difference of the philosophical poles of adversarial representation (common law lawyers) and neutral provision of a public services (civil law notaries), a parallel distinction can be drawn relative to the timing of formal verification of the adequacy of the constitution of a priority claim in collateral to assure repayment of a loan that is retained in the possession of the debtor.

The formal verification as to the adequacy of constitution of a security interest and its associated priority under the UCC Article 9 approach, comes in the context of litigation in which the creditor will assert the priority against some combination of further creditors and the debtor. Such litigation may be in the context of simple foreclosure and debt collection efforts, as well as in the context of debtor insolvency proceedings. How well the parties and their lawyers did their work at the time of constitution of the security interest and its priority, is established in the context of the litigation arising from a dispute. Such litigation, if it ever occurs, may transpire long after the initial extension of credit. The court in which the dispute unfolds is required to master the relevant substantive law and establish the salient underlying events in order to ascertain which creditors' claims to the collateral will have priority.

In contrast, a requirement to involve a civil law notary in the constitution of a security interest and its priority means that an impartial professional, with a duty of technical competence, is involved at an early date in the parties' transaction. Should litigation arise about the security interest, the court benefits from the presentation of documents prepared by the notary. In addition to their preparation by a neutral professional with a duty of competence, such documents benefit from "public faith", meaning that there is no question of proof as to the existence of the act into which the parties entered in the presence of the notary.

Accordingly, one way to distinguish systems which rely on the UCC Article 9 model from those which rely on the notarial model for the creation of non-possessory security interests is to consider allocation of the burdens and of the timing of verification. The criterion of allocation of burdens pertains to the identity of the party on whom they place the burden of providing the professional services to ensure that a priority in collateral is duly constituted. The criterion of timing of verification pertains to when the verification of the due constitution of a security interest is contemplated, that is, whether the verification occurs at the time of creating the interest, or at the time of litigating about it in connection with a default in repayment and perhaps a contest among creditors as to which of the creditors' claims to the collateral have priority. Systems without notaries place a higher burden on the parties and their advisors at the time of constituting the priority, and later on courts at the time of litigation. Systems with notaries burden transactions more at the time of constitution of the priority, but afford a court at the time of litigation an evidentiary basis potentially more solidly grounded in reliable documentation upon which to address resolution of the dispute. In systems with notaries, the parties benefit from the support of the notary in assuring the technical correctness of the constitution of the security interest. Although this support may increase the cost burden on the parties, it leaves them less margin to make mistakes in the constitution of the security interest than under the UCC Article 9 model simply because the notary as a neutral professional is an additional control on what the parties undertake.

The UCC approach to security interests differs from that of most other jurisdictions in another important way as well. The UCC as a system offers a simple, universal conception of security interests for all kinds of personal property. This conceptual simplicity stands out in contrast to the many jurisdictions that for a variety of historical reasons offer systems with a high degree of conceptual fragmentation for the constitution and management of security interests. This conceptual fragmentation may manifest itself as the existence of a variety of legal instruments for the establishment of security interests within a legal system, which may vary in applicability according to the kind of collateral as well as in underlying theory. It may also manifest itself, as it does in the European Union, as the survival of approaches varying by territories that are increasingly incorporated into one economic space. For example, European Union Member State frameworks for publicity of security interests range through: (i) complete denial of publicity (Germany); (ii) notification as the means of publicity (France for security assignments); (iii) asset-based registries (France, Italy and Spain for select assets); (iv) debtor-based registries (England for floating charges); and (v) registration systems intended to establish the transaction date (Dutch silent pledge, Spanish and Italian "date certain").[231]

In the context of the European Union as a supranational organization seeking to build a common internal market, this observation of fragmentation might be attributed two kinds of significance. On the one hand, the conceptual fragmentation represents a clear obstacle to the construction of a true internal market without national boundaries. On the other hand, its existence may derive, unsurprisingly, from the history of independent national development of financial law. But even at the national level, conceptual fragmentation abounds. For example, even following the recent French reform, tangible moveable property is subject to a pledge known as a *"gage"*, while a pledge of intangible property is known as a *"nantissement"*, notwithstanding that each is now accomplished with reference to the same registry system. Even such banal terminological fragmentation introduces a further burden for any foreigner, but especially one not versed in the official language or languages of the relevant legal system. Hence, the adoption of the UCC across each of the jurisdictions comprising the United States stands out relative to the situation in Europe and elsewhere in the world, both because of the UCC's universal conception of the concept of security interest (at least in respect of its broad concept of "personal property") and because of the very fact of its wide adoption.

The requirements as to what is filed in a registry, and the language of filing itself, are each significant elements of the linguistic burden which a legal system may impose on transnational commercial and financial deals that involve collateral. Requirements that documents underlying the security interest be presented in an official language and that such documents be "notarized" as "public writings", as well as general operative inadequacy of registry systems, may significantly burden such transactions. Mexico and Brazil are examples of countries at the extreme end of the spectrum in respect of the linguistic burden of what must be presented and its notarization. They differ in that Mexico is well along in the establishment of a national computerized registry, whereas Brazil's registries remain uncoordinated and in many instances not computerized. The United States and, following its recent reform, France, are examples of countries which impose a relatively light burden in this regard.

1. *Mexico, Brazil, Argentina – maximum linguistic burden*

Mexico is a jurisdiction which affirmatively involves its notaries in the creation of security interests generally. In 2000, Mexico reformed its laws on secured lending.[232] Since then, it has made substantial progress in the creation of a computerized national registry for commercial documents, including security interest documentation.[233] Nonetheless, Mexico's secured lending framework remains burdensome for those whose language is not Spanish. And, even for those whose language is Spanish, its establishment of notarization as a key foundational prerequisite to the constitution of security interests adds a step and a burden not present in other jurisdictions. Various provisions of Mexican law work to assure that the registration of security interest documentation to establish a priority of claim occurs only relative to Spanish-language materials, and no special provision is made for the languages of Mexico's indigenous communities.

One might argue that notarization requirements for the constitution of security interests are a desirable means of limiting the scope of proceedings in Mexican courts. It might further be argued that such a limitation is congruent with the historical diffidence directed beginning in the mid 1800's towards the work of state courts in Mexico that led their final judgments to be reviewable in federal courts pursuant to *amparo* petitions.[234] In brief, the Mexican system allows a party against whom a final judgment is issued by any court, to petition a federal court for *amparo, i.e.* protection, from enforcement of the judgment. Such protection will be granted if the federal court determines that the challenged judicial action improperly infringes on the constitutional rights of the party against whom it is issued. The opening of any final state court judgment to review in a federal court through the mechanism of an *amparo* proceeding reflects the historical distrust by Mexico's federal authorities of state authorities to conform to federal norms. Mexico's implementation of the notarial system can be argued as further reflecting a concern that its courts, particularly its state courts, not assume unduly broad responsibilities, such as delving into factual questions about the constitution of lien priorities.

The notarization requirement clearly reduces the scope of a court's fact finding role and its consequent margin of discretion relative to the eventual outcome of its decision, because of the heavy presumption of authenticity of notarized documentation. In a centralizing federal system where the concern to limit the independence of state courts was so great that their final judgments were made subject to review by federal courts on the simple request of a disgruntled litigant for consideration of an *amparo* recourse, the notion that judicial resolution of commercial and financial disputes be limited to a highly formalized documentary foundation is not entirely surprising. Whether now to lighten the linguistic burdens of constitution of a security interest imposed by the requisite of notarization as presently applicable merits evaluation in view of significant changes in Mexico. These changes include the ongoing reform of Mexico's federal and state courts that is widely recognized as improving the quality of their work, and the increasing sophistication of its economy as it further opens to international commerce and finance.

The Federal Code of Commerce, which governs commercial transactions throughout Mexico, mandates that, in order to be recorded in the public registry, a document evidencing one of the principal forms of security interest, namely the *prenda sin transmisión de posesión* (pledge without transfer of possession) and the *fideicomiso de garantía* (guarantee trust), must be either a "public instrument granted before a *notario* or *corredor público*"[235] or a private document "ratified" before a *notario* or *corredor público*.[236] Moreover, the federal *Ley General de Títulos y Operaciones de Crédito* (General Law on Securities and Credit Transactions) provides that for effectiveness relative to third parties, the parties to a *prenda sin transmisión de posesión* (pledge without transfer of possession) and a *fideicomiso de garantía* (guarantee trust) must ratify their signatures before a *notario* or a *corredor público* if the transaction concerns property of value of at least 250,000 *unidades de inversión* (about US$64,000) or in the case of a *fideicomiso de garantía* if it includes real property.[237]

The mentioned statutory provisions that require the involvement of a *notario* or *corredor público* are mandates for the preparation of documentation in Spanish. Each of the *corredor público* and the *notario* work within statutory frameworks which promote that their work be in Spanish. Federal law regulates the activity of a *corredor público* and provides that its work "be prepared in Spanish, including documents presented in foreign language".[238] Each of Mexico's states and federal district has its own law that defines the requirements for notarization. The Notarial Law of the Federal District[239] is representative of the corresponding laws of the Mexican states. It provides that a notarial instrument is void if not prepared in Spanish.[240] The Notarial Law of the Federal District provides for the ability of a notary to notarize the signature of documents not prepared in Spanish without their translation into Spanish (unless the law requires that they be in Spanish).[241]

However, there really is no loophole to the necessity to prepare security interest documentation in Spanish. The cited provisions of the Federal Code of Commerce require that security documentation to support establishment of a priority lien, in excess of amounts that are *de minimis* for transnational business and finance, be prepared in Spanish by virtue of the requirement of ratification of signatures before a *notario* or a *corredor público*. Moreover, simply to register security interest documentation, and therefore assure the priority of the relevant interest against third parties, requires Spanish-language documentation. Notably, the Federal Civil Code mandates that foreign language documents may be registered only if first translated by an expert translator and filed in notarial records.[242] Although the Federal Civil Code does not extend to the real property registries maintained by Mexico's thirty-one states (in which filing is required relative to immoveable property),[243] it is the model for their civil codes, which generally impose similar requirements as to any filing in their registries.

The heaviness of the burden on transnational commercial and financial deals involving Mexican collateral is not simply or even principally the requirement to use Spanish in conjunction with the filing. Rather, it is the requirement to file the actual instrument of pledge, rather than simply to provide the identity of the parties and an adequate description of the collateral, as would be the case in conjunction with the notice filing model of Uniform Commercial Code Article 9. In addition, the two steps of notarization and then registration of the actual instrument of pledge are more costly to the parties than a system that contemplates just the step of registration.

Secured lending in Argentina and Brazil remains burdensome primarily for reasons other than language. In each case, the solution of present challenges other than language burdens, would make apparent the further challenge of language burdens as a weight on secured lending.

In Argentina, lenders remain dependent on cumbersome judicial mechanisms to foreclose upon collateral. They are accordingly reluctant to grant credit based upon collateral other than significant real property collateral as security, the value of which justifies the cost of the judicial proceedings necessary to accomplish foreclosure.[244] In addition to the concern to employ Spanish in connection with meeting the requirements to give notice to prospective further creditors by registration of non-possessory security interests, there is a significant litigation burden to accomplish foreclosure. It is unlikely that a prudent lender would further complicate eventual foreclosure by attempting to employ security documentation intended to be enforced in Argentina in a language other than Spanish.

In Brazil, issues include the lack of a unified national registry for security interests in movable and intangible property (or even a coherent set of readily searchable local registries), the heterogeneity of forms of security interest, and the burdens of achieving a successful definitive foreclosure.[245] Were these issues resolved, the issue of language and associated documentary burdens might emerge as a more critical burden. In fact, the registrations required to establish security interests opposable against third parties and the need to make recourse to courts, are each triggers of the obligations to present Portuguese language documents or translations into Portuguese of documents originally written in other languages.

2. Belgium, Switzerland, Italy, Spain – multiple official languages

In all the systems here examined, notaries will typically work only in an "official" language, requiring translation of documents from other languages into an "official" language. Each of the cluster of countries here considered features multiple official languages. At least in some instances, this may facilitate transactions across borders with parties from places that share one or more of the official languages. For example, a German or an Austrian party may find the status of German as an official language in Belgium, or in Italy's province of Bolzano, an aid to doing business there. Among other consequences of the status of German as an official language in those places, aspects of transactions which require notarization of documents can be accomplished in such a party's preferred language, without translation.

Thus, in Belgium, secured lending that involves notarization and registration of documents to establish the security interest and its priority may be accomplished with recourse to any one of Belgium's three official languages of Dutch/Flemish, French or German. A Belgian notary can notarize a document in any one of the three official languages (Dutch, French or German), provided that the notary and the parties (in the case of the parties with a translator if necessary) understand the relevant content. In contrast, documents not drafted in one of the three official languages must in any event be translated into one of those languages as a condition to registration.[246] Nonetheless, the multiplicity of official languages likely facilitates transactions with parties from other jurisdictions that share at least one of the official languages.

The Swiss system is similar in this regard, with the difference that notaries must use the language or languages of their canton. The Swiss Federal Civil Code, adopted in 1907, provides that the cantons cannot impose special forms for the validity of a transaction if federal law does not do so.[247] However, it leaves to each canton the establishment of the norms, including relative to language, for the creation of public acts, such as those required to convey interests in property.[248] Hence, to create a security interest such as a mortgage on real property and establish its priority with the services of a notary of a particular canton, demands compliance with the language requirements of the canton involved.

Italy and Spain share the existence of old, never formally repealed notarial legislation that mandates use of one national language. However, in each country subsequent constitutional developments relative to regionalization (in Italy, the growing importance of its *Regioni*, and in Spain, the consolidation of its *Comunidades Autónomas*) over-ride such legislation so as to allow use of other constitutionally-favored languages.

Notaries run Italy's system of registration of real property and commercial documents. It is a highly computerized system, consultable on a national basis.[249]

The Italian rules relative to notarization create a strong incentive to the preparation of relevant documentation in Italian, with translation into other languages, as deemed necessary. The Italian law no. 89 of February 16, 1913, was proclaimed after little more than fifty years of existence of the Italian state. It defines the role of the notary as to receive acts among living parties and to attribute them public faith, and it mandates that notarial acts be written in Italian.[250] Pursuant to the law, the notarial act can also be simultaneously accomplished in another language, should the parties declare not to know Italian, provided that the notary and witnesses understand it.[251] In addition, the notarial act can be simultaneously accomplished in a foreign language and in Italian with the aid of a translator, if the notary does not know the foreign language.[252] However, the special provisions for language of Italy's special statute regions have constitutional status and supersede the provisions of the 1913 national law on notaries. Thus, for example, notaries in the province of Bolzano, part of the special statute region of Trentino-Alto Adige/Südtirol, are required to be bilingual in German and Italian.[253] Likewise, notarial acts in the special statute region of Valle d'Aosta can be prepared in French as well as Italian.[254]

The limited openness of the 1913 notarial law to languages other than Italian reflects the nation-building effort in course at the time of its adoption, with emphasis on the use of Italian, as a key element of national identity. Some of the historical importance of the notarial role derives not only from the significance attributed to language as an element of nation-building in the context of the prevailing use of dialects that varied significantly from place to place, but also from the concern that contracts be made binding in a society with historically limited extent of literacy in the general population. Interestingly, the view of notarial services as an exercise of governmental monopoly is evolving in Italy. Recently, notaries have been required to compete as to their professional fees, rather than adhere to a national fee schedule.[255]

Spain is accommodating of Spanish and "the other Spanish languages."[256] Although there are limited instances where a "public writing" before a notary is not required to create a security interest enforceable against third parties, in general such a writing is necessary, as well as entry in an appropriate registry.[257] The national notarial law of 1862 requires public writings to be in Spanish.[258] Nonetheless, the Constitutional provision for official status of the "other Spanish languages" allows such languages to be used in the autonomous community to which they correspond. Thus, for example, the *Estatuto de autonomía de Cataluña*, the charter of the autonomous community of Catalonia, provides citizens with the "right of linguistic option". The right is that each citizen may choose whether to interact with a notary in either Spanish or *Catalán*, as well as the requirement that notaries and their staff demonstrate adequate knowledge of *Catalán*.[259] Catalonia's *Ley de Política Lingüística* mentioned above is a further source of the mandate that notaries and the registries pertinent to establishment of security interests be capable of working in both languages.[260]

3. France – an effervescent adoption of notice filing

France recently reformed its security interest laws, creating a new Book IV of its Civil Code.[261] The innovations of the reform have the incidental effect of lightening in a number of ways the burden of language imposed on a foreign lender seeking to establish a priority claim to collateral in a borrower's possession in France. For jurisdictions such as Argentina, Brazil, Italy, Mexico and Spain, the French reform raises the question of what justifies the continuing insistence in those countries on generally burdening secured credit transactions with the requirements of notarization and recordation of documentation, that extend beyond what is minimally necessary to identify the debtor, the creditor, and the collateral in which an interest is claimed. The French reform posits that French courts are competent to sort out questions of fact relative to the constitution of security interests and questions of fraud. The implicit assumption of the requirements of notarial involvement in Argentina, Brazil, Italy, Mexico and Spain is that the notarial process shoulders the preponderance of the burden in this regard in advance of disputes, thereby affording courts a firmer foundation of documents endowed with "public faith" in the event of an eventual contest among claimants to collateral. The consequence is to impose a heavier burden on all parties at the commencement of a transaction, while perhaps lightening the burden on a court deciding a specific dispute.

One of the French innovations is to allow a form of non-judicial foreclosure for security interests in tangible moveable property and for real property. The reform reverses the prior prohibition under French law of a so-called *pacte commissoire*, whereby a debtor agrees that, upon default in payment of a loan, ownership of collateral passes automatically to the creditor.[262] The allowance of a *pacte commissoire* for tangible moveable property and for real property is accompanied by protections for the debtor, namely that: (i) a *pacte commissoire* may not be applied to a debtor's principal residence, (ii) there be either an appraisal or an organized market by which to value the collateral at the time of transfer; and (iii) any surplus value be returned to the debtor.[263] Further, recent case law declines to extend the legislative innovation to allow the constitution of a security interest by formal transfers of title prior to default.[264] In addition, the *pacte commissoire* is not allowed for the creation of non-possessory security interests in the inventory of businesses.[265] Notwithstanding these limitations, the opportunity to avoid judicial foreclosure through the mechanism of a *pacte commissoire* reduces the need to make recourse to French courts using, of course, French.

Further relevant innovations of the reform are express provision for the creation of non-possessory security interests in moveable tangible collateral (*gage sans dépossession*)[266] and in the inventory of businesses (*gage des stocks*).[267] Such pledges are accomplished by a simple writing that designates the debt guaranteed, the quantity of goods pledged and their nature.[268] Such a pledge becomes effective relative to third parties by publicity, which can be accomplished by its registration,[269] rather than the prior (and still valid) mechanism of transfer of possession from the debtor to the creditor.

The system for registration of the newly-recognized non-possessory pledges is in the style of the model of Uniform Commercial Code Article 9. Indeed, to search for filings by debtor name, the recently-established national computerized registry for the *gage sans dépossession* is consultable through an English-language interface, as well as in French.[270] The registry is maintained through an official who, as a representative of the State, works in French, namely, the *greffier* of the *tribunal de commerce*, a public and ministerial officer appointed by the Minister of Justice, but under the supervision of the prosecutor's office.[271] Generally, pledges of intangible property (*nantissement de meubles incorporels*) may be recorded in the same registry and with the same formality of a simple writing, that is, a writing not prepared through a notary.[272] The registration of a *gage des stocks* is accomplished in a registry of the *greffe* of the *tribunal* where the debtor has its seat or domicile.[273]

Although France's new provisions on security interests do not directly address the question of language, they reduce the linguistic burden for a party seeking to establish or enforce significant categories of liens on French collateral that might be associated with a transnational commercial or financial transaction. Of course, the combination of the requirements of publicity to make security interests effective against third parties and the continued requirement to make recourse to a notary in respect of real property interests, creates an ongoing bias for the use of French in the relevant documentation. Moreover, the eventual need to turn to the court system to enforce security interests in the event of contested foreclosure, with the associated requirement of dealing with the courts in French, is additional motivation to use French-language documentation in respect of the agreements made and of what is recorded in the relevant registry. However, by simplifying the process of establishing creditor priority in collateral held by a debtor as security for repayment of a loan, the new provisions pertaining to the creation of priority security interests significantly increase the linguistic-friendliness of the French system to transnational business.

D. Recognition of the "languages of international finance" – Securities law

The European Union approach to the language of documentation for the public offering of securities recognizes that to require preparation of offering documentation in all official languages, or even only all official languages of the countries in which an offering is made, imposes an unacceptable economic burden. The determination implicit in the European Union approach on this point is that the importance of broad capital markets to the creation and maintenance of a common market outweighs any concern that a prospective investor be able to review offering documentation prepared in that investor's primary language.

European Union law, applicable of course to the European Union Member States of Belgium, France, Italy, Luxembourg, and Portugal here discussed as well as the balance of the European Union, allows a Member State to require that a public offering of securities made by an issuer for which it is the "home" state be drawn up in a language "accepted by the competent authority of the home Member State."[274] However, where an offer to the public is made in one or more Member States other than the home Member State, "the prospectus shall be drawn up either in a language accepted by the competent authorities of those Member States or in a language customary in the sphere of international finance, at the choice of the issuer . . . . The competent authority of each host Member State may only require that the summary be translated into its official language(s)."[275]

Thus for example, in accord with the European Union law, Portugal allows that public offering documentation may be written "in a language commonly used in international financial markets" if prepared as part of an offer made in multiple states, or if the issuer is organized under foreign law. The maximum linguistic burden in each such instance that Portugal's Securities Commission may require is preparation and distribution of a Portuguese-language summary.[276] These measures in compliance with the European Union mandate supersede Portugal's baseline requirement for purely domestic solicitation of investment. That baseline is that solicitation be undertaken in Portuguese, unless Portugal's Securities Commission makes a specific finding that "the interests of investors are protected".[277]

Brazil's Securities Law offers an example of a more aggressive approach to use of a national language. It requires registration of debt securities issued abroad by a Brazilian company, including debt securities that are convertible into stock. The documents required by the foreign jurisdiction to accomplish the offering must be registered in the Brazilian Real Property Registry, accompanied by a sworn translation in Portuguese.[278]

The European Union approach to language of offering documentation is to allow issuers to work predominantly in a language widely-spoken by sophisticated investors. In practice this means that offering documentation is widely prepared in English. The Brazilian approach is to require everything to be translated into the national language, even in the case of an offering by a Brazilian entity exclusively to non-Brazilian investors that is made entirely outside of Brazil. Although there is no express United States federal mandate that English be used in securities offering documentation, the potential liability risk in the United States associated with claims that non-English offering documentation would be misleading in some way to actual or prospective investors is strong deterrence to use of languages other than English. The substantive review by state regulators of the terms of securities offerings pursuant to so-called Blue Sky laws is further incentive for the use of English in relevant offering documentation. Although "covered securities", meaning essentially securities listed on the major securities exchanges and other securities of equal or senior rank offered by their issuers, securities of domestic governmental issuers, and federally-qualified private placements, are exempt from substantive review under state Blue Sky laws, offerings of small and medium size issuers are typically subject to such review.[279]

Solid grounds may exist for both the approach of using a "language customary in the sphere of international finance" and the approach of mandating either expressly or indirectly, use of one national language. The linguistic heterogeneity of the European Union implies that any mandate to translate securities offering documentation into a less widely-spoken language as a condition of soliciting its speakers to invest would likely lead to determinations by issuers not to make the investment opportunity available to such speakers. The cost of translation would simply be too great. Moreover, if the target investors have sufficient sophistication and resources either to speak a "language customary in the sphere of international finance", for example, English, themselves or to be assisted by competent English-speaking advisors, the cost of translation into a less-widely spoken language for purposes of protecting actual and prospective investors becomes less justifiable. Brazil's more restrictive policy that requires filing of a full prospectus in the national language even if the offering is made abroad, may be justified on grounds of the different context that it addresses.

In Brazil, the predominance of Portuguese among the domestic community is such that any solution other than the mandate of Portuguese translation of the offering documentation could well be argued to deprive domestic stakeholders, be they investors, creditors, tax authorities, unions or others, of material information. Similar reasoning can be advanced relative to the pressure within United States capital markets to use English.

NOTES TO CHAPTER IV

61. Manley O. Hudson, *Languages Used in Treaties*, 26 AM. J.INT'L L. 368 (1932) (taking issue with claim of established primacy of French as a rule of customary public international law).

62. Statistics Canada, www.statcan.ca.

63. Law no. 1349 of Dec. 31, 1975 (Law *Bas-Lauriol*), J.O.R.F. of Jan. 4, 1976, at 189, and *Circulaire* of March 14, 1977, J.O.R.F. of March 19, 1977, at 1483. *See* Thomas E. Carbonneau, *Linguistic Legislation and Transnational Commercial Activity: France & Belgium*, 29 AM. J. COMP. L. 393 (1981). For overview and history of language regulation in France starting with foundation of the *Académie Française*, see Marc Frangi, *État, langue et droit en France*, 119 REVUE DU DROIT PUBLIC 1607 (2003).

64. Law no. 665 of Aug. 4, 1994 relative to the employment of the French language, art. 2, J.O.R.F. of Aug. 5, 1994.

65. Constitutional law no. 92-554 of June 25, 1992, J.O.R.F. of June 26, 1992, at 8406.

66. Constitution, art. 61-1.

67. Constitution, art. 61.

68. Decision no. 94-345 of July 29, 1994, J.O.R.F. of Aug. 2, 1994, at 11240.

69. Decision no. 99-412 of June 15, 1999, J.O.R.F. of June 18, 1999, at 8964. On the Charter, see text *infra* at note 175.

70. *See* Marie Landick, *French courts and language legislation*, 11 FRENCH CULTURAL STUDIES 131 (2000) for a non-lawyer's summary of examples of such cases.

71. *See* text *infra* at note 164.

72. Case C-366/98 (*Criminal proceedings against Yannick Geffroy and Casino France SNC. Reference for a preliminary ruling: Cour d'appel de Lyon – France*), [2000] ECR I-6579.

73. FPS Economy - Directorate-general Statistics Belgium, www.statbel.fgov.be.

74. Bruno de Witte, *Regional autonomy, cultural diversity and European integration: the experience of Spain and Belgium*, in Sergio Ortino, Mitja Žagar and Vojtech Mastny, eds., THE CHANGING FACES OF FEDERALISM: INSTITUTIONAL RECONFIGURATION IN EUROPE FROM EAST TO WEST (2005).

75. Articles 4 and 18, respectively.

76. Law of Feb. 24, 1984 on the "*régime des langues*", MÉMORIAL (J.O. GRAND-DUCHÉ DE LUXEMBOURG) A - RECUEIL DE LÉGISLATION no. 016 of Feb. 24, 1984, at 196-197.

77. *See* Nicholas Kasirer, *Lex-icographie mercatoria*, 47 AM. J. COMP. L. 653 (1999).

78. Enacted as Schedule B to Canada Act (U.K.)1982, c. 11, effective April 17, 1982.

79. Interpretation Act, §§ 8.1 and 8.2, R.S.C. 1985 c. I-21, as amended by Federal Law—Civil Law Harmonization Act, No. 1, S.C. 2001, c. 4, s. 8.

80. Constitutional law of 1867, art. 133.

81. The Constitution Act, 1982, articles 16(2), 16.1, 17(2), 18(2), 19(2) and 20(2).

82. Manitoba Act, 1870, 33 Vict., c. 3 (Canada), section 23 (confirmed by the Constitution Act, 1871).

83. *Re Manitoba Language Rights*, [1985] 1 S.C.R. 721. *See* Ruth Sullivan, *The Challenges of Interpreting Multilingual, Multijural Legislation*, 29 Brooklyn J. Int'l L. 985 (2004).

84. L.R.Q. chap. C-11(1977, chap. 5).

85. L.Q., 1991, c. 64.

86. *See* Sullivan at 1026, *supra* note 83.

87. For example, see the cases discussed in text, *supra* note 60.

88. *See* http://www.justice.gc.ca/eng/dept-min/scc-csc/faq.html.

89. *Traité Relatif à l'Harmonisation en Afrique du Droit des Affaires* (JO Ohada N° 4 of Nov. 1, 1997, at 1), signed at Port-Louis (Mauritius), Oct. 17, 1993, deposited with Senegal, and effective since January 1998.

90. Guinea-Bissau is also a member of the CPLP. *See* text *infra* at note 107.

91. OHADA Treaty, art. 10.

92. *Id.*, art. 14.

93. *Id.*, art. 42.

94. Art. 42, *Traité portant Révision du Traité relative à l'Harmonisation du Droit des Affaires en Afrique, signé à Port-Louis (Ile Maurice), le 17 Octobre 1993, available at* www.ohada.com.

95. *See* Nelson Enonchong, *The Harmonization of Business Law in Africa: Is Article 42 of the OHADA Treaty a Problem?*, 51 J. African L. 95 (2007). The comparison that he draws with Canada as also a bilingual English- and French- speaking country overlooks Cameroon's national ethnic and linguistic realities that predate, and survive along with, its colonial legacies.

96. *Available at* www.ohada.org.

97. *See* Félix Onana Etoundi, *Les Principes d'UNIDROIT et la sécurité juridique des transactions commerciales dans l'avant-projet d'Acte uniforme OHADA sur le droit des contrats*, x Uniform Law Review/Revue de Droit Uniforme 683 (UNIDROIT 2005-4).

98. www.unidroit.org.

99. Conclusions of the Colloquium at Ouagadougou (Burkina Faso), Nov. 15-17, 2007, *The Harmonisation of Contract Law within OHADA, available at* www.unidroit.org.

100. *See, e.g.* Mainassara Maidagi (Justice of the Common Court of Justice and Arbitration of OHADA), *Le défi de l'exécution des décisions de justice en droit OHADA*, 35 (116) Recueil Penant 176 (2006), highlighting the challenges in practice for member states to internalize and effectively implement the OHADA uniform law on execution of judgments; Pierre Meyer, *La sécurité juridique et judiciaire dans l'espace OHADA*, 35 (116) Recueil Penant 151 (2006), observing that concerns of judicial impartiality and competence persist within and among the OHADA member states.

101. Lucy Riall, GARIBALDI: INVENTION OF A HERO 135-36 (2007).

102. Italian Constitution, art. 6. *See* Louis Del Duca and Patrick Del Duca, *An Italian Federalism? — the State, its Institutions and National Culture as Rule of Law Guarantor*, 54 AM J. COMP. L. 799 (2006).

103. *See infra* at note 210.

104. Law no. 482 of Dec. 15, 1999, GAZZ. UFF. no. 297 of Dec. 20, 1999. Friulian, Ladino and Romansche are related Rhaeto-Romanic languages with roots in Latin. Occitan and *Provençal* are closely-related Romance languages.

105. *E.g.*, the article 12 provision of Brazil's Constitution for naturalization after one year of residence of those originating from Portuguese-speaking countries, and Portugal's Organic Law no. 2 of April 17, 2006, DIÁRIO DE REPÚBLICA-I SÉRIE-A no. 75, at 2776, of April 17, 2006, which although tightening prior standards, grants naturalization as a right, without the otherwise applicable six-year requirement for naturalization, to those who ever had Portuguese citizenship or a grandparent who never lost Portuguese citizenship, and allows the government to grant naturalization, also without the six-year residency requirement, to those considered "descendants of Portuguese persons" and to "members of communities of Portuguese ascendancy," a mechanism for persons from the former Portuguese enclave of Goa, now part of India, to pursue Portuguese citizenship.

106. *See* Paulo Canelas de Castro, *A Comunidade dos Países de Língua Portuguesa — Para um Discurso Jurídico sobre a sua Identidade e um seu Programa de Acção*, in COLÓQUIO DE DIREITO INTERNACIONAL: COMUNIDADE DOS PAÍSES DE LÍNGUA PORTUGUESA 23-106 (Livraria Almedina, Coimbra 2003).

107. www.cplp.org.

108. Constitution, art. 13.

109. Constitution, art. 159.

110. Joint declaration of the Government of the People's Republic of China and the Government of the Republic of Portugal on the question of Macao (1987), http://www.imprensa.macau.gov.mo/bo/i/88/23/dc/en/.

111. Christopher Tanner, *Law-Making in an African Context: The 1997 Mozambican Land Law*, FAO LEGAL PAPERS ONLINE #26 (March 2002), illustrates the importance and challenges of law reform in a post-colonial, post-conflict state.

112. *See* CPLP web site, www.cplp.org.

113. *Id.*

114. *See* www.iilp-cplp.cv.

115. *See* text *infra* at section VII.B.4.b.

116. *Global Results of By-Census 2006*, DIRECÇÃO DOS SERVIÇOS DE ESTATÍSTICA E CENSES, *available at* www.dsec.gov.mo, at 219 and 221.

117. *See, e.g., Financing Macau*, MACAU BUSINESS (Sept. 1, 2007) (US$6 billion estimated investment since initiation of liberalization of gaming in 2002, with estimated US$30 billion more to come by 2012).

118. Jian En Ci, *Desenvolvimento da Localização e Modernização do Direito Comercial de Macau* 6 Perspectivas do Direito (1999), *available at* www.macaulaw.gov.mo.

119. *Available at* www.imprensa.macau.gov.mo.

120. Constitution, art. 13.

121. Art. 11 of the Portuguese constitution adopted in 1974 with the overthrow of the authoritarian regime.

122. For Portugal: Law no. 24 of July 31, 1996 (Consumer Protection Law), art. 7(3) as amended by Decree Law no. 67 of April 8, 2004; Decree Law no. 67 of April 8, 2003, art. 9(3) (consumer good warranties); Decree Law no. 68 of March 25, 2004, art. 6 (technical information on housing). European law may also limit these requirements. *See* text at notes 71 and 164. For Brazil: *Código de Defesa do Consumidor*, Law no. 8078 of Sept. 11, 1990, art. 31.

123. Constitution, Art. 37.

124. Código Comercial, art. 96. However, the purpose of a company registered for commercial purposes must be correctly stated in Portuguese. Código das Sociedades Comerciais, restated by Decree Law no. 76-A of March 29, 2006, art. 11(1).

125. Art. 365.

126. Law no. 10406 of Jan. 10, 2002, the Brazilian Civil Code, art. 224, provides: "Documents prepared in foreign language must be translated into Portuguese in order to have legal effects in the Country."

127. Law no. 6015 of Dec. 13, 1973, articles 129(6) and 221(iii) respectively.

128. Law no. 10406 of Jan. 10, 2002, Brazil's Civil Code, art. 215(3).

129. Law no. 6015 of Dec. 13, 1973, art. 148, provides that any

"documents and papers written in foreign language, ... in order to be legally enforceable in Brazil and against third parties, shall be translated into Portuguese and have the translation registered, which is also applied to powers of attorney executed in foreign languages."

130. Law no. 10406 of Jan. 10, 2002, art. 104.

131. *Id.*, art. 112.

132. *See* text *supra* at note 51.

133. *Superior Tribunal de Justiça*–2004, REsp 151079/SP–*Recurso Especial* 1997/ 0072063-2.

134. *See* http://buscon.rae.es/draeI/.

135. *See* text *infra* at notes 206 and 244.

136. Diario Official of Aug. 14, 2001, First Section, at 2-4.

137. Ana Luisa Izquierdo and Manuel González Oropeza, *Indigenous Autonomy in Mexico*, 45 Voices of Mexico 17 (1998).

138. Constitution, art. 1.

139. *Id.*, art. 2.

140. *Id.*

141. *Id.*, art. 2(A)(IV).

142. *Id.*, art. 2(B).

143. *Id.*, art. 2(A)(VIII).

144. *See* text *infra* at note 216.

145. http://oaxaca.gob.mx/economia/index.php?seccion=cifras&id=demografia.

146. Constitución Política del Estado Libre y Soberano de Oaxaca, art. 16, *available at* www.congresooaxaca.gob.mx.

147. *Id.*

148. Constitution of Spain, art. 3.

149. Act no. 1 of Jan. 7, 1998, DOGC no. 2553 of Jan. 9, 1998.

150. *Id.*, articles 2(2), 14, 15, 17, 30, 31, and 33.

151. *Sentencia* no. 46 of Feb. 28, 1991.

152. Treaty of Lisbon amending the Treaty on European Union and the Treaty establishing the European Community, signed at Lisbon, Dec. 13, 2007, OJ C 306 (Dec. 17, 2007), fully ratified November 2009. *See* http://europa.eu/lisbon_treaty/index_en.htm.

153. Case C-213/89 (*The Queen v Secretary of State for Transport, ex parte: Factortame Ltd and others*), [1990] ECR I-2433.

154. *See* La Pergola and Del Duca, *supra* note 28.

155. Commission of the European Communities, *Communication from the Commission to the Council, the European Parliament, the European Economic and Social Committee and the Committee of the Regions: A New Framework Strategy for Multilingualism*, COM(2005) 596 final, Nov. 22, 2005.

156. Consolidated Version of the Treaty on European Union, art. 55 (*ex* art. 53 TEU); Consolidated Version of the Treaty on the functioning of the European Union, art. 358 (*ex* art 314 TEC).

157. Consolidated Version of the Treaty on the functioning of the European Union, art. 24 (*ex* art. 21 TEC).

158. *See* Bruno de Witte, *Language Law of the European Union: Protecting or Eroding Linguistic Diversity?* in Rachael Craufurd Smith, ed., CULTURE AND EUROPEAN UNION LAW (2004). On costs of the Community's translation infrastructure, see Richard L. Creech, *supra* note 19 at 26-32.

159. *See, e.g.* de Witte, *supra* note 158, at 221; Richard L. Creech, *supra* note 19 at 24-26.

160. *See* Creech, *supra* note 19, at 49-67.

161. *See* text *infra* at note 274.

162. Case C-361/01P (*Cristina Kik v. Office for Harmonisation in the Internal Market (Trade Marks and Designs) (OHIM)*), [2003] ECR I-8283.

163. *Id.* at paragraphs 93 and 94.

164. Case 120/78 (*Rewe-Zentral AG v. Bundesmonopolverwaltung fur Branntwein ("Cassis de Dijon")*), [1979] ECR 649. *See also Casino, supra* note 71.

165. *See* de Witte, *supra* note 158 at 240-41.

166. Respectively, Case 379/87 (*Groener v. Minister for Education and the Dublin Vocational Education Committee*), [1989] ECR 3967, and Case C-281/98 (*Angonese v. Cassa di Risparmio di Bolzano*), [2000] ECR I-4083.

167. For further discussion of notarial involvement relative to security interests, see Section IV.C.

168. *See* OJ C 303/1 (Dec. 14, 2007).

169. Consolidated Version of the Treaty on European Union, art. 6 (1) (*ex* art. 6).

170. Protocol to the Lisbon Treaty on the Application of the Charter of Fundamental Rights of the European Union.

171. Consolidated Version of the Treaty on European Union, art. 3 (*ex* art. 2).

172. *Id.*, art. 6 (*ex* art. 6).

173. Consolidated Version of the Treaty on the functioning of the European Union, art. 218.

174. *Available at* www.conventions.coe.int. For introduction to the European Court of Human Rights, *see* Michael D. Goldhaber, A PEOPLE'S HISTORY OF THE EUROPEAN COURT OF HUMAN RIGHTS (2007).

175. *Available at* www.conventions.coe.int.

176. OJ C 364/1 (Dec. 18, 2000).

177. Corte cost. judgment nos. 348, 349 of Dec. 22, 2007, Gazz. Uff. of Oct. 31, 2007.

178. *Available at* conventions.coe.int.

179. Council of Europe, *Explanatory report, European Charter for Regional or Minority Languages*, ¶10, *available at* http://conventions.coe.int/Treaty/en/Reports/Html/148.htm.

180. Articles 9 and 10, European Charter for Regional or Minority Languages, *available at* conventions.coe.int.

181. Part III, *id.*

182. Article 1, *id.*

183. Articles 4 and 5, *id.*

184. Status *available at* conventions.coe.int.

185. Declarations *available at* conventions.coe.int.

186. ALI/UNIDROIT PRINCIPLES OF TRANSNATIONAL CIVIL PROCEDURE, adopted 2004 by ALI and UNIDROIT, Section 6.

187. *See* NOUVEAU CODE DE PROCÉDURE CIVIL, articles 23 (judge not obligated to use interpreter if judge knows language in which the parties express themselves), 688-6 (recipient of notification of foreign act in language not understood by defendant entitled to translation at plaintiff's expense), 740 (questions posed by parties and their counsel, even if foreigners, and responses, to be accompanied by translation), and 1499 (arbitral awards not prepared in French to be presented with certified translation by registered translator). Art. L123-22 of the CODE DE COMMERCE requires accounting documentation to be kept in French.

188. Portugal's Código de Processo Civil, as revised in 2003, provides that proceedings be accomplished in Portuguese, and that foreigners who do not know Portuguese may be assisted as necessary by a sworn translator. Art. 139.

189. Nouveau Code de Procédure Civil, art. 23.

190. *See* Mitchel Lasser, *The European Pasteurization of French Law*, 90 Cornell L. Rev. 995 (2005); Pierre Birnbaum, The Heights of Power: An Essay on the Power Elite in France (1982); Ezra N. Suleiman, Politics, Power, and Bureaucracy in France: The Administrative Elite (1974).

191. The Constitution Act, 1867, art. 133, continued in force by The Constitution Act, 1982.

192. *Id.*, art. 14.

193. Charter of the French Language, art. 7.

194. Código Federal de Procedimientos Civiles, art. 180.

195. *Id.*, art. 271.

196. *Id.*

197. Law no. 1 of Jan. 7, 2000 of *Enjuiciamiento Civil*. http://noticias.juridicas.com/base_datos/Privado/l1-2000.html.

198. Art. 142.

199. *Id.*

200. *Id.*

201. Articles 142 and 143.

202. Art. 122.

203. Art. 4.

204. Brazil's Civil Procedure Code allows judges to consider documents written in foreign languages, provided that a Portuguese translation by a sworn translator is available. Código de Processo Civil, Law no. 5869 of Jan. 11, 1973, art. 157.

205. *E.g.* Portugal's Código de Processo Civil, Art. 140. A Brazilian court may call upon a translator for assistance in further understanding the significance of any foreign language documents, even if already translated. Código de Processo Civil, Law no. 5869 of Jan. 11, 1973, art. 151.

206. Código Procesal Civil y Comercial de la Nación, Law no. 17454 of Sept. 20, 1967, Boletín Oficial no. 21308 of Nov. 7, 1967, art. 115.

207. *Id.*, art. 123.

208. Art. 122, Code of Civil Procedure, adopted by R.D. no. 1443 of Oct. 28, 1940, Gazz. Uff. no. 253 of Oct. 28, 1940, and much amended.

209. *Id.*

210. Art. 123.

211. DPR no. 670 of August 31, 1972, Gazz. Uff. no. 301 of Nov. 20, 1972, art. 100.

212. Constitutional Law no. 4 of Feb. 26, 1948, Gazz. Uff. no. 59 of March 10, 1948, art. 38.

213. Art. 144.

214. *Id.*

215. Código Federal de Procedimientos Civiles, art. 132.

216. *Id.*, art. 180.

217. Código Procesal Civil y Comercial de la Nación, Law no. 17454 of Sept. 20, 1967, Boletín Oficial no. 21308 of Nov. 7, 1967, art. 115.

218. *See* text *infra* starting at note 385.

219. Código Procesal Civil y Comercial de la Nación, Law no. 17454 of Sept. 20, 1967, Boletín Oficial no. 21308 of Nov. 7, 1967, Book Six.

220. Art. 67, *available at* http://www.sice.oas.org/DISPUTE/COMARB/argentina/regarb2.asp.

221. Law no. 9307 of Sept. 23, 1996, art. 37. *See* Joaquim T. de Paiva Muniz and Ana Tereza Palhares Basilio, Arbitration Law of Brazil: Practice and Procedure (2006).

222. Carlos Calvo (1824-1906) was an Argentine diplomat who wrote a treatise on international law, published in five editions in French and Spanish between 1868 and 1896. The Calvo Doctrine, drawn from his work, asserts that foreigners are to be treated on a plane of absolute equality with the nationals of a given country. Foreigners should not lay any claim to diplomatic protection or intervention by their home countries since this would only provide a pretext for violations of the territorial sovereignty and judicial independence of the less powerful nations. Carlos Calvo, 1 Le Droit International Théorique et Pratique (4TH ed., 1887) (*"dans leurs démêlés avec les États américaines, les nations européennes sont toujours intervenues contre les faibles et ne sont jamais attaqués aux forts et aux puissants."* [in their disputes with American States, the European nations have always intervened against the weak ones and have never attacked the strong and the powerful] *Id.* at 349.).

223. Const. art. 27 limits acquisition of "lands and waters" to Mexican companies and citizens. Exception is made to foreigners who accept a Calvo clause and agree that its breach means forfeiture of the property at issue. Const. art. 27(I).

224. D.O., Jan. 4, 1989.

225. D.O., Jul. 22, 1993. Mexico's Commercial Code Book 5, Title 4 is "On Commercial Arbitration." Cód. Com. art. 1415-1463.

226. *Id.*, art. 1436 and art. 1438, respectively.

227. *Id.*, art. 1438.

228. *Id.*, art. 1415.

229. *See* Del Duca, *supra* note 27.

230. *Ley del Servicio Público de Energía*, art. 45, as amended by D.O., Dec. 23, 1992 and Dec. 22, 1993 (CFE); *Ley Orgánica de Petróleos Mexicanos y Organismos Subsidiarios*, art. 14, as amended by D.O., Dec. 22, 1993 (Pemex).

231. Eva-Marie Kieninger, *Evaluation: a common core? Convergences, subsisting differences and possible ways for harmonization*, in Eva-Marie Kieninger, ed., Security Rights in Movable Property in European Private Law 647, 670 (2004),

lays out the heterogeneity of European national legal frameworks for secured lending based on case study examination of fifteen European Union Member States, plus South Africa and the United States.

232. Patrick Del Duca and Rodrigo Zamora Etcharren, *Mexico's Secured Lending Reforms*, 33 UCC L.J. 225 (2000).

233. *See* www.siger.gob.mx.

234. On the Mexican writ of *amparo*, see Del Duca, *supra* note 27, at 98-105.

235. CÓDIGO DE COMERCIO, art. 25(I).

236. CÓDIGO DE COMERCIO, art. 25(III).

237. Articles 365 and 404.

238. *Ley Federal de Correduría Pública*, art. 19(V).

239. *Ley del Notariado para el Distrito Federal*, GACETA OFICIAL DEL DISTRITO FEDERAL of March 28, 2000.

240. *Id.*, art. 162(IV). Although the notary is to prepare a notarial instrument in Spanish, the instrument may use foreign language terms that are generally used as specific terms of science or art. *Id.*, art. 102. Foreign language materials are to be included in their original copy, but with translation into Spanish by a recognized translator. *Id.*, art. 102(XVII). Persons with insufficient knowledge of Spanish appearing before a notary may name an interpreter to assist them. *Id.*, art. 107.

241. *Id.*, art. 135.

242. CÓDIGO CIVIL FEDERAL, art. 3006.

243. *Ley General de Títulos y Operaciones de Crédito*, art. 388. CÓDIGO DE COMERCIO, art. 25(I).

244. *See* Julio A. Kelly, *Argentina* in INTERNATIONAL SECURED TRANSACTIONS (2003); Heywood W. Fleisig and Nuria de la Peña, *Argentina: Cómo las Leyes para Garantizar Préstamos Limitan el Acceso a Crédito* (Center for the Economic Analysis of Law, 1996).

245. *Doing Business in Brazil* (The International Bank for Reconstruction and Development / The World Bank, 2006); Sergio Spinelli Silva Jr., Daniel Calhman de Miranda, Camila Leal Calais and Katerine Yuka Tsuchitori, *Brazil* in INTERNATIONAL SECURED TRANSACTIONS (2007).

246. As to notarization and language, see http://www.notaire.be/info/acheter/421_acte_notarie_langue.htm. As to registration, see Thierry Bosly, Thierrry Lohest, Gilbert Nyatanyi and Vincent Moyhy, *Belgium* in INTERNATIONAL SECURED TRANSACTIONS 9 (2005).

247. Swiss Federal Civil Code, art. 10.

248. *Id.*, art. 55 of the Final Title (on the entry into force and application of the Civil Code).

249. *See* description of "Notartel" service, *available at* www.notariato.it.

250. Law no. 89 of Feb. 16, 1913, art. 54, GAZZ. UFF. no. 55 of March 7, 1913.

251. *Id.*

252. *Id.*, art. 55.

253. *See* text *supra* at note 211; www.notai.bz.it/italiano/diventareNotaio.php (website of *Consiglio notarile di Bolzano*).

254. *See* text *supra* at note 212.

255. D.L. no. 223 of July 4, 2006, art. 2(a), Gazz. Uff. no. 153 of July 4, 2006, rectified Gazz. Uff. no. 159 of July 11, 2006, converted into law by Law no. 248 of Aug. 4, 2006, Gazz. Uff. no. 186 of Aug. 11, 2006, ord. supp., coordinated text Gazz. Uff. no. 186 of Aug. 11, 2006 ord. supp.

256. *See* text *supra* at note 148.

257. José A. de Bonilla Pella, *Spain* in International Secured Transactions 7-9 (2003).

258. Law of May 28, 1862 as amended (*del Notariado*), art. 25.

259. Statute of Autonomy of Catalonia 2006, art. 33.

260. Act no. 1 of Jan. 7, 1998, *supra* note 149, articles 2, 4, 12, 14, and 15 (especially 14(5)).

261. Civil Code articles 2284 through 2488, as amended by *Ordonnance* no. 346 of March 23, 2006, J.O.R.F. of March 24, 2006, at 4475.

262. Code Civile, art. 2348 (as to tangible, moveable property), art. 2459 (as to real property).

263. *Id.*

264. Cass. Com., *arrêt* no. 1500 of Dec. 19, 2006, *SARL DIVA v. Caisse fédérale du crédit mutuel du Nord de la France, available at* www.courdecassation.fr.

265. Code de Commerce, art. L527-2.

266. Code Civile, articles 2333-2350.

267. Code de Commerce, articles L527-1 to L527-11.

268. Code Civile, art. 2236 (*gage sans dépossession*); Code de Commerce, Art. L527-1 (*gage des stocks*).

269. *Id.*, art. 2238.

270. *See* www.infogreffe.fr.

271. Decree no. 2006-1804 of Dec. 23, 2006, J.O.R.F. no. 303 of Dec. 31, 2006, at 20368.

272. Code Civile, articles 2355 and 2356. Special rules apply to pledges of accounts receivable. *Id.*, articles 2356-2366.

273. Code de Commerce, art. L527-4.

274. Directive 2003/71/EC of the European Parliament and of the Council of Nov. 4, 2003, OJ L 345/64 (Jan. 31, 2003), art. 19(1), 19(3). For discussion of models of harmonization specific to securities law, see Patrick Del Duca, *Uniform law, federated jurisdictions and an example from U.S. and EEC securities regulation* in Int'l Uniform Law in Practice 470 (UNIDROIT, 1988).

275. Directive 2003/71/EC, art. 19(2), supra note 274.

276. Código dos Valores Mobiliários, art. 163-A.

277. Código dos Valores Mobiliários, art. 6. *See also* articles 147-A requiring a tender offer to be made in Portuguese unless the Securities Commission

otherwise decides that the "interests of investors are protected", and 389 defining failure to provide materials also in Portuguese as a lesser offence.

278. *Lei das Sociedades por Ações,* Law no. 6404 of Dec. 15, 1976, amended by Law no. 9457 of May 5, 1997, art. 73(3).

279. 15 U.S.C. §77r.

Map Six - Community of Portugese Language Countries

V. PARTY WORK-AROUNDS TO GOVERNMENTAL IMPOSITIONS OF LINGUISTIC BURDENS

Savvy international lawyers routinely work around legal norms that transaction parties find troublesome. To minimize exposure to unwelcome norms of a legal system, they structure transactions by parceling them among various agreements and entities. As part of this parceling, portions of transactions may be allocated to agreements among specially-created entities in other jurisdictions that do not feature the troublesome norms. The goal is to place the relevant portions of the transaction as much as possible beyond the scope of application of the norms of concern. In particular, international lawyers undertake such structuring with a view to mitigate the challenges to performance and enforcement of transactions in the face of undesired norms of a legal system, whose application might be triggered either by a disgruntled party or by a governmental authority of its own initiative.

Adroit structuring of relationships, specification of entities, and contractual drafting of governing law and mechanism for dispute resolution provisions can blunt the impact of requirements of governmental authorities that encourage or mandate the conduct of particular interactions with governmental authorities in an official language. Because of such savvy lawyering, governmental requirements to promote a language by mandating that interactions with governmental authorities in support of transnational business be conducted in a particular language may do little to achieve actual promotion of the language. Likewise, they may have only limited impact on the conduct of a transaction and its enforceability notwithstanding the choice of the parties to employ a disfavored language for all or a predominant part of their dealings. What follows here is an exposition of opportunities for parties to transnational commercial and financial deals, with particular attention to the issue of language, to work around governmental strictures that they find uncongenial.

A. Two generations of US judicial response to party work-arounds

Legislators, civil servants, and judges are capable of considerable ingenuity in articulating and enforcing peremptory governmental policies on the one hand, while transaction parties and their legal counsel can be just as ingenious in navigating and evading them on the other. Examples addressed by two generations of the United States Supreme Court illustrate this ingenuity and the modern trend of recognizing that parties to transnational deals will use their creativity to evade uncongenial norms. Indeed, the trend is not only to recognize their creativity, but in some measure to encourage it. Although neither of the two cases directly concerns the parties' choice of language, the two cases taken together illustrate the increasing respect on the part of United States courts of choices of all types made by parties to transnational deals. One source of this respect is the recognition that parties to such transactions do have means available to work around governmental strictures that they do not find congenial. A further source is the recognition that in many instances no useful purpose is served by disrespecting party choices.

Justice Brandeis in 1930, in the first of the two cases, *Home Insurance Company v. Dick*, addressed an effort by an insurance policy beneficiary to collect the proceeds of a fire insurance policy issued in Mexico by a Mexican insurance company to cover a tugboat.[280] The plaintiff was not the original Mexican insured, but rather an assignee. The ability to bring a legal action in Mexico against the issuer based on the policy was barred by expiration of the statute of limitations in Mexico. Having subsequently taken up residence in Texas, the plaintiff brought the case in Texas, on the basis of a Texas statute mandating provision in insurance policies of at least a two-year period to bring claims.

The defendants named were New York insurance companies with which the Mexican insurer had procured reinsurance coverage. The plaintiff attempted to obtain jurisdiction over the New York insurance companies by serving the agents for service of process that the New York insurance companies had appointed in Texas in connection with qualifying to do business there. The New York insurance companies thusly targeted through this tenuous, but artfully traced chain, were alleged to have a duty to pay the plaintiff under New York law.

Justice Brandeis wrote for the unanimous court to conclude that the Texas statute was overreaching in that the state "may not abrogate the rights of parties beyond its borders having no relation to anything done or to be done within them." Had the dispute originated in facts with greater links to Texas, the two-year requirement of the Texas statute would conceivably have governed. The Court was not persuaded by the plaintiff's efforts to bring the matter under Texas law. Indeed, this case can be understood as principally about turning back an aggressive plaintiff by careful analysis of the parameters of a transaction concluded by the original parties with intent to rely entirely upon Mexican law. In a sense, the original parties to the insurance contract "chose" governing law other than Texas law simply by having nothing whatsoever to do with Texas. The United States Supreme Court in its conflict of law analysis upheld their choice against the assertion of a countervailing policy claimed to be embodied in Texas law.

Justice Burger, writing for the United States Supreme Court a generation later in the *Bremen* case, addressed a different, but related subject, namely the respect of express party choices about how to manage legal issues arising in connection with business conducted across borders. In its *Bremen* decision of 1972, the United States Supreme Court upheld a choice of forum clause in a contract between the American owner of a drilling rig and the German company engaged to tow it from Louisiana to Italy.[281]

The Court ruled that it would enforce respect of the parties' initial choice of the High Court of Justice in London as the place to resolve disputes unless the protesting party met the "heavy burden of showing that its enforcement would be unreasonable, unfair, or unjust." This ruling frustrated the American owner's effort to sue in courts in the United States after a storm damaged the rig at the beginning of the towing process and resulted in unanticipated docking in Florida. The Court in so doing reversed lower court determinations that

> "agreements in advance of controversy whose object is to oust the jurisdiction of the courts are contrary to public policy and will not be enforced."[282]

Justice Burger, ratifying the approach of the RESTATEMENT (SECOND) OF THE CONFLICT OF LAWS §80 (1971), motivated the majority holding in *Bremen* as follows:

> "The expansion of American business and industry will hardly be encouraged if, not-withstanding solemn contracts, we insist on a parochial concept that all disputes must be resolved under our laws and in our courts. Absent a contract forum, the considerations relied on by the Court of Appeals would be persuasive reasons for holding an American forum convenient in the traditional sense, but in an era of expanding world trade and commerce, the absolute aspects of the doctrine of the *Carbon Black* case have little place and would be a heavy hand indeed on the future development of international commercial dealings by Americans. We cannot have trade and commerce in world markets and international waters exclusively on our terms, governed by our laws, and resolved in our courts."

Justice Burger left open the possibility of invalidating a choice of forum clause in select instances, observing:

"A contractual choice-of-forum clause should be held unenforceable if enforcement would contravene a strong public policy of the forum in which suit is brought, whether declared by statute or by judicial decision."

Justice Burger's endorsement of the RESTATEMENT (SECOND)'s soft multilateral approach of deference to party autonomy absent a "strong public policy" to the contrary, confirms the inherent uncertainty about what private international law rules a court of any given legal system might apply in a specific instance. Justice Burger's ruling underlines the opportunity, and indeed invites, the thoughtful identification of governing law and mechanism for dispute resolution by transnational deal parties, as well as structuring of their transactions, so as to carefully define what parts of them are exposed to any particular legal system and such of its requirements as may be potentially of concern.

The issue of working around governmental policies favoring the use of an official language, like the international "conflict of law" cases addressed by Justices Brandeis and Burger, is very much shaped by the lack of a "supreme" court to judge whether application of the policy is founded in a given instance. Indeed, each of Justices Brandeis and Burger wrote for the Supreme Court of the United States on a distinct topic, the former to restrict the application of a law of a state of the United States and the latter to subordinate, or at least soften, the law of the United States so as to allow deference to, and application of, the parties' choice of law at the time of contracting. However, neither was in the position of a truly supreme international court able to impose its resolution of the issue on all relevant legal systems. Accordingly, the lack of a universal court is at the root of both Supreme Court decisions.

In the absence of a universal and monist legal system, the issue of how governmental authorities and transaction parties confront governmental policies favoring the use of an official language, has common ground with the machinations of the legal team of the plaintiff before Justice Brandeis. The commonality is the opportunity to work around such policies by the thoughtful structuring of transactions, the careful identification of governing law, and the astute selection of forum in which to raise disputes.

B. Party techniques to overcome challenging language policies

1. Bifurcated transactions

The simplest way to avoid troublesome requirements of a legal system is not to conduct business within the legal system. Behind the extremism of this seeming tautology, is the common practice of conducting business through off-shore entities. Although the term "off-shore" evokes an island-haven where transactions can be accomplished out of sight of mainland authorities, it is used in the present context to refer to any location of an entity outside the jurisdiction of the legal system of concern. Transactions are often structured using pre-existing or newly-constituted entities that are created outside the jurisdiction of concern and that avoid to undertake activity that would subject them to the norms of a jurisdiction of concern. Issues that would be subject to problematic treatment under the legal system of concern are instead routinely addressed in agreements between entities that remain outside the reach of the jurisdiction of concern.

One path to division of a transaction among jurisdictions is the creation of entities in multiple jurisdictions, each of which handles a portion of the transaction. A Luxembourg subsidiary of a French company that the parent company uses as a conduit to issue bonds to be traded on the New York Stock Exchange, is an example. Alternatively, parties to a joint venture might constitute a joint venture entity in a jurisdiction that they deem congenial for any number of reasons, including language, substantive law, taxation and quality of legal institutions, among others. The joint venture entity would then own assets in other jurisdictions. The result is to divide among jurisdictions, on the one hand, the issues related to governance of the joint venture, and on the other, the law applicable to the revenue-generating activity. In each instance part of a transaction is accomplished in other jurisdictions to benefit from favorable corporate, tax, bankruptcy, securities or other legal norms, or more favorable market conditions. Although a governmental authority might attempt to apply its norms extra-territorially to regulate such activity in any event, any such attempt, to have effect, must overcome the challenge to the governmental authority of learning about what happens outside the jurisdiction. Such a challenge is most likely to be overcome if the governmental authority benefits from the cooperation of authorities in the off-shore jurisdiction, if one of the parties becomes disgruntled and accordingly informs the governmental authority, or if a competitor of the parties with knowledge of the offshore structure decides to inform the relevant governmental authority.

Transactions involving cross-border secured lending further illustrate the opportunities and the limitations of how deals can be structured to avoid the strictures of jurisdictions with norms perceived as problematic by the parties. Cross-border credit transactions are often bifurcated between (i) agreements related to the extension of credit and (ii) the steps necessary to constitute priority liens in collateral under the law of the jurisdiction where the collateral resides. The borrower and the lender parties can agree to organize the loan documentation to fall under the law of just about any jurisdiction, although such agreements are often under New York or English law as centers where transnational lenders are based and which have correspondingly well-developed commercial and financial law. However, the part of the deal pertaining to the borrower's provision of collateral to guarantee repayment needs to be under the law of the jurisdiction where the collateral is located because of the need to insure effective enforcement of the lien priority against third party creditors. Linguistically, the agreements that speak to the extension of credit and the terms of its repayment are often English-language agreements, whereas the documentation of the collateral package is ineluctably subject to the language requirements imposed by the governmental authorities with which its creation and enforcement relative to the debtor and third party creditors necessitate interaction.

The bifurcation of cross-border transactions is routinely pressed to include the formulation of inter-creditor agreements under the law of the jurisdiction "off-shore" relative to the location of the collateral. Thus, it is common for multiple lenders who extend credit to a borrower in, for example Mexico, on the basis of collateral in Mexico in which the borrower grants them a lien in reliance on procedures of Mexican law, to make agreements among themselves in the form of an English-language agreement prepared under New York law. Such inter-creditor agreements may address (i) the terms of subordination among themselves of their relative claims, (ii) the procedures by which decisions among them will be made about when to foreclose, and (iii) conditions of eventual forbearance in the event of a borrower default. Should one of the creditors contracting with the others in this sense fail to adhere to its bargain, it would be subject to actions for specific performance and damages by the other creditors party to the inter-creditor agreement in the offshore jurisdiction under the law of that jurisdiction, all transpiring in the language of that jurisdiction and not the official language of the jurisdiction where the debtor and the collateral are located. The presence of many lenders in such places as London and New York facilitates the making of these kinds of agreements with English or New York choice of law and forum clauses. The presence of the creditors party to an inter-creditor agreement in these jurisdictions makes it unlikely that English or New York courts would decline jurisdiction and generally obviates potential concerns that there would be a lack of available assets against which to enforce an eventual judgment against one or more of them.

These inter-creditor agreements work because they attempt to define rights only among the parties to them, not third parties. In this sense the inter-creditor agreements share a characteristic of agreements between commercial parties to resolve contract disputes by arbitration. Take for example a transaction involving multiple lenders based in New York that are extending credit to a borrower in Mexico, based on the borrower's grant of a priority claim to collateral in Mexico as security for the borrower's repayment of the loan. The parties' ability to establish in English the priority of their claims to collateral against third parties, by contractual documentation that they agree be subject to the law of an English-speaking jurisdiction, and perhaps even an English-language arbitration, is almost certainly limited. The parties must establish the security interest in the collateral under the law, and accordingly using the language, of the non-English speaking jurisdiction of the collateral's location, *i.e.* Mexico, in order that the priority claim of the creditors be effective against third parties who might make recourse to Mexican courts. However, among themselves the parties have the flexibility to make to each other such contractual undertakings as they choose, using English or New York law, and English or New York courts as the forum in which to resolve eventual disputes.

Because of the general need in the context of foreclosure (and bankruptcy proceedings) to be able to enforce obligations regarding collateral in the jurisdiction where the collateral resides, governmental policies mandating the use of a particular language for the drafting of the documentation which constitutes and establishes the priority of such interests, may well prove effective in the sense that parties desiring to accomplish their transaction will need to adhere to the requirements of such policies. However, such policies will nonetheless become counter-productive if burdensome to the point of directing transactional activity elsewhere. Such policies are likely to be effective because the creation of the security interest and the establishment of its priority require registration in some form of government-sanctioned data base accessible to the public in order to establish a priority defensible against third parties. Sound reason for requirements to impose the use of a language relative to the establishment of the priority of a security interest in collateral is to achieve the goal of publicity that is the motivation of the registration system. Imposition of language requirements may serve to make the content of the registry intelligible to the relevant public, and to allow the governmental personnel concerned to understand enough so that the registration and related indexation can be implemented.

2. *Choice of law and forum for dispute resolution*

Astute structuring of contract clauses to address choice of law and mechanism for dispute resolution may work to mitigate the limitations that public policies uncongenial to the intentions of the parties would impose, including policies favoring a language not of their choice. These structural approaches that turn on choice of law and forum for dispute resolution seek to move the resolution of disputes to a forum that will disregard or obviate the troublesome provision. For example, the parties might choose New York law as the governing law, and New York courts as the forum for dispute resolution, relative to a contractual relationship that they prefer to establish in English, but that French law and French courts might characterize as an employment relationship, falling within the Toubon legislation's requirement that such a contractual relationship be documented in French as a condition of its enforceability.

In general, most legal systems are likely to agree that the parties' agreement to choice of law for dispute resolution is to be respected, at least as long as the parties or their transaction have some substantial relationship with the relevant jurisdiction or there is a reasonable basis for such agreement. The significant exception to the otherwise widespread respect of party choice of governing law concerns matters of "fundamental policy." As the RESTATEMENT SECOND, CONTRACTS relative to United States law frames the issue, the parties' choice of governing law will not be respected if:

> "application of the law of the chosen state would be contrary to a fundamental policy of a state which has a materially greater interest than the chosen state in the determination of the particular issue and which . . . would be the state of the applicable law in the absence of an effective choice of law by the parties."[283]

The trend is likewise to defer to party choice of forum for the resolution of disputes, as recognized for example in the American Law Institute/UNIDROIT PRINCIPLES OF TRANSNATIONAL PROCEDURE.[284]

The absence of the parties' specification in a transnational contract of what law governs the contract, together with conflicting law of relevant national legal systems, can create considerable uncertainty about how, substantively and procedurally, a dispute about their contract might be resolved. The further absence of an agreement on choice of forum for resolution of disputes additionally exacerbates this uncertainty. The outcome of a dispute might indeed by determined by which party first makes recourse to a court and by the court chosen by that first moving party. There are, however, "soft law" efforts to address this problem of private international law in coordinated fashion through the technique of restatements.

The American Law Institute/UNIDROIT PRINCIPLES OF TRANSNATIONAL PROCEDURE employ the term "substantial connection" for use in determining what law should govern a contract in the absence of agreement by contract parties on the point. The PRINCIPLES OF TRANSNATIONAL PROCEDURE define "substantial connection" with reference to the criteria of where a "significant part" of the transaction occurred, where a defendant habitually resides, where a defendant is organized or has its principal place of business, and where property is located.[285] Courts generally will make their determination by considering factors of this sort, as also indicated by the American Law Institute's domestic United States work, the RESTATEMENT SECOND, CONTRACTS. The RESTATEMENT SECOND, CONTRACTS uses similar terms with reference to the concept of substantial connection, for example, the places of contracting, contract negotiation and contract performance, location of the contract subject matter, and domicile, residence, nationality, place of incorporation and place of business of the parties. [286] These are all criteria embraced by Justice Burger in the discussion above of the *Bremen* case, through his reference to them via the RESTATEMENT SECOND, CONFLICT OF LAWS.[287]

The "fundamental policy" exception, also noted by Justice Burger, is a further variable that parties might take into account as they make agreements about choice of law and choice of forum. Parties to a cross-border transaction might well seek by a contractual choice of forum clause to place eventual disputes between them in the hands of the courts that are least likely to accept an imposition of law that the parties find burdensome as a "fundamental policy", in which a relevant state might have a "materially greater interest". Staying away from courts that are more likely to accept a troublesome provision as a "fundamental policy" because it is a policy of their own legal system, is a common aspect of party efforts to protect the autonomy of their agreements.

Whether techniques of using choice of law and choice of forum work at all to protect the autonomy of party agreements is in part rooted in the underlying substance at issue. As here suggested, they might well not work with respect to constitution of an interest in collateral intended to be the object of foreclosure in the event of a borrower default in the repayment of a loan. For example, the purported constitution of a priority security interest in English in contradiction of the law of the jurisdiction where the collateral is located that would require such interests be constituted in a non-English official language of the jurisdiction, would likely be ineffective against claims of creditors in that jurisdiction. A court of that jurisdiction would likely find that the third party creditors had neither actual nor constructive notice of the purported priority creditor's claim because of the use of a language not recognized in the jurisdiction. Moreover, a court before which the dispute was brought via an agreement of the parties might well decide to recognize the existence of a fundamental policy as to language, for example to alert third party creditors, that the state of location of the collateral has a "materially greater interest" in promoting.

In short, notwithstanding any agreements of a debtor and creditor regarding priority of liens, the determination of who holds the highest priority security interest in collateral is one instance where party choices of law and forum other than that of the state where the collateral is located, would likely not be respected as determinative of any relationship except the relationship directly between the parties themselves. In such an instance, the state where the collateral is located would likely deem itself as having a materially greater interest in the dispute than any other state whose law or courts the parties might choose. The provisions of the Restatements and Principles mentioned recognize this prospect. Indeed, if the question of what law governed the priority of a security interest in collateral came before a court other than of the location of the collateral, or before an arbitrator, such a court or arbitrator might likewise determine that the law of the place of location of the collateral, regardless of any agreement of the creditor and debtor, embodies a "fundamental policy of a state which has a materially greater interest" in the application of the policy.

How well approaches of party definition of choice of law and choice of forum work, depends on the weight that a designated forum gives to the choice of the parties, and also on the ability of a party acting as a plaintiff to enforce the resulting resolution in jurisdictions that likewise will disregard the troublesome provision. French courts, for example, might well refuse to enforce either a foreign judgment or an arbitral award against a French employee, if based on an agreement found to be an employment contract prepared, in violation of the Toubon legislation, in a language other than French.

3. *Arbitration*

A further tool for parties to cross-border transactions to maximize assurance of the autonomy of their agreements is for the parties to agree to arbitration of any disputes that may arise. The widespread adoption of the New York Convention and other treaties supporting party choice of international arbitration is a major constituent of the trend to respect the choices of parties to transnational deals about how they wish to conduct their business, including their choices about the language in which to define and conduct their relationship. Because states by their ratification of such treaties accept arbitration, it is unlikely that arbitrators, or a national court considering the enforcement of an arbitral award, would reach questions of whether party choice of language in which to conduct either the initial transaction or subsequent arbitral proceedings, violates a "fundamental policy" as to language. Moreover, party agreement to arbitration is a way to limit the challenges raised by submitting, for example, an English-language contract to dispute resolution processes that would involve courts and others not fluent in English and particularly English-language legal terminology such as the parties might have employed in their agreements. Of course, for purposes of such matters as the establishment and enforcement of a priority creditor claim to collateral to secure repayment of a loan, which collateral was left in the possession of the borrower, the issue of compliance with the law of the jurisdiction of where the collateral is located remains, because of the inability of the parties in their arbitration agreement to limit the rights of third party creditors to make direct recourse to the relevant courts.

The New York Convention on the Enforcement and Recognition of Foreign Arbitral Awards is in force among more than 140 countries, including almost all of those named in this investigation.[288] The New York Convention and various conventions addressing the same subject matter, but of regional or bilateral scope, for example, the Inter-American Convention on International Commercial Arbitration (the "Panama Convention"),[289] establish the agreement of the ratifying states to respect and enforce arbitral awards resolving disputes between parties from different states. Parties who agree to such arbitrations in their contracts at the time they are made, or subsequently, can entrust the resolution of the dispute to arbitrators whom they believe competent to deal with the language and terminology of their transaction and its documentation. Indeed, the arbitration clauses used in such contracts often specify that the arbitrators must have fluency in the language in which the parties have chosen to conduct their relationship, for example, English, and satisfy further requisites of subject matter expertise relevant to address the contract interpretation issues that may arise.

A further option for potential disputes between a foreign investor and a host country government, as distinguished from a dispute between two private parties, is arbitration through the International Center for the Settlement of Investment Disputes ("ICSID"), pursuant to any of the ICSID convention, a Bilateral Investment Treaty by which a host country accepts such arbitration, or an *ad hoc* agreement.[290] Typically the provisions relative to enforcement of arbitral awards resulting from such dispute resolution between a state and a foreign investor are either established to be those of the New York Convention, or are substantially analogous to them.

There are only limited exceptions under the terms of the New York Convention pursuant to which a ratifying state may decline to enforce a qualifying arbitral award.[291] The grounds to decline enforcement are: (i) incapacity of the parties to make the arbitration agreement; (ii) failure of due process to allow the losing party to present its case; (iii) that the arbitral award exceeds the scope of the agreement to arbitrate; (iv) improper constitution of the arbitral panel; (v) failure under applicable law of the arbitral award to bind the parties; and, (vi) that the country in which enforcement is sought does not allow arbitration of the dispute, or recognition of the award would be contrary to its public policy.

International arbitration under the New York Convention and other analogous treaties raises the same limitations as domestic arbitration relative to ability to appeal a contested arbitral award, that is, that an arbitral award is ordinarily not subject to appeal for errors of fact or law as would be a judgment by a court of first instance. However, in the international context, the limited grounds to contest enforcement of the award constitute a substantial incentive to the parties to elect arbitration rather than litigation before national courts. The limited ability to contest an arbitral award is precisely one of its principal attractions. By adopting an arbitration clause enforceable by treaty in all relevant national legal systems, that further benefits by virtue of the treaty ratification from a strong assurance of enforceability of an ensuing award, the parties largely avoid issues of national procedure. Further, they avoid the limitations of national courts relative to language and perhaps also concerning substantive knowledge of the parties' business transaction and its context.

One negative aspect of the trend to arbitration of transnational commercial and financial disputes is that arbitration deprives national court systems of activity. Instead of public resolution of such issues in the courts, the procedures associated with arbitration remain opaque from public view, and the ultimate resolution and the grounds for such resolution adopted by the arbitrators remain private to the parties directly involved.[292] By subtracting consideration of significant cross-border commercial and financial matters from such court systems, arbitration deprives them of an opportunity to confront challenging issues, and accordingly to articulate further and clarify commercial and financial law relevant to purely domestic as well as transnational deals. As parties to cross-border deals weigh the competing merits of commitments to each other to resolve their disputes by arbitration rather than in courts, they do not consider the implications of their choices for the further development of the law and institutions of national legal systems.

The specification in a contract that the law governing a transaction be a law that allows the transaction to be conducted in, for example, English, would constitute further protection against any policy of another relevant legal system mandating or encouraging that some part of the transaction depend upon a national law requiring use of a language other than English. Moreover, providing that the forum for resolution of disputes and enforcement not be a jurisdiction whose conflict of law and substantive policies are problematic, would diminish the likelihood of any judicial invocation of the troublesome national provisions.

The courts of the place of arbitration agreed by the parties typically assert jurisdiction over judicial actions arising from an arbitration. A party who chooses to raise one of the grounds to challenge an arbitral award under the New York Convention, may well bring that challenge in the courts of the place of arbitration. For example, in the *Metalclad* arbitration between the Metalclad company and the Government of Mexico that gave rise to one of the initial North American Free Trade Agreement ("NAFTA") Chapter 11 arbitral awards, the parties had agreed that British Columbia would be deemed the place of arbitration. When Mexico challenged the validity of the arbitral award against it, the British Columbia court of first instance issued an opinion that could be read to demonstrate considerable willingness to revisit the substance of the award that was contested before it. Although the matter was eventually resolved with a payment by Mexico to *Metalclad* in conformity with one of the grounds identified by the arbitrators for their award, the willingness of the British Columbia court to revisit the substance of the award, as perceived in its opinion on the matter, may have, at least for a period of time, discouraged drafters of arbitration clauses, and the parties agreeing to them, from selecting British Columbia as a place of arbitration.[293]

The simple reason why parties would exercise care in establishing what courts could review an arbitral award, is to be as certain as practicable that the eventual award is upheld. As a result of the exercise of such care, a national court of the jurisdiction of the troublesome provisions would only have the opportunity to consider the parties' choices as to use of language in the context of determining whether to enforce a foreign judgment or, even better for purposes of diminishing the likelihood of consideration of the troublesome provision, the arbitral award. In that context, it would reach the issue of the parties' choices in respect of language only if it made rather improbable determinations. The essence of such determinations would be that the law of the court's country mandated the application of norms flaunted by the parties. Such a conclusion could be reached either because the national choice of law provisions led to application of norms of the court's country that so provided, or because a public policy of sufficient import of the court's country so mandated, even if the national choice of law provisions otherwise pointed to, or respected the parties' choice of, the law of another country as governing.

In particular, under the New York Convention, a national court would need to find that the violation of the mandate that an official language be used for a particular interaction between the parties or with a governmental authority caused the award to fall within the New York Convention exceptions of violation of public policy/public order or deprivation of due process. Such a finding would allow the national court not to enforce the award. Although conceivable, for example as to issues of claims in collateral located within the instant jurisdiction and similar issues, such a finding would be otherwise aggressive. To the extent that enforcement were sought against assets of the losing party outside the jurisdiction mandating the use of a particular language, a similar such finding by a court of another jurisdiction would be even more improbable.

A particularly potent combination of choice of law and choice of forum for dispute resolution in order to avoid potentially troublesome peremptory national policies, is an agreement to arbitrate in conjunction with a choice of governing national law that includes application of the UNIDROIT PRINCIPLES OF INTERNATIONAL COMMERCIAL CONTRACTS.[294] It is quite unlikely that an arbitrator would find ground to quarrel with such a choice, and even more unlikely that a national court in the context of enforcement proceedings under the New York and analogous conventions would find ground to second guess an arbitrator's acceptance of the choice. The UNIDROIT Principles themselves accord the parties broad freedom to determine the content and form of their contract.[295] As to language, the only express reference of the UNIDROIT Principles is a common-sense preference for interpretation of an agreement in the language in which it was originally prepared, if versions in multiple languages are otherwise contractually deemed to be of equal authority.[296]

4. Linguistically-neutral forum

Yet another way to manage the challenge of a jurisdiction unwelcoming to a deal conducted and documented primarily in a non-"official" language is to provide for dispute resolution in a jurisdiction which employs that language. For example, if the non-"official" language that the parties choose to employ is English, they might designate an English-speaking jurisdiction as the place for dispute resolution. Such a jurisdiction is "easiest" for an English-language deal if the jurisdiction is English-speaking, and the jurisdiction of both one of the parties and of the governing law of the contract. In so far as the jurisdiction is the home of the party against whom the deal is to be enforced, the likelihood that any mandate of the plaintiff's jurisdiction in favor of a language other than English would have significance is reduced. In so far as parties act on the incentive to pick an English-language jurisdiction for dispute resolution in reaction to a non-English-speaking jurisdiction's hesitation to enforce any aspect of an English-language deal (or in reaction to its imposition of burdens of translation relative to accomplishing such enforcement), they further marginalize the non-English-speaking jurisdiction. In addition, this action further frustrates any policies that it may have to promote the use of its language. This phenomenon exemplifies the benefit of facilitating party choice relative to language, rather than seeking to impose use of a language.

An additional alternative is to pick a jurisdiction for dispute resolution which is, for example, English-speaking, and accordingly most likely a common law jurisdiction, but which has little or no relationship with either of the parties. Jurisdictions such as California[297] and New York,[298] for instance, have statutory provisions that accept for their courts to resolve such disputes. However, a judgment arising from such a dispute resolution mechanism would not benefit from the New York Convention's provision for recognition of international arbitral awards by the courts of countries that have ratified the New York Convention. The eventual entry into force of the new Hague Convention on Choice of Court, discussed below, would change this.[299] In the meantime, the parties would need to rely on the availability of assets against which to seek enforcement in jurisdictions that would recognize the judgment. Under the full faith and credit clause of the United States constitution, such a judgment by a California or New York court, for example, or by a federal court to which such a dispute might be removed under diversity jurisdiction, would be recognized throughout the United States. Although such a judgment might face challenges to enforcement in the home country jurisdiction that purported to mandate the choice of language of the underlying contract (where obviously the "full faith and credit" clause of the United States constitution would have no relevance), a defendant party active in transnational commerce and finance might well have a sufficient presence in jurisdictions such as New York that would recognize the judgment, to enable meaningful enforcement.

Within the European Union, the extension by Member State courts of full faith and credit to judgments of other Member State courts is available for commercial judgments pursuant to European Community Regulation no. 44/2001, which further mandates respect of party agreements of forum for dispute resolution.[300] Accordingly, the strategy of seeking a linguistically neutral forum appears to have viability within the European Union as well.

C. Indicia of when international harmonization of law efforts may prove fruitful

Parties to transnational commercial and financial deals and governmental authorities share an interest in the existence of frameworks to support the conduct of such transactions in ways that provide certainty of outcomes and that minimize transaction costs. Parties to such transactions and governmental authorities that share a language have particular common ground to desire that legal frameworks relevant to transnational commercial and financial deals allow them to work in their common preferred language. Frameworks that permit this can facilitate lower costs, improve the quality of transactions, encourage more transactions, and refine the capacities of national legal systems and their institutions.

Parties and governmental authorities, together with other stakeholders in the rule of law, share further reason to give active attention to the role of language in law reform efforts that address frameworks for cross-border transactions. Legal frameworks to support cross-border transactions that address issues of language can facilitate fuller participation of transaction parties of many languages in the globalizing economy in their language of choice. Benefits also arise from the ability of transnational business participants to find frameworks keyed to their needs when they necessarily interact with governmental authorities in the languages of such authorities, which may not be the language chosen by the parties for the conduct of their deal. These benefits work to increase interactions with governmental authorities and therefore increase the constituencies pressing for their efficient and transparent functioning.

Considering the divergent perspectives of transaction parties and governmental actors, transaction parties will attempt to "game the private international law rules" through forum shopping among jurisdictions in order to achieve the bargain they wish to make, while governmental actors will attempt to impose their policies. Hence, for example, faced with government leverage over the creation and establishment of priorities in loan collateral as a tool for requiring use of a particular language in relevant documentation, parties may make greater recourse to bifurcation of their transaction so as to pair down to an absolute minimum the portion of their deal subject to the government leverage. In so doing, they expand the domain of party autonomy in a transnational financial deal, notwithstanding the force of the government's leverage to constrain the domain of such autonomy as to the collateral package aspect of the transaction.

In so far as the cost to parties of using the techniques outlined to work around troublesome governmental requirements is low, such governmental strictures will have little impact. Parties will simply do as they choose. Moreover, to the extent that governmental authorities fail to deem implementation of their requirements as to language to be priorities, there will be even less incentive for the establishment of meaningful internationally-coordinated frameworks.

To the extent the contrary is true, that the cost to parties of working around troublesome governmental requirements is significant and that governmental authorities deem implementation of the policies underlying the requirements to be priorities, there is fertile ground to establish such frameworks of international coordination of national norms. Parties and governmental authorities in this hypothesis would share strong incentives to collaborate in the development of frameworks that give each category what it seeks. Parties would desire a low-cost, reliable way to make and enforce their transactions. Governmental authorities desire not only to stimulate transactions, but also to achieve policy goals relative to use of language. Such policies might include language requirements designed to permit the efficient provision of a government service, assure speakers of the target language adequate information and minimum burdens of translation, and promote both the language and the ability of its speakers to participate in transactions, among others.

By way of example, the ready availability of enforceability of agreements to arbitrate lessens the incentive to address national procedural requirements as to language that may be overbearing or unnecessary, for example, certification or notarization of translations. Thus, transaction parties and a governmental authority concerned with the interests of parties from its jurisdiction would have diminished incentive to seek to initiate or support a process of reform that might lead to unification or harmonization of requirements.

An example in the contrary sense, that is, an instance of substantial incentive to implement a harmonized framework, is the Cape Town Convention on International Interests in Mobile Equipment, discussed below, to address security interests in mobile collateral, notably aircraft.[301] The ready identifiability and mobility of collateral such as aircraft served to outweigh the interests that cause national legal systems to be the relevant source of the norms on publicity that enable one creditor to obtain effective priority of its claims to collateral relative to those of other creditors. The particular characteristics of aircraft (they are big, expensive and mobile) distinguish them from other tangible collateral. The necessary prevalence of national law and courts in connection with the establishment of satisfaction of the requirements of publicity to achieve priority of liens against third party claims in ordinary tangible collateral, gives governmental authorities significant leverage to impose their requirements on the parties, leverage that governmental authorities do not have relative to aircraft. Moreover, in respect of ordinary tangible collateral, governmental authorities generally concur in the policy priority within their respective territories of enforcing their own norms relative to the establishment of security interests and the priority of such security interests in collateral. These requirements impose significant costs on the parties, and governments typically perceive little benefit in harmonizing them precisely because of the limited ability of parties to work around them.

However, the highly mobile nature of the transport vehicle kinds of collateral object of the Cape Town Convention, and in particular of the aircraft object of the protocol to it on matters specific to aircraft equipment, exacerbates the costs to parties of uncoordinated requirements of various jurisdictions to the point that economic activity apparent as important to governmental authorities may be limited. To wit, the risks to a creditor of encountering uncoordinated proceedings relative to seizure of an aircraft by foreclosing creditors in Colombia and the United States, which have a significant element of fortuity attached to them depending on where the aircraft happens to be when governmental authorities acting at the creditor's instance seek to seize it, that is, whether authorities in Bogota or Los Angeles are the ones to grab it at the instance of creditors, are quite high. Indeed, they are high enough that they may effect the provision of competitive flight services between the two cities. They are also high enough that one leading lender in the financing of aircraft, the United States Export-Import Bank, offered a one third reduction in the exposure fee that it would otherwise charge in connection with the financing of large commercial aircraft in countries that implement the Cape Town Convention.[302] These circumstances contributed to the adoption of the Convention and its protocol on matters specific to aircraft equipment with the support of transaction party and governmental stakeholders, and relatively prompt recognition, by each of Colombia (not coincidently a major market for the sale of aircraft manufactured in the United States) and the United States (and the growing list of further parties to the Convention, including China, the European Union and India) of the value of its ratification.[303]

NOTES TO CHAPTER V

280. *Home Insurance Company v. Dick*, 281 U.S. 397 (1930).

281. *The Bremen v. Zapata Off-Shore Co.*, 407 U.S. 1 (1972).

282. *See Carbon Black Export, Inc. v. The Monrosa*, 254 F.2d 297 (5th Cir. 1958), *cert. dismissed*, 359 U.S. 180 (1959).

283. RESTATEMENT, SECOND, OF CONTRACTS (1981), §187.

284. ALI/UNIDROIT PRINCIPLES OF TRANSNATIONAL CIVIL PROCEDURE, *supra* note 186, section 2.4.

285. *Id.*, section 2.

286. RESTATEMENT, SECOND, OF CONTRACTS (1981), §188.

287. *See* text *supra* at note 281.

288. The exceptions as to countries named in this investigation are: Angola, Cape Verde, Chad, Comoros, Congo, Democratic Republic of the Congo, East Timor, Equatorial Guinea, Guinea-Bissau, Sao Tome & Principe and Togo. *See* www. uncitral.org.

289. Jan. 30, 1975, 104 STAT. 449, PAN-AM. T.S. 42.

290. *See, e.g.* Campbell McLachlan, Laurence Shore and Matthew Weiniger, INTERNATIONAL INVESTMENT ARBITRATION: SUBSTANTIVE PRINCIPLES (2007); Antonio R. Parra, *The Development of the Regulations and Rules of the International Centre for Settlement of Investment Disputes*, 41 THE INT'L LAWYER 47 (2007).

291. New York Convention, art. V.

292. *See* Jack J. Coe, Jr., *Transparency in the Resolution of Investor-State Disputes — Adoption, Adaptation, and NAFTA Leadership*, 54 U. KAN. L. REV. 1339 (2005-2006).

293. *United Mexican States v. Metalclad Corporation*, 2001 BCSC 664 (British Columbia Sup. Ct. May 2, 2001). *See, e.g.*, Charles H. Brower II, *Investor-State Disputes Under NAFTA: The Empire Strikes Back*, 40 COLUM. J. TRANSNAT'L L. 28 (2001-2002).

294. Michael Joachim Bonell, *Soft Law and Party Autonomy: The Case of the UNIDROIT Principles*, 51 LOYOLA LAW REV. 229-252 (2005).

295. UNIDROIT PRINCIPLES, articles 1.1 and 1.2.

296. *Id.*, art. 4.7.

297. California CODE OF CIVIL PROCEDURE §410.40 provides in pertinent part:

Any person may maintain an action or proceeding in a court of this state against a foreign corporation or nonresident person where the action or proceeding arises out of or relates to any contract, agreement, or undertaking for which a choice of California law has been made in whole or in part by the parties thereto and which (a) is a contract, agreement, or undertaking, contingent or otherwise, relating to a transaction involving in the aggregate not less than one million dollars ([US]$1,000,000), and (b) contains a provision or provisions under which the foreign corporation or nonresident agrees to submit to the jurisdiction of the courts of this state.

California CIVIL CODE §1646.5 provides in pertinent part:

Notwithstanding Section 1646, the parties to any contract, agreement, or undertaking, contingent or otherwise, relating to a transaction involving in the aggregate not less than two hundred fifty thousand dollars ([US]$250,000), including a transaction otherwise covered by subdivision (a) of Section 1301 of the Commercial Code, may agree that the law of this state shall govern their rights and duties in whole or in part, whether or not the contract, agreement, or undertaking or transaction bears a reasonable relation to this state. This section does not apply to any contract, agreement, or undertaking (a) for labor or personal services, (b) relating to any transaction primarily for personal, family, or household purposes, or (c) to the extent provided to the contrary in subdivision (c) of Section 1301 of the Commercial Code.

298. New York GENERAL OBLIGATIONS LAW §§ 5-1401 and 5-1402.

299. *See* text *infra* at note 385.

300. *See* text *infra* at note 334.

301. *See* text *infra* at note 363.

302. *See* http://www.exim.gov/news/highlights/capetown.cfm.

303. UNIDROIT, as depositary of the Convention and its protocols, maintains current information on ratification. *See* www.unidroit.org.

Map Seven - Spanish-speaking Countries and Places

VI. ROLE OF LANGUAGE IN CURRENT MODELS FOR DEVELOPMENT OF LEGAL FRAMEWORKS TO SUPPORT TRANSNATIONAL COMMERCIAL AND FINANCIAL DEALS

The focus of this section is on how stakeholders, including private sector interests, governments, and others concerned with the rule of law and legal frameworks to support transactional commercial and financial deals, can intervene to achieve continued and augmented benefits of linguistic diversity. The goals are to facilitate inclusion of potential parties no matter what language they might speak and to diminish the marginalization of legal systems that arises from the linguistic burdens imposed by governmental authorities working with outdated and uncoordinated norms. A further goal is to render the international frameworks for the unification and harmonization of law that are relevant to transnational commerce and finance, as fully as practicable open to multiple languages.

Three well-established models of internationally-coordinated frameworks for efforts to harmonize and unify law relevant to transnational commercial and financial deals are sketched with an emphasis on how language and the promotion of language figures in each.[304] Each of the models discussed here, in its own fashion, is not only a well-established path for the elaboration of solid and widely-diffused international frameworks for the conduct of transnational commercial and financial deals, but also potentially presents two kinds of opportunities as to language, as follows.

The models here discussed can each be worked to diminish the linguistic burdens that impede participation of legal systems and languages in the frameworks, and the conduct, of transnational commercial and financial business. One opportunity for stakeholders in a particular legal system and in an associated language is to deal in one of the official languages of the framework in respect of the formulation of the framework itself. That is, such stakeholders are well served if they can make their legal system and its official language the base of the transnational framework. Some languages and legal systems because of their weight in the world are obviously easier points of departure than others for this purpose.

A second potential opportunity, particularly suited for languages and legal systems not as widely diffused, is to seek to assure that the transnational framework opens the door to support of transnational commercial and financial deals conducted in a language in addition to the predominant language of the framework. The door opening occurs by virtue of integrating to the international framework a legal system operating in an official language other than the languages in which the international framework is established. Such integration can be assured at several levels. One level is to undertake the integration by thoughtfully translating the operative instruments of the international framework into the official language or languages of the target legal system. A further level would then be to adopt the substance of such translation as national law.

A yet further level of potential integration is associated with the formulation of the transnational framework, even if such formulation does not occur in an official language of the relevant jurisdiction. Those working in the official language of the target legal system miss, perhaps obviously, a significant opportunity if they are not a critical part of the formulation of the international framework in its "official" languages. The opportunity that derives from participation in the formulation effort is to shape the international framework, including its structure, concepts, and vocabulary, so as to enable the international framework and the target legal system, with its own official language, to integrate well together. Thus, for example, the German law concept of *nachtfrist*, an obligation of the contract party to demand assurance of performance prior to cancellation of a contract on grounds of anticipatory breach, is incorporated in the Vienna Convention on the International Sale of Goods, for which German is not an official language.

A.   International conference model

The model of international "conferences" for the development of private international law to support transnational deals is one of expert preparation of texts of proposed treaties and model laws, followed by their acclamation at a periodic meeting of relevant states, after which states may or may not formally adhere to them by following national ratification procedures. The process involves the creation of substantial consensus among experts, through a process of dialog without formal voting, and the extensive participation of non-governmental organizations with insight into the issues of concern. The process differs from that characteristic of bodies directly focused on public international law, such as the General Assembly of the United Nations, where the process is more overtly political and issues are routinely decided by vote over the protest of vocal minorities.[305] In addition to bringing expert legal advice to bear in connection with the preparation of the relevant texts, the international conference model seeks to create multilateral momentum for the ratification of such texts. It works well with respect to subject matters and areas that lack effective cross-border communities otherwise able to promote the development and implementation of coordinated frameworks.

A limitation is the rigidity of the multilateral treaty process, namely the difficulty of securing widespread ratification of amendments, as well as the initial ratifications. Part of this rigidity derives from the typical national requirements for ratification of a treaty, which generally include signature of the treaty by a head of government or state, plus some form of "advice and consent" by at least part of the legislative branch of government. A further aspect of the rigidity is the requirement for coordination not only of ratifications among multiple states, but also of the amendments that would have effect only in the measure that each pertinent state would ratify them.

The Hague Conference on Private International Law, tracing its roots to 1893, involves some sixty states meeting every four years to act on proposals of approval of treaties for ratification, in English and French.[306] Between 1951 and 2005, the Hague Conference promulgated for ratification thirty-five conventions, of which the most widely ratified concern: abolition of legalization; service of process; taking of evidence abroad; access to justice; international child abduction; inter-country adoption; conflicts of laws relating to the form of testamentary dispositions; maintenance obligations; and, recognition of divorces.[307] The most recently promulgated conventions to emerge from the Hague Conference are from 2005 and not yet ratified by the minimum number of states required for their entry into force. They address topics directly relevant to transnational commercial and financial deals, namely, the Convention on the Law Applicable to Certain Rights in respect of Securities Held with an Intermediary, and the Convention on Choice of Court Agreements.

Working in a similar vein, the Inter-American Specialized Conferences on Private International Law ("CIDIP"), held every four years under the auspices of the Organization of American States, have produced nine conventions on private international law topics and a model law on secured transactions, prepared in the official languages of English, French, Portuguese and Spanish.[308] The model law on secured transactions has been influential in the reform of the secured lending laws of Chile, El Salvador, Guatemala, Mexico and Peru.[309] The model law on secured transactions, as well as proposed model regulations for the operation of the registries of filings of security interests that are critical to implementation of the model law (and that have the ambition of producing an internationally-searchable registry system for secured transactions across Latin America),[310] reflect a degree of fluidity in the international conference model. That is, the international conference model is not strictly limited to the production of treaties, but rather can employ additional instruments, such as model laws and regulations, that work around the rigidity inherent to the treaty process.

Nonetheless, the international conference model in its pure form, as well as in its variant of propagating model laws and other texts, contrasts with the potential dynamism of a supranational process, such as that achieved by the European Union. The European Union, like other supranational communities such as OHADA, offers institutions capable of implementing ongoing legislative reform, without the need for recourse to the procedures of treaty amendment and the associated requirements of national ratification. In addition, in the case of the European Union, much legislative activity can be accomplished without the requirement of unanimous assent of the affected states. The requirement of unanimity is instead an inherent element of treaty amendment. That is, considering a treaty as an agreement among states, the agreement is not fully changed until each party to it, *i.e.* each state, has completed its procedures to fully accept the revised text of the treaty.

In addition, each of the European Union and OHADA, as a supranational community, offers a coordinated, diffuse system for judicial application and interpretation of the legislation through national courts, that is led by high courts established directly as institutions of the supranational community. In the case of the European Union, such courts are its General Court (formerly known as the Court of First Instance) and the European Court of Justice. In the case of OHADA, it is OHADA's Common Court of Justice and Arbitration. In contrast, the treaties that emerge from the international conference model do not in general contemplate the creation of new international institutions to update, implement and apply their terms without the unanimous assent of the ratifying states.

The Vienna Convention on the International Sale of Goods,[311] dealing with unification of a portion of contract law, is a widely adopted convention, initially promoted by the United Nations Commission on International Trade Law ("UNCITRAL"). It springs from the international conference model. Notwithstanding the rigidity of the international conference model relative to a supranational legal system, the adoption of the Convention of the International Sale of Goods in some seventy states achieves an approximation of universalism that so far no supranational entity approaches in the realm of law relevant to transnational commercial and financial deals. Further, it can be argued that its form as a treaty is part of the reason for its widespread adoption, on the theory that the heterogeneity of the commercial law of the legal systems which have adhered to the Convention was so great, ranging across civil, common and "socialist" (a reference principally to was the form of organization of the component parts of the former Soviet Union and of the states whose economic systems emulated it) systems, that a model law embracing its content would have had less wide, and likely less uniform, adoptions.

The Vienna Convention on the International Sale of Goods illustrates how a specific treaty can enhance party options to deal with the topic of language. It offers, for example, a United States seller and a Mexican buyer of goods the option to elect, either expressly or simply in their silence by default, for the governance of their contract, a "unified" body of law to address specific issues related to the formation, and consequences of breach, of their deal. The Convention's ratification by the United States and Mexico removes, within the scope of its subject matter, the "conflict of law" issue, thereby facilitating enforcement of the terms of the parties' transaction in either country under the same metric of substantive law.

As a United Nations convention, the Vienna Convention on the International Sale of Goods is available in equally authoritative English and Spanish texts. Therefore, regardless of whether a United States and a Mexican party transact their business in English or Spanish, it offers each, or at least their respective lawyers, equally authoritative texts in the official language corresponding to each party's legal system so as to permit direct understanding of the applicable legal norms that it lays out. For those concerned with languages beyond the six official languages in which its text exists by virtue of being a United Nations treaty (Arabic, Chinese, English, French, Russian and Spanish), a number of thoughtful expert translations have been prepared, including in Czech, Danish, Dutch, Farsi, Finnish, German, Italian, Japanese, Norwegian, Polish, Portuguese and Swedish.[312] The number of these translations evidences recognition of the importance of accessibility by parties that undertake transnational commercial and financial matters, in the language most familiar to them, to frameworks such as that established by the Convention on the International Sale of Goods. However, the widespread translation of the Convention on the International Sale of Goods reflects more than just the benefit of its accessibility to populations speaking diverse languages.

When the Convention on the International Sale of Goods was elaborated in the 1980's, the world's legal systems most germane to international transactions were divided principally among civil law, common law, and socialist legal systems. The text of the Convention offers familiar aspects for both civil and common law lawyers. Like a civil law code, its text is meant to be an all-encompassing framework, and gaps in its text are to be filled with reference to the "general principles on which it is based."[313] At the same time, courts are to interpret it with regard "to its international character and to the need to promote uniformity in its application", a mandate that in the common law tradition lends persuasive value to decisions of other courts.[314] Although the socialist legal systems, by virtue of their model of economic organization, did not have domestic law pertinent to market transactions, they did participate in international trade, and the Convention on the International of Sale of Goods was prepared to be acceptable for their ratification of it. In consequence, many countries with socialist economic systems ratified it. As the socialist economies evolved to market economies that demanded domestic commercial law, the accordingly familiar Convention on the International Sale of Goods often inspired their domestic legislation.[315]

The collaboration of experts from many jurisdictions, the quality of their work, and the consequent breadth of its adoption yielded a vocabulary and conceptual framework that could be and has been broadly appreciated, as evidenced not only by the wide ratification of the Convention on the International Sale of Goods itself, but also its use as a source of inspiration for the content of national law reforms and as the conceptual root of further harmonization initiatives, such as the UNIDROIT PRINCIPLES OF INTERNATIONAL COMMERCIAL CONTRACTS, the Principles of European Contract Law, and the EU Common Frame of Reference of Contract Law.[316] The high quality translation of the Convention on the International Sale of Goods into many languages is further evidence of the ability to appreciate the importance of its vocabulary and conceptual framework.

In many instances, experts involved in the drafting of the Vienna Convention on the International Sale of Goods have contributed directly to the translations of it into other languages. No doubt, their deep familiarity with the Convention by virtue of having participated in its elaboration improved their ability to produce a translation of it. However, regardless of whether a translation is prepared by one of them or some other expert in a particular national legal system, the design of the Convention with cognizance of the diverse realities into which it must be inserted, facilitates its translation into various languages without loss of meaning. That cognizance means that the Convention fits better with a variety of legal systems and even that it incorporates concepts more intelligible to such legal systems. The result is the ability to provide conventional translation of the text of the Convention for use in such legal systems with greater precision. The Convention is a stellar example of a harmonization effort that integrates productively with a range of existing legal systems. It is likewise a premier success of the working of the international conference model.

B. Restatement/expert association/ model law

The rubric "restatement/expert association/model law" describes a series of approaches to international harmonization of law that share the core characteristic of availing themselves of expert knowledge as a driver of the reform process. The kinds of initiatives considered under this rubric share with the international conference model the attribution of importance to expert knowledge. However the "restatement/expert association/model law" approach differs from the international conference model in privileging direct access to expert knowledge on the part of economic and governmental actors, without the intermediation of the treaty process. The associated refinement of the restatement/expert association/model law approach relative to the other models is its focus on the process of preparation and update of a reform as a continuing process, with recognition that the ongoing process of expert consideration of reform is also part of the process of implementation of the reform. The restatement/expert association/ model law approach accordingly has an intensified focus, because of the way it uses experts, on how the proposed reform integrates into its target legal systems.

A challenge of any effort to harmonize law across borders is to propose reform that would integrate productively with existing legal systems. The insight, for example, of the design of the European Union's two principal legislative instruments as Directives and Regulations, is recognition of this challenge.[317] Regulations have immediate direct application, whereas Directives are to fix goals that the Member States to whom they are addressed must achieve by a deadline. The margin of discretion in the mechanisms of implementation left to Member States in respect of a Directive is precisely to allocate to each Member State the burden of undertaking the task of ascertaining how best to integrate the mandate of the Directive with its particular legal system.

In the European Union system, the combination of the European Commission's role as a technocratic expert with the power of normative proposal and the ongoing legislative process in which the Commission, Parliament and Council collaborate, provides an engine of continuing reform. In contrast, the international conference model tends to stall once the text of a treaty has been promulgated for ratification by states. That is, there may be a considerable delay prior to a treaty collecting a sufficient number of state ratifications in accordance with its terms so as to enter into force simply because of the slow pace of ratification by individual states. In addition, in the European Union system, there are institutional mechanisms, including actions by the European Commission and Member States before the European Court of Justice, to pressure a Member State which is slow to implement obligations of European Union law. The analogous provisions of public international law in respect of pressuring a state to honor its treaty obligations are far more limited. One consequence is that the treaties produced by the international conference model tend to be drafted as largely self-executing. That is, they are drafted so that once ratified, limited further implementing action is intended to be required.

The concept of Heisenberg's uncertainty principle of quantum mechanics, to the effect that attempts to measure parameters might change them,[318] is at the core of what propels implementation of the model of restatement/expert association/model law. This model seeks to instill the kind of dynamism that the European Union's supranational legislative process demonstrates with some regularity. This model posits that appropriately-structured expert consideration of legal issues can lead to law reform. In this model, the process of consideration of reform by well-placed and well-qualified experts is made precisely the impetus and instrument for ongoing reform. The expert review and analysis of the phenomena to be observed, in the ideal working of the model, changes the otherwise existing status quo by creating understanding of the opportunity for improvement. A further challenge to harmonization of law efforts is to diffuse and implement the proposed reform such that the reform is actually used. As to this as well, the process of expert consultation itself can create channels for the diffusion of the reform. What the various kinds of instruments considered here in conjunction with this model share, is preparation by a diverse group of recognized experts, and their diffusion, application, and updating through decentralized channels in which the experts are meant to have an ongoing role.

Five examples of the "restatement/expert association/model law" approach are used to sketch how it works and the opportunities that it offers for incorporation of attention to issues of language. The implementation of the Uniform Commercial Code ("UCC") and its ongoing updating within the United States constitutes a first and particularly effective example of the process. In addition, each of the UNIDROIT PRINCIPLES OF INTERNATIONAL COMMERCIAL CONTRACTS, the Draft Legislative Guide on Secured Transactions of the United Nations Commission on International Trade Law ("UNCITRAL"), the Model Law on Secured Lending of the Organization of American States ("OAS"), and the soft law approaches of such instruments as INCOTERMS and the

UNIFORM CUSTOMS AND PRACTICE FOR DOCUMENTARY CREDITS of the International Chamber of Commerce ("ICC"), represents a different way of seeking to use the ongoing work of experts to implement reform. The UNIDROIT PRINCIPLES OF INTERNATIONAL COMMERCIAL CONTRACTS, first promulgated 1994 and updated 2004, are not a treaty, but rather a restatement of contract law that parties may elect to apply to their transactions. The Draft Legislative Guide on Secured Transactions, in preparation since 2002 by a working group of experts from diverse backgrounds under the auspices of UNCITRAL, fits broadly within the expert working group model.[319] The OAS Model Law on Secured Lending presents a specific text intended to be adopted as legislation by OAS member states.[320] INCOTERMS and the UNIFORM CUSTOMS AND PRACTICE FOR DOCUMENTARY CREDITS are texts prepared by a business organization, to be used at the choice of transaction parties.

The UCC is a highly successful model law now adopted in each of the states of the United States. It was initially prepared, and on a continuing basis is updated, under the auspices of the Uniform Law Commission, formerly known as the National Conference of Commissioners on Uniform State Laws, in collaboration with the American Law Institute.[321] Founded in 1892, the Uniform Law Commission is comprised of some 300 lawyers, including legislators, practicing lawyers, and law professors appointed by state governments to research, draft and promote enactment of uniform state laws on a *pro bono* basis, *i.e.* without compensation.[322] The American Law Institute, founded 1923, is a self-perpetuating organization of legal experts including judges, lawyers and law professors, limited to 3000 members and known for its law reform projects, particularly its restatements of various topics of common law in the United States.[323] The success of these two organizations in promoting and elaborating this and other uniform laws on a wide range of topics, and as to the American Law Institute, its various restatements of American law, suggests the benefit of investment in the activities of these and similar organizations working internationally. Critical to the success of the two organizations is their consistent success in accessing a deep reservoir of technical expertise. In addition, the Uniform Law Commission, in part by virtue of the selection of its members by state legislatures, has maintained the confidence of state legislatures such that they are receptive to adopt the texts that it promulgates. Similarly, the American Law Institute and its restatements, in part because of the association of its membership with the legal establishment in the United States, have been consistently credible to courts in the United States, often referenced with approval in judicial opinions as clarifying and properly stating relevant law.

With the multilateral conference model for the adoption of conventions, the UNIDROIT PRINCIPLES OF INTERNATIONAL COMMERCIAL CONTRACTS share the favorable attribute of mobilizing professional expertise and being founded on a firm ground of widely-held consensus of relevant actors. However, as a restatement, the UNIDROIT principles are more readily updateable because there is no issue of ratification, as there would be for a treaty arising out of the multilateral conference model for the adoption of conventions. The UNIDROIT Principles are available in UNIDROIT's official languages of English, French, German, Italian and Spanish, with thoughtful expert translations available in Chinese, Korean, Romanian, Russian, Portuguese, Serbian, Turkish and Vietnamese.[324] As mentioned in connection with the discussion of the Vienna Convention on the International Sale of Goods, such translations and their relevance to the legal systems of reference, as well as to those who speak the corresponding languages, are enhanced by the involvement of experts from such jurisdictions in the formulation of the underlying text and its substance. The core of experts guiding the formulation of the UNIDROIT principles has been consistently distributed among a panel of experts from a heterogeneous group of legal systems, working in various languages. For example, the Working Group for the preparation of a third revision of the Principles of International Commercial Contracts, present at the opening of its first session on May 29, 2006, comprised a group of experts each with a national prominence in legal and governmental circles and collectively representing a cross-section of the world's legal systems and associated languages with significant relevance to international trade, namely: Guido Alpa (Italy), M. Joachim Bonell (UNIDROIT), Paul-André Crépeau (Canada), Samuel Kofi Date Bah (Ghana), Benedicte Fauvarque-Cosson (France), Paul Finn (Australia), Marcel Fontaine (Belgium), Michael Philip Furmston (United Kingdom), Henry D. Gabriel (United States), Sir Roy Goode (United Kingdom), Arthur Hartkamp (Netherlands), Alexander Komarov (Russian Federation), Ole Lando (Denmark), Takashi Uchida (Japan), João Baptista Villela (Brazil), Pierre Widmer (Switzerland), Zhang Yuqing (China) and Reinhard Zimmermann (Germany).[325]

The UNCITRAL Draft Legislative Guide to Secured Transactions offers an alternative approach to the mobilization of expert knowledge in support of harmonization of law. It adopts a "recipe book" approach. Rather than offer a complete text of relevant law, it lays out the elements which legislation would address. It offers experts of the relevant jurisdiction and target language, a tool in order to create, in the format and language of the jurisdiction, a framework supportive of an important aspect of many transnational commercial and financial deals. As an illustration of the political savvy that is a requisite to the actual implementation of harmonization of law initiatives, it focuses narrowly on the elements essential to a system to support secured lending, including the conceptualization of what is a security interest and the establishment of priority of claims based on non-possessory security interests through filings in public registries, indexed by name of the debtor. It wisely does not directly tackle the justification for involvement of civil law notaries, and its associated costs, in the creation and registration of security interests. Its goal is not only to provide guidelines for the legislative reform of the positive law relative to creation of security interests and the establishment of their relative priority, but also to facilitate the adoption of actual legislation that incorporates its substance. To raise the notion of a cost-benefit calculation to assess the desirability of requirement for notarial involvement, would likely provoke political debate that would sidetrack the core of the reform sought by the Draft Legislative Guide to Secured Transactions.

In contrast to the "recipe" approach of the Draft Legislative Guide, the OAS model law is meant to work in the sense of the Uniform Commercial Code. Like the UCC, the OAS model law is a text meant to be adopted in multiple jurisdictions. Also like the UCC process, its preparation and diffusion involves experts from the relevant jurisdictions who, in addition to their initial expertise, are meant to have positions from which to instigate consideration of the model law's adoption. Whether the organization of the OAS experts is as effective in producing the adoption of the OAS text as that of the UCC experts remains an open question that will in time be assessed against the track record created of legislative implementation of the OAS model law.[326]

Further analogous soft law instruments include INCOTERMS and the UNIFORM CUSTOMS AND PRACTICE FOR DOCUMENTARY CREDITS, each prepared by the International Chamber of Commerce. These are expert texts prepared by an association of the private sector actors which use them. INCOTERMS, the International Chamber of Commerce's standard trade definitions, was first issued 1936, and is now in its sixth revision, INCOTERMS 2000, available in Arabic, Bosnian, Chinese (Cantonese), Chinese (Mandarin), Croat, Czech, Dutch, English, Estonian, Finnish, French, German, Italian, Japanese, Russian, Serb, Slovak, Slovene, Spanish, Swedish, and Vietnamese. INCOTERMS offers standard definitions that parties may incorporate into their agreements in order to establish when title passes between parties, to allocate risk of loss between parties, and to determine responsibility for shipment and delivery arrangements. The UNIFORM CUSTOMS AND PRACTICE FOR DOCUMENTARY CREDITS was first published by the International Chamber of Commerce in 1933 and is now in its sixth revision, updated to conform to current practices of communication with banks by internet. Like the INCOTERMS, it is prepared through the International Chamber of Commerce with extensive and broad input from industry participants. The UNIFORM CUSTOMS AND PRACTICE FOR DOCUMENTARY CREDITS is widely used by parties to letter of credit transactions in support of transnational commerce. The UNIFORM CUSTOMS AND PRACTICE FOR DOCUMENTARY CREDITS that entered into force July 1, 2007, known as UCP 600, is available in English and French from the International Chamber of Commerce, with additional translations through International Chamber of Commerce affiliates made into various other languages, including Arabic, German and Spanish.

The success of the instruments here considered is evidenced both by the widespread commercial adoption of some of them, and by the broad influence of all of them on legislative and regulatory processes, as well as by the extent of their translation to make them as widely-accessible as possible. This model of continuing expert interaction lends itself to the process of diffusion not only through widely-spoken languages, but also through the integration of less-spoken languages and their legal systems, during both the phases of preparation of the framework in the widely-spoken languages and in its translation to the less-spoken languages and their legal systems.

C. Supranational legislation: European Union law

The European Union and the *Organisation pour l'Harmonisation en Afrique du Droit des Affaires* ("OHADA" – Organization for the Harmonization in Africa of Business Law)[327] each exemplify models for the adoption and application of supranational legislation that overcome the rigidity of the international convention model, while offering binding law in a way that restatement and other private initiatives do not. Each provides a supranational process to adopt and revise substantive law. The case of the European Union is especially noteworthy because of the longstanding impulse to increase the reliance on qualified majority voting of the Member States as part of the legislative process. The reforms achieved by the November 2009 completion of the ratification by all the European Union's Member States of the Lisbon Treaty will intensify the recourse to qualified majority voting, but the law of the European Community, now fully subsumed as part of the European Union, from its earliest days has valued qualified majority voting as an essential component of the furtherance of European integration. Moreover, each of OHADA and the European Union provides a supranational judicial mechanism that embraces national judges as partners with the supranational judicial bodies in the interpretation and application of the supranational law.

The common story of the European Union and of OHADA as supranational organizations is that each was born of critical economic, political and social challenges. The Member States of each established the new tools of supranationalism to deal with daunting challenges of constructing something entirely new and without knowing fully how the new supranational organization would evolve. The European Union's present generality of purpose, its extended history and success, and the dimension of the economy that it concerns, might be argued as grounds to assert that the European Union's commercial and financial law may be of greater global significance than OHADA's. Indeed, at the present time OHADA is focused specifically on business law, while the European Union addresses a far broader range of issues. Further, OHADA has only a decade of existence, while the European Union has celebrated the fiftieth anniversary of the founding of its predecessor, the European Economic Community.

However, for each of OHADA and the European Union, the substance of its commercial law, the path-breaking mechanisms to adopt such law, the procedures to assure such law's application, and its approach to language exemplify legal innovation to support transnational commerce and finance in support of broader political and social goals. Each of these two supranational communities and its substantive law is accordingly of significant interest. OHADA's Uniform Acts are enumerated above in connection with the introduction of OHADA and its approach to language.[328] The sketch which follows of the European Union's relevant norms indicates not only the scope of the Union's achievements relative to harmonization of law relevant to commercial and financial deals, but also both the magnitudes of its ambition and of the remaining challenges of supporting transnational commerce and finance yet to be confronted.

The outline that follows of the kinds of European Union achievements in respect of harmonization of norms relevant to cross-border commerce and finance within the European Union touches on: (i) choice of forum for litigation to enforce contracts; (ii) substantive choice of governing law for contracts; and, (iii) indication of the European Union's increasing achievements in the establishment of uniform, or at least harmonized, substantive law. It serves as foundation for subsequent discussion of the European Union's emerging role in international harmonization of law efforts generally, *i.e.* not only the harmonization of law within the European Union, but also the European Union's participation in efforts to harmonize law in the world as a whole.[329]

1. Choice of forum

The operative European Union norm on choice of forum for the resolution of commercial disputes is Council Regulation no. 44/2001 of December 22, 2000 on jurisdiction and the regulation and enforcement of judgments in civil and commercial matters.[330] The European Union commenced its effort to offer uniform rules on jurisdiction and recognition and enforcement of judgments in commercial and civil matters with the 1968 Brussels Convention, extended in 1988 by the Lugano Convention to the states of the now superseded European Free Trade Association that had begun its existence as a competing alternative to the European Economic Community, including at its peak the United Kingdom as a key member. The European Union's current effort on the topic, Council Regulation no. 44/2001, applies to all its Member States except Denmark. The Convention on jurisdiction and the recognition and enforcement of judgments in civil and commercial matters, signed October 30, 2007, is intended to succeed each of the Brussels and Lugano conventions as to Community Member State Denmark, and each of Iceland, Norway, and Switzerland, all without prejudice to the application otherwise within the European Union of Regulation no. 44/2001.[331]

An advantage of the Regulation as a legal instrument is that it is directly effective without national implementing action; whereas, a treaty, even after ratification by the Member State in question, may require further national implementing action to the extent that its provisions are not so precise as to be self-executing. Moreover, a Regulation can be updated through the European Union's established legislative process, rather than requiring the further burden of ratification by each state involved. The initial recourse to treaty to address the subject matter of choice of forum for resolution of commercial disputes was associated with concern that at the time the then-applicable European Community framework did not support addressing the topic under the then-existing treaty provisions, the perceived challenge of imposing a self-executing text on Member State legal systems (which is the significance of a European Regulation), and the political sensitivity of imposing common rules for the subject matter without a national ratification process. The European Union with the adoption of Regulation no. 44/2001 has moved beyond these concerns.

The substantive essence of Regulation no. 44/2001 is that a person domiciled in a Member State is subject to suit in the courts of that Member State. Regulation no. 44/2001, among its further "special rules", provides that a person domiciled in a Member State may also be sued "in the courts for the place of performance of the obligation in question."[332] Such rules also include that proceedings concerning the existence of companies and the validity of decisions of their bodies are to be decided by the courts of the Member State in which the company has its seat, as determined by such courts' application of their Member State's private international law.[333] Interestingly, Regulation no. 44/2001 provides that a company is domiciled at the place where it has its statutory seat, central administration or principal place of business.[334] Further, it provides for respect of party choice of forum agreements, including by parties none of whom have domicile in the European Union.[335] The basic thrust of the Regulation as to use of a language is that doing business in a place means to accept the risk of defending a suit in the courts of that place, using the language of that place, unless arrangements are otherwise made, such as for example, agreement for an arbitration in an agreed language or agreement on use for dispute resolution of the courts of a particular jurisdiction.

2. *Choice of law*

As was the case for the migration of the choice of forum rules from a treaty to a European Regulation, the operative European Union rules on choice of law applicable to contractual obligations are now as of 2008 set forth in a European Regulation, binding on all subjects of European Union law without national implementing action.[336] The initial establishment of European Community norms on choice of law was the Rome Convention on the law applicable to contractual obligations, originally opened for signature in 1980,[337] and subsequently extended by amendments to include provision for its interpretation by the European Court of Justice and ratification by the further Member States of the European Community.[338] The currently operative European Union Regulation, like the Rome Convention that it succeeds, sets uniform rules for the establishment of the law governing contractual obligations in any situation involving a choice between the laws of different countries, although it excludes from its scope obligations arising from negotiable interests, arbitration agreements and agreements on choice of court, company law matters, family law matters, trusts, evidence and procedure. It allows the contracting parties freely to select the law to govern their agreement, including of a state that is not a member of the European Union, with the fallback, in the absence of an agreement as to choice of law, being the law of the country with which the contract is most closely connected. That law is presumed for most commercial and financial contracts to be the law of the habitual residence of the party which is to effect the performance "characteristic" of the contract.

3. Substantive law

There is a significant and growing body of European Union legislation that defines substantive European contract law pertinent to commercial and financial transactions, available of course in equally authoritative texts in the various official languages of the European Union. This body of law includes measures in respect of: payment systems;[339] commercial agents;[340] product liability;[341] electronic commerce;[342] financial services;[343] securities;[344] and collection on default judgments issued by courts in commercial matters.[345]

Much of the European Union law in such areas as banking, bankruptcy and securities is in the form of European Directives. These directives mandate harmonization of Member State legal requirements so as to eliminate barriers to cross-border activity, many of them working on a "reciprocal recognition" principle. The single license concept of the second banking directive,[346] for example, allows a financial institution to rely on regulation by its home country, presumably in its preferred language, to enable it to operate throughout the European Union. The proposed

Regulation on a statute for a European Private Company would employ a modified single license concept, in that the owners of a business could choose to organize it as a company under the Regulation with the benefit of its rules relating to limited liability, capital structure and corporate governance, but would otherwise be subject to the national law of the country where the company maintains its registered office.[347] As a Regulation rather than a Directive, it would once adopted have effect without any subsequent implementing action under national law.

There is ongoing consideration of what might be involved in efforts to produce a unified, or at least harmonized, European substantive contract law, which would be a step beyond the Rome Convention rules establishing a common basis for choice of governing national rules and the partial harmonization thus far achieved as to specific, relatively narrow, subject matters. The effort consists in part in the production of a European restatement of contract law principles common to the European Union's Member States in each of the common law and civil law traditions.[348] Because the restatement is not formal Community legislation, its production is thus far confined to two languages, English and French, corresponding to opposite sides of the common law/civil law divide. More controversial for the moment is the notion that the European Union might be well-served to adopt a European Civil Code in preemption of current national law pertinent to commercial and financial matters. [349]

The model of supranationalism, as embodied in the European Union law here reviewed, but also in OHADA's work, establishes a framework to support law reform by adoption of binding legislation and its enforcement through courts. The supranational institutions of each of the two organizations and their Member States participate in the supranational legislative process and in the judicial application of such law, although in varying degrees. Within the officially multilingual European Union, the involvement of stakeholders from its component legal systems, working in and with the languages of those systems, is an essential component of law reform activity. The limitation for broader application of this model of supranationalism is the restricted number of countries outside of Europe and francophone Africa that are willing to accept the limitation of national sovereignty inherent in the process. Nonetheless, its adoption through the foundation of OHADA and its growing success in the context of the European Union confirm its importance. In particular, its growing success in the European Union context is most recently evidenced by the expansion of the Union to twenty-seven Member States, the update through the Lisbon Treaty of the mechanisms for the expanded Union's governance, and the continued interest of additional states of geopolitical significance on the margins of Europe to join the European Union, for example, Macedonia, Morocco, Turkey and Ukraine.

NOTES TO CHAPTER VI

304. José E. Alvarez, INTERNATIONAL ORGANIZATIONS AS LAW-MAKERS, ch. 5 (2005) describes, along the lines here contemplated, models of UN treaty-making conferences and treaty-making by experts.

305. *See* Hal Burman, *Private International Law*, 43 THE INT'L LAWYER 741, 757 (2009).

306. *See* www.hcch.net.

307. *Id.*

308. OEA/Ser.K/XXI.6, CIDIP-VI/RES. 5/02, 41 I.L.M. 1038 (2002). The Inter-American Convention on the Law Applicable to International Contracts, OAS TREATY SERIES no. 78, 33 I.L.M. 732 (CIDIP V) is in force between Mexico and Venezuela, with Bolivia, Brazil and Uruguay having signed but not yet ratified it. Its respect for party choice of law, and, in the absence of such a choice, the imposition of the law of the country with which the contract is mostly closely connected, reflects an approach similar to that of the Rome Convention. The Inter-American Convention on Conflicts of Laws concerning Commercial Companies is in force among Argentina, Bolivia, Guatemala, Mexico, Paraguay, Peru, Uruguay and Venezuela and in general provides that corporate governance matters are to be handled under the law of the country under which the company is organized, much as the full faith and credit clause of the United States constitution allows corporate entities formed and governed under the laws of the individual fifty states to contract and otherwise conduct business throughout the United States.

309. Boris Kozolchyk and Dale Beck Furnish, *The OAS Model Law on Secured Transactions: A Comparative Analysis*, 12 SOUTHWESTERN J. OF LAW AND TRADE IN THE AMERICAS 101, 105-107 (2006).

310. *See* Burman at 748, *supra* note 305.

311. (1988) 1489 UNTS 3 (Registration no. 25567) 1489. The Convention is adopted by each of the European Union Member States, except Ireland, Malta, Portugal and the United Kingdom.

312. *See, e.g.* http://www.cisg.law.pace.edu/cisg/text/text.html.

313. Vienna Convention, art. 7(2), *supra* note 311. On the civil and common law aspects of the Convention, see Vivian Grosswald Curran, *A Comparative Perspective on the CISG*, in Harry M. Flechtner, Ronald A. Brand, and Mark S. Walter, eds., DRAFTING CONTRACTS UNDER THE CISG 49-61 (2008).

314. Vienna Convention, art. 7(1), *supra* note 311.

315. Peter H. Schlechtriem, *25 Years of the CISG: An International* lingua franca *for Drafting Uniform Laws, Legal Principles, Domestic Legislation and Transnational Contracts*, in Harry M. Flechtner, Ronald A. Brand, and Mark S. Walter, eds., DRAFTING CONTRACTS UNDER THE CISG 167-187 (2008).

316. *Id.*

317. Treaty on the functioning of the European Union, art. 288 (*ex* art. 249 TEC, *ex* art. 189 Treaty of Rome).

318. Werner Heisenberg, THE PHYSICAL PRINCIPLES OF QUANTUM THEORY (1930, Carl Eckart and Frank C. Hoyt, trans.).

319. *See, e.g.* United Nations General Assembly document A/CN.9/WG.VI/ WP.31/Add.1 (Nov. 22, 2006).

320. Organization of American States, model law on secured lending,. *See* Boris Kozolchyk and Dale Beck Furnish, *Supra* note 309.

321. For an overview of UCC Article 9 written with a European reader in mind, see Harry C. Sigman, *Security in movables in the United States – Uniform Commercial Code Article 9: a basis for comparison* in Eva-Marie Kieninger, ed., SECURITY RIGHTS IN MOVABLE PROPERTY IN EUROPEAN PRIVATE LAW 54 (2004).

322. *See* www.nccusl.org.

323. *See* www.ali.org.

324. *See* http://www.unidroit.org/english/principles/contracts/main.htm.

325. *Available at* www.unidroit.org.

326. *See supra* note 309.

327. *See* text *supra* at note 89.

328. *See* text *supra* at note 97.

329. *See* text *infra* at section VII.B.4.a.

330. OJ L 12/1 (Jan. 16, 2001), replacing the Brussels Convention on Jurisdiction and Enforcement of Judgments in Civil and Commercial Matters within the European Community, except in regard to Denmark.

331. OJ L 339/3-41 (Dec. 12, 2007).

332. *Id.*, art. 5(1).

333. *Id.*, art. 22(2).

334. *Id.*, art. 60.

335. *Id.*, art. 23.

336. European Parliament and Council Regulation no. 593 of June 17, 2008, OJ L 177/6 (June 18, 2008). An analogous measure for non-contractual obligations is European Parliament and Council Regulation no. 864 of July 11, 2007, OJ L 199/40 (July 11, 2007).

337. Convention on the Law Applicable to Contractual Obligations, opened for signature in Rome, June 19, 1980 (80/934/EEC), OJ L 266/1 (Oct. 9, 1980).

338. *See* Council Decision no. 856 of Nov. 8, 2007 concerning the accession of the Republic of Bulgaria and of Romania to the Convention on the Law applicable to Contractual Obligations, OJ L 347/1 (Dec. 29, 2007).

339. Directive 2009/44/EC of the European Parliament and of the Council of May 6, 2009 amending Directive 98/26/EC on settlement finality in payment and securities settlement systems and Directive 2002/47/EC on financial collateral arrangements as regards linked systems and credit, OJ L 146/37 (June 10, 2009); Directive 2007/64/EC of the European Parliament and of the Council of November 13, 2007 on payment services in the internal market amending Directives 97/7/EC, 2002/65/EC, 2005/60/EC and 2006/48/

EC and repealing Directive 97/5/EC, OJ L 319/1 (Dec. 5, 2007); Directive 2000/35/EC of the European Parliament and of the Council of June 29, 2000 on combating late payment in commercial transactions, OJ L 200/35 (Aug. 8, 2000); Directive 98/26/EC of the European Parliament and of the Council of May 19, 1998 on settlement finality in payment and securities settlement systems, OJ L 166/45 (June 11, 1998).

340. Council Directive 86/653/EEC of Dec. 18, 1986 on the co-ordination of the laws of the Member States relating to self-employed commercial agents, OJ L 382/17 (Dec. 31, 1986).

341. Council Directive 85/374/EEC of July 25, 1985 on the approximation of the laws, regulations and administrative provisions of the Member States concerning liability for defective products, OJ L 210/29 (Aug. 7, 1985) amended by Directive 1999/34/EC of the European Parliament and of the Council of May 10, 1999, OJ L 141/20 (June 4, 1999).

342. Directive 2000/31/EC of the European Parliament and of the Council of June 8, 2000 on certain legal aspects of information society services, in particular electronic commerce, in the Internal Market (Directive on electronic commerce), OJ L 178/1 (July 17, 2000); Directive 1999/93/EC of the European Parliament and of the Council of Dec. 13, 1999 on a Community framework for electronic signatures, OJ L 13/12 (Jan. 19, 2000).

343. Directive 2000/12/EC of the European Parliament and of the Council of March 20, 2000 relating to the taking up and pursuit of the business of credit institutions, OJ L 126/1 (May 26, 2000) (capitalization of credit institutions); Directive 2002/83/EC of the European Parliament and of the Council of Nov. 5, 2002 concerning life assurance, OJ L 345/1 (Dec. 19, 2002), as amended; Council Directive 92/49/EEC of June 18, 1992 on the co-ordination of laws, regulations and administrative provisions relating to direct insurance other than life assurance and amending Directives 73/239/EEC and 88/357/EEC (Third Non-Life Insurance Directive), OJ L 228/1 (Aug. 11, 1992).

344. Directive 2001/34/EC of the European Parliament and of the Council of May 28, 2001 on the admission of securities to official stock exchange listing and on information to be published on those securities, OJ L 184/1 (July 6, 2001), as amended; Directive 2003/71/EC of the European Parliament and of the Council of Nov. 4, 2003 on the prospectus to be published when securities are offered to the public or admitted to trading and amending Directive 2001/34/EC, OJ L 345/64 (Dec. 31, 2003), as amended; Directive 2004/39/EC of the European Parliament and of the Council of April 21, 2004 on markets in financial instruments amending Council Directives 85/611/EEC and 93/6/EEC and Directive 2000/12/EC of the European Parliament and of the Council and repealing Council Directive 93/22/EEC, OJ L 145/1 (April 30, 2004).

345. *See infra* note 366.

346. Directive 2006/48/EC of the European Parliament and of the Council of June 14, 2006 relating to the taking up and pursuit of the business of credit institutions, OJ L 177/1 (June 30, 2006), as amended (recast text of the "second

banking directive", Second Council Directive 89/646/EEC of Dec. 15, 1989, OJ L 158/87 (June 23, 1990)).

347. *Commission Proposal for a Council Regulation on the Statute for a European Private Company*, COM 396/3 (June 25, 2008).

348. *See, e.g.* Commission of the European Communities, *Communication from the Commission to the Council and the European Parliament on European Contract Law*, COM(2001) 398 final (July 11, 2001). *See also* Ole Lando & Hugh Beale, (eds.), THE PRINCIPLES OF EUROPEAN CONTRACT LAW PART I: PERFORMANCE, NON-PERFORMANCE AND REMEDIES (1995), and Isabelle de Lamberterie, Georges Rouhette & Denis Tallon, (eds.), LES PRINCIPES DU DROIT EUROPÉEN DU CONTRAT: L'EXÉCUTION, L'INEXÉCUTION ET SES SUITES (1997). For current efforts in this sense, see www.copecl.org, the web site of the Joint Network on European Private Law, which aggregates a number of initiatives focused on the presentation of Common Principles of European Contract Law.

349. *See* Jan Smits, *The Draft-Common Frame of Reference for a European Private Law: Fit for Purpose?*, 15 MAASTRICHT J. EUR. & COMP. LAW 145 (2008); Encarna Roca Trias, *The Process of Codifying the European Legal System*, in Mauro Bussani and Ugo Mattei, eds., OPENING UP EUROPEAN LAW: THE COMMON CORE PROJECT TOWARDS EASTERN AND SOUTH EASTERN EUROPE 101 (2007).

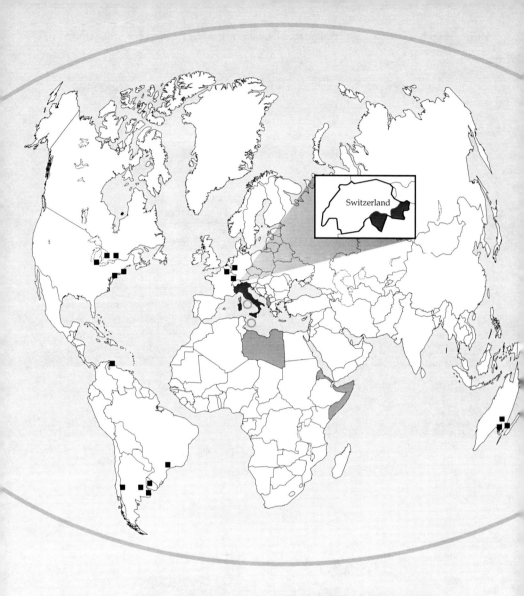

Map Eight

Italian speakers in the world

■ Native language
■ Secondary language or non-official
■ Italian-speaking communities

Map Eight - Italian Speakers in the World

VII. EFFECTIVE STRATEGIES TURNING ON LANGUAGE

L anguage is only one challenge to transnational commercial and financial deals, but an important one because of the costs of all kinds associated with navigating it. Governmental policies geared simply to promote a language by mandating its use, or just as significant, simply to ignore the issue of how requirements for the use of language in the context of party interactions with governmental authorities burden cross-border transactions, are likely ill-conceived for several reasons. Along the same lines, inattention to how the language of national law, including its concepts and vocabulary, fits with the language and frameworks preferred by participants in transnational deals likely results in the structuring of deals so as to avoid engagement with national law and institutions.

First, inattention to the issue of language fails to recognize the burden that requirements for the use of language impose on transaction parties who for their own reasons would prefer to conduct their business in a different language. Such reasons may include the belief that they understand each other better in the language of their choice or that the language better corresponds to a legal or market reality that the parties face. Second, policies that overlook the burdens associated with mandates to use an official language overlook that their implementation as a practical matter is confined to impositions by governmental authorities that an official language be used in interactions with such authorities. Among themselves, parties will do as they please. Third, a governmental policy to mandate use of a language in some heavy-handed fashion appears likely to be unproductive because it overlooks the considerable ability of parties to work around it by appropriately structuring their transactions. Indeed, the intensity of procedures involving use of an official language not consonant with the parties' choice of language magnifies the incentive of the parties to work around the governmental mandate of those procedures, using the techniques of bifurcated transactions and astute specification of governing law and procedures for dispute resolution discussed above.[350]

The requirements relative to use of language in interactions with governmental authorities imposed by the various jurisdictions that include populations divided among languages vary in design, in degree of burdensomeness, and in substantive outcome. These variations are instructive for the formulation of linguistically sensitive approaches to investment in efforts to harmonize relevant legal frameworks transnationally. The collective experience of the various jurisdictions considered here suggests widespread contemporary recognition that, rather than mandating use of language by sophisticated parties to transnational commercial and financial matters, facilitating use of language is more productive of promoting both business and the use of a target language. The trend appears to be that legal systems offer opportunities to use language by providing frameworks that support the conduct of business in the language of interest, rather than that legal systems mandate use of a language. Although governmental authorities do not typically extend themselves to work in non-official languages, there is a great deal that they can do to lighten the linguistic burden of interactions with them, even by parties who prefer to conduct their business in a non-official language.

A more nuanced and defensible governmental approach to policy to the use of a language in respect of transnational commercial and financial deals, and to the promotion of a language in general, is one that considers: (i) what might be done to make a language an attractive choice for parties; and, (ii) what are the minimum governmental requirements relative to language that are required for those governmental actions with one or more of the parties that cannot be avoided. Parties are much more likely to employ a language if they actually have good reason to want to use it, such as that they speak the language fluently, legal frameworks in the language support their deals, and governmental interactions in the language are not unduly burdensome. Indeed, if the relevant governmental interactions are perceived by the parties as facilitating implementation of the deal desired by the parties, the parties will more fully embrace them. Further, some potential parties may be precluded from participation in transactions if the costs associated with the linguistic burdens of governmental interactions are excessive. Governments share an interest with such parties in working to ensure that costs associated with language burdens are not factors contributing to their exclusion from the opportunity to engage in transnational business. Thoughtful governments will seek to provide the parties legal frameworks that are consonant with the language and economic needs of the parties. Further, it will often be the case that the parties prefer a language other than an "official" language to conduct their dealings, notwithstanding the ineluctability of some interactions with governmental authorities in a mandated official language. In those instances, to minimize the linguistic burden of such required interactions will diminish the burdens, on otherwise desirable transactions, of conventional translation to accomplish the interaction with governmental authorities.

So, if the goal of a government is to promote the use of a language for transnational commercial and financial deals, what are some effective ways to do so? Useful answers to this query should take into account: (i) the reality and consequences of parties' ability to make creative exercise of party autonomy as to choice of law and forum for dispute resolution and as to the structure of their transactions among jurisdictions; (ii) the negative effects not only for the transaction parties, but also for governmental institutions, of burdening transactions with national private law and private international law rules that seek to frustrate the exercise of party autonomy; and, (iii) the costs of governmentally-mandated procedures involving the use of language which simply make it harder for the parties to conduct their business. An enlightened route to promoting the use of an official language might be to lower the barriers to transnational commercial and financial contracting, by minimizing the linguistic burdensomeness of required governmental interactions. Just as important, is active participation of the full breadth of stakeholders—governmental and private, in the elaboration and the implementation of, the available international conventions, model laws, restatements, supranational legislative frameworks, and the like. As a legal system's norms and institutions conform to international standards, there will be less reluctance to using such norms and the associated official language. Such conformity may well do more to promote an official language than a direct mandate to employ it. Likewise, the benefit of minimizing the linguistic burden of governmental interactions that must necessarily take place in an official language, is to lift a barrier to participation in transnational commercial and financial deals that otherwise weighs upon economic actors subject to the legal system.

There are many ways for governments to minimize the language barriers to transnational commercial and financial contracting, while simultaneously promoting well-grounded national policy goals. Such goals may include promoting the use of a language within and beyond national borders, the efficient delivery of government services, the participation of speakers of a language in transnational commerce and finance, and the protection of the interests of such speakers as they do so. Broadly speaking, what governmental authorities may do in these regards falls into categories of unilateral action and of participation in multilateral initiatives of law reform.

A.   Unilateral action

Unilaterally, governmental authorities may require that interactions with them be in an official language, for example when parties deal with national courts, pursue administrative authorizations or registrations, or seek to avail themselves of public procurement opportunities. Governmental requirements as to the constitution of priority creditor claims to collateral to secure repayment of a loan retained in the possession of a borrower, perhaps to support generation of the revenue stream intended to be dedicated to repayment of the loan, and as a condition to the offer to the public of stock, bonds or notes are respectively examples of registrations and authorizations that governmental authorities can unilaterally impose. As governmental authorities seek to mandate use of language in these interactions, they frequently offer exceptions or escape valves to avoid unduly burdening transnational commercial and financial deals.

For example, many jurisdictions limit a mandate that an official language be used in a contract as a condition to the validity of that contract to instances when a governmental entity itself is a counterparty. Indeed, France, if the transaction is entirely outside France although nonetheless with some instrumentality of the French government, dispenses with the requirement to use French entirely. Mexico in the cases of its national electric and petroleum monopolies goes even further than France in this regard. It allows the parties, one or the other of CFE and PEMEX on the one hand, and a party doing business with one of them on the other, the free choice of use of a language (and of choice of governing law and forum for dispute resolution) for "international" matters, including those which may well involve significant performance in the country.

The widespread allowance of agreements to arbitrate is a further example of how governments lighten the language burden on transnational commercial and financial deals. Although all countries impose the burden of translation into an official national language as a condition of making recourse to the national courts to enforce an agreement, most countries allow parties to avail themselves of the New York Convention and other similar conventions on the enforcement of arbitral awards. Parties who do so significantly mitigate the burden of requirements to use an official language in interaction with national courts by agreeing to specify the language of the arbitration and the language abilities which their arbitrator or arbitrators must have. In essence, the burden is reduced to the translation of the arbitral award in conjunction with efforts to enforce it. Although the initial negotiation of such conventions as the New York, Inter-American and ICSID conventions was certainly a multilateral initiative, they are sufficiently established for the present analysis to consider a national determination to adhere to them to be in effect a unilateral measure.

A further set of examples of unilateral governmental action to lighten the linguistic burden of governmental interactions pertains to security interests. Jurisdictions such as the states of the United States with the adoption of Article 9 of the Uniform Commercial Code, and France with its recent reforms, embrace notice filing systems for the establishment of priority claims to loan collateral. In doing so, they provide a less linguistically burdensome regime than jurisdictions such as Brazil and Mexico which require notarization of security agreement documentation as a precondition to, and as a part of, filing in a public registry.

These examples, however important they may be to facilitating transnational commercial and financial deals, are only part of what governments can potentially achieve to facilitate the conduct of transnational business. They are limited in the sense that they are unilateral actions of governmental authorities to allow parties the space to undertake transactions on the terms of the parties' choice. These unilateral actions of governmental authorities recognize that the efforts of parties to transnational commercial and financial deals invested in "working around" peremptory government policies frustrate the implementation of such policies. They further recognize that such policies also burden the economic and social value otherwise created through the transnational business.

However, the unilateral governmental actions do not directly reach the core challenge of designing and implementing frameworks that support what the parties would do in the exercise of their autonomy. In addition, they do not fully exploit the opportunity to motivate the parties to exercise their autonomy in ways that bring the conduct of transactions within frameworks that not only promote the achievement of governmental policies, but also work through, rather than around, governmental institutions. Paradoxically, the collaboration of governmental authorities in the establishment of multilaterally-coordinated frameworks for transnational commerce and finance can bolster the role of governmental authorities in ways that unilateral assertion of impositions does not.

B.   Multilateral action

The stakeholders in economic growth have long recognized the importance of defining common, or at least compatible, frameworks within which parties to transnational commercial and financial contracts can reach agreements as to which a party's enforcement efforts will not yield unexpected outcomes. Further, they seek opportunities to strengthen the rule of law, particularly in emerging economies, and the associated values of foreseeability and transparency. Unilateral action may prove an ineffective tool to promote and regulate transnational commercial and financial deals. Indeed, it may simply suppress or divert to other places otherwise desirable economic activity.

Efforts to create legal frameworks that are coordinated multilaterally are potential wins for all stakeholders. Such frameworks obviate much of the need for transaction party efforts to create their own transaction-specific frameworks. Stakeholders benefited by such frameworks include not only transaction parties who desire efficiency and certainty in their transactions, but also governments and others interested in promoting (i) the rule of law through the development of effective institutions and (ii) substantive governmental policies, for example, the policies for the promotion of language here considered.

In emerging as well as developed economies, working through courts and other governmental institutions, rather than around them, can reinforce the effectiveness of such institutions, including key components of the rule of law, namely the foreseeability and transparency of their actions. Such a result contributes to the development of critical governmental institutions, such as courts, registries and regulatory bodies. That such institutions work effectively is preferable to party evasion of them, either because they do not exist, or because they are either ineffective or affirmatively harmful to either or both of the parties' intended business and to more general economic and social objectives. It is likewise preferable to a common stopgap, namely the imposition of private standards and agreements through transnational supply chains, although such imposition may be of some value where government regulation fails, notably in emerging-market jurisdictions.[351]

The examination of the national (and supranational) systems here considered is consistent with recognizing the obvious benefit of development of frameworks in languages that are widely-spoken. However, it further suggests the benefits of efforts to engage with a language less widely-spoken as well. Such efforts may range from simply making the framework accessible to speakers of such a language, to actually rendering the framework into such a language. The goal of these efforts overall is to promote broad participation in transactions, without a potential party's preferred language constituting an impediment.

The tools to accomplish this goal extend through a range of options. At the simplest end, they begin with simple conventional translation and progress to bilingual provision of services in varying degrees. At a more sophisticated level that seeks engagement with international efforts to harmonize law relevant to transnational commercial and financial deals, they include active involvement of speakers of the relevant less widely-spoken language in the process of establishing the framework. Such persons who are expert in both the language and the corresponding legal system, can play a critical role by participating in the establishment of content of the framework in the more widely-spoken language so that it integrates with the less widely-spoken language and its legal system. They may also play a key role in stimulating the input of, and acceptance by, political constituencies that may be essential to assuring governmental action to adopt and implement the framework.

What follows are three kinds of proactive options, roughly in increasing order of challenge, by which stakeholders with an interest in how transnational commercial and financial deals are conducted can intervene to use language as a fulcrum to advance the goals initially identified, namely, to (i) promote transnational deals by reducing the burden of working around inadequate and uncoordinated legal systems; (ii) advance rule of law goals by strengthening the role of legal institutions; and, (iii) promote the languages in which such systems function.

1. *Participation in international norm implementation*

Languages and frameworks for transnational commercial and financial norms benefit from use. As transaction parties and their advisors come to know and understand them, they more readily and more fully make recourse to them. Likewise, as transaction parties and their advisors interact with governmental authorities through frameworks meant to support transnational commercial and financial deals, their recourse to such authorities creates incentives and pressures for such authorities to function well.

Accordingly, investments in education to promote the understanding and diffusion of coordinated transnational frameworks in support of cross-border transactions are high return activities. The people who give life to language and law include public administrations, professional organizations, economic actors, and universities. Experience with, for example, the Convention on the International Sale of Goods, now in force for twenty years, suggests the value of concerted efforts to diffuse knowledge of a framework for transnational business through writings that explain the framework, and also practice developments and possibilities under it, as its use evolves.[352] It further suggests that law schools and the practicing bar benefit from concerted educational efforts to make them aware of the opportunities offered by a new normative framework, and even more so of how and when to use the framework in conjunction with or in lieu of more established options. Appropriate targets of such activities are not only seasoned practitioners but also the rising generation of professionals and students. Universities and professional organizations, such as bar associations, are prime partners in the diffusion of new frameworks. Their role need not be limited simply to education. They may also be key partners in assuring the implementation of the framework by helping to instigate the necessary legislative, regulatory and administrative actions to achieve such implementation.

A further way to engage educational, professional, governmental and economic actors in a framework is to give them the opportunity to work with the framework and its further elaboration. This opportunity can be established more broadly than simply the opportunity of parties to employ a framework in connection with their transactions. Thus for example, the Convention on the International Sale of Goods includes a mechanism to involve courts, lawyers and academics in an active way with its implementation on a global basis. Its Article 7 includes an exhortation for its uniform interpretation. It provides:

> "In the interpretation of this Convention, regard is to be had to its international character and to the need to promote uniformity in its application and the observance of good faith in international trade."[353]

As a matter of drafting, this exhortation makes the decision of any court in the world of potentially persuasive value to a court (or arbitrator) called to resolve a dispute to which the Convention applies. It co-opts the parties, their counsel and the court into working with the framework in its full breadth. Energetic counsel will seek to have understanding not only of prior decisions of whatever court before which litigation might be pending, but also of courts elsewhere, including of other legal systems. The treaty reference to promotion of uniform application thereby creates the incentive to collect and analyze the decisions of actors in many jurisdictions, as a number of well-prepared and maintained web sites in fact do, notably of UNCITRAL and UNIDROIT, but also of private sector institutions, for example, Pace University in the United States.[354] As one example of the international character of the interpretation of the Convention on the International Sale of Goods, the Pace University web site identifies a decision of the French Court of Cassation as of persuasive value in assessing how other courts would rule on the question of whether China's ratification of the Convention includes extension of its effects to Hong Kong in view of Hong Kong's status as a Special Administrative Region of China (the view of the Court of Cassation is that the Convention does not extend to Hong Kong).[355]

Mechanisms by which national courts refer questions to a supranational court are another instance of co-opting a range of actors across countries to participate in the application and evolution of a framework. The European Court of Justice has jurisdiction to provide authoritative answers to questions posed to it by Member State courts.[356] It has used this jurisdiction not only to elaborate an ambitious and potent body of jurisprudence, but also to deputize Member State courts as partners in the implementation of European Union law, with the attendant powers and duties. The European Court of Justice's *Factortame* decision, in which it declared the power of English courts when acting to enforce European Union law to enjoin the English public administration, a power such courts lacked as a matter of purely English law, is but one example.[357] In that instance, the European Court of Justice found the exercise of the power that it declared to be an obligation on the part of the English courts, so as to assure the implementation of European Union law. OHADA's provision for jurisdiction of its high court not only to hear appeals from national courts, but also to answer interlocutory questions from lower courts, is a further example in this sense.

2. *Participation in international norm drafting*

International conventions, model laws, mutual recognition, soft law "principles", international restatements, and the like provide common frames of reference to parties and courts by offering harmonized substantive law. In so doing, they also increase party choice of language options through their use of multiple official languages and their establishment of common concepts for translation into national languages.

The texts of international conventions, model laws and analogous instruments typically exist in multiple languages in equally authentic versions in which considerable expert thought has been invested to assure quality of translation. The United Nations conventions, such as the Vienna Convention on the International Sale of Goods, exist in the six official languages of the United Nations. The Inter-American conventions on private international law are prepared in the OAS languages of English, French, Portuguese and Spanish. Moreover, such conventions and guidelines are often translated into other languages with similar quality of expert attention, for example, the German and Italian translations of the Vienna Convention on International Sale of

Goods. The International Organization for the Unification of Private International Law (UNIDROIT) provides the UNIDROIT PRINCIPLES OF INTERNATIONAL COMMERCIAL CONTRACTS not only in UNIDROIT's official languages, but also in the languages of a substantial number of its members.[358]

The opportunity for a country to invest in the collective effort to draft multilateral harmonization and unification frameworks so as to coordinate them with its policy priorities, even if its language is not one of the official languages of the framework, is of considerable value. The country's participation in the collective effort can assist in creating the path for transnational commercial and financial deals to flow through, rather than around, its institutions. Such participation can assure that the multilateral framework is crafted to fit the perhaps unique realities of that country's institutions. Moreover, any thoughtful translation of the framework into an official national language is a high return investment in involving the country's economic and professional actors in the framework in their preferred language. This is even more so true if the language of interest to the particular country is not one of the official languages of the relevant framework.

Commitment of resources to the restatement/expert association/model law approach discussed above,[359] like the commitment of resources to education, is a potentially high return activity. As mentioned, this approach frequently transpires through institutions outside the bounds of traditional governmental structures. This approach is helpful not only to formulate, but also to engage and diffuse across languages, the understanding of frameworks of transnational commercial and financial norms.

Internationally, for example, the American Law Institute's work relative to insolvency law among the North American Free Trade Agreement parties of Canada, Mexico and the United States has likewise been associated with significant law reform, notably Mexico's bankruptcy legislation.[360] The instances of reform of Mexican and United States law relevant to insolvency are examples of progress towards a common substantive frame of reference, while preserving the linguistic diversity of the relevant legal systems. The collaboration of Mexican and United States experts in the work preparatory to the reform yielded a law, which although of course Spanish-language legislation adapted to the reality of Mexico, is conceptually much more coherent with United States federal bankruptcy law than its predecessor, thereby among other benefits, offering a stronger foundation for transnational commercial and financial deals. Not to be overlooked on the point of coherency between Mexican and United States insolvency legislation, is the incorporation by each country of the 1997 UNCITRAL Model Law on Cross-Border Insolvency, in Mexico in 2000 and in the United States in 2005.[361] These are further examples of the multiple paths by which governmental authorities and transaction parties can achieve the benefit of harmonized frameworks to support transnational commercial and financial deals while continuing to enjoy the benefit of linguistic diversity. In the present instance, the benefits of linguistic diversity are manifested in the intensified vitality of the use of Spanish with respect to insolvency proceedings in Mexico and of English with respect to insolvency proceedings in the United States. Indeed, the vitality of each language is augmented precisely because of the reforms coordinated in the two systems.

3. Reduction of the burden of interaction with governmental authorities: filing office/ intelligent forms

The concept of approaches based on simplified filing office formalities and intelligent forms is to limit the linguistic and other procedural burdens of interaction with governmental authorities by reducing the complexity of the interaction. In this approach, the role of governmental authorities is configured to cast the interaction, to the extent practicable, as one of routine processing of forms. Adopting such an approach signifies some measure of trust in the sophistication of parties and in the integrity of both party and governmental actors.

In respect of a transaction among sophisticated parties, their sophistication is reason for greater confidence in their ability to protect themselves even in the absence of external controls and hence less need to incur the costs of procedures to ensure that they understand the consequences of business that they undertake. Likewise, having an institutional reason to trust other governmental actors diminishes the need independently to verify the conclusions of their work. These two inter-related premises of sophistication and trust underlie respectively the UCC Article 9 framework for secured lending and the recently adopted French provisions relative to non-possessory liens, each discussed above, and the European Union provisions relative to recognition of judgments of other Member States in civil and commercial matters.

The UCC Article 9 framework and the recent French reforms relative to non-possessory liens in moveable and intangible property share a trust in the sophistication of the parties and in the work of the courts that may be called upon to resolve disputes among creditors as to lien priorities. Unlike the systems of Argentina, Brazil, Italy, Mexico and Spain, they do not require notarization and filing of the agreements between a debtor and the intended preferred lien creditor as a condition of the establishment of lien priorities relative to the pertinent kinds of collateral. The lack of interjection of the notary as a neutral professional charged (i) with assuring the proper form of the relevant documentation and (ii) to create a record accorded "public faith" for purposes of proof of the relevant details of the relationship between the debtor and the intended preferred creditor, implies greater institutional trust of the initial parties to bear responsibility for correctly establishing their relationship and of the courts eventually to sort out claims of competing creditors to collateral over which one creditor claims to have received a priority interest.

The UCC Article 9 framework carries the concept a step further than the recent French reform with respect to the elaboration of a coordinated choice of law framework. The federal character of the United States, as contrasted to the unitary character of France, establishes the basis for the UCC Article 9 to do this. This framework addresses the identity of the state in which notice filings should be made to establish a priority interest in collateral. Under the Commerce Clause of the United States Constitution, the United States enjoys a substantially national marketplace. Accordingly, the traditional allocation of the subject matter of commercial law to the fifty states, in the context of a national marketplace, poses the question not only of where to file to establish a priority claim in collateral. It also raises the question of where a potential creditor should search to determine whether to extend additional credit based on borrower offers of liens in its personal property assets. As discussed above, UCC Article 9 in its present elaboration provides that the relevant registry is that of the state of organization of the debtor.[362]

In effect, the UCC Article 9 example of a coordinated specification of relevant law by multiple jurisdictions offers an example of how at an international level the management of linguistic burdens might be ameliorated by multilateral harmonization of law. Such harmonization would be based on coordination of choice of law provisions, the substantive requirements of which are calibrated to moderate their linguistic burden, for example, requirements which approximate the UCC Article 9 notice filing requirements.

The Cape Town Convention on International Interests in Mobile Equipment,[363] promoted by UNIDROIT, is an international convention that adopts this filing office/intelligent forms approach. In so doing, it sidesteps the additional requirement of notarial involvement widely present in respect of the creation of security interests under the civil law systems prevailing in much of the world. The Cape Town convention provides a unified framework for the recordation of security interests in aircraft, rolling stock, and eventually other kinds of mobile equipment. Compliance with the terms of the Convention, for example, enables a lender to know that its lien against an aircraft has priority whether the aircraft is in Bogota or Los Angeles, notwithstanding the differences of Colombian and US law relative to foreclosure on collateral and contests among creditors. The mechanism for establishing priority of a lien is a filing similar in concept to that of UCC Article 9, that is, what matters is the notice provided by the fact of filing rather than the linguistic content of the filing. In essence, the registrar's role does not extend to any involvement with the substance of what is registered. The Cape Town Convention accordingly not only seeks to eliminate "conflict of law" issues in respect of its subject matter, but also substantially mitigates the burden of choice of language that might otherwise challenge accomplishment of the desired financial transaction.

Coordinated multilateral arrangements to accord full faith and credit to judgments of courts of other jurisdictions can also be considered a tool in the management of linguistic burden. The European Union's Regulation no. 44/2001 on jurisdiction and the regulation and enforcement of judgments in civil and commercial matters approximates the full faith and credit clause of the United States constitution in that it mandates that a relevant judgment given in a Member State be recognized in other Member States without "any special procedure being required", except in limited circumstances such as if "manifestly contrary to public policy in the Member State in which recognition is sought" or if it is a default judgment reached without due process notice to the defendant.[364] Regulation no. 44/2001 also establishes simple, standard forms by which a judgment of one Member State once drawn up or registered as an "authentic instrument" in such State, is to be recognized in another Member State.[365] One of the rationales of these forms is to mitigate the burdens of having to work in multiple languages.

Regulation (EC) no. 805/2004 of the European Parliament and of the Council of April 21, 2004 creates a European Enforcement Order for uncontested claims, that is, for default judgments, that works on a similar model.[366] The Regulation applies among all Member States except Denmark, and for qualifying judgments obviates the requirement of national *exequatur* proceedings as a prerequisite to the enforcement of such judgments. The Regulation reduces the national judicial role in connection with enforcement of a qualifying foreign default judgment to that of processing pre-established forms almost in the style of the familiar international driver's license. In so doing, this Regulation unburdens judges and other governmental officials, as well as the contract party attempting enforcement across borders of a default judgment on a contract, from much of the weight of divergent language and legal concepts.

The London Agreement, in force since May 1, 2008, manifests a desire by a number of European states to lessen the linguistic burdens of patent protection under the European Patent Convention ("EPC").[367] It is a further variant to the approach of recognizing documentation approved by another governmental authority without translation into a national official language. Under the London Agreement, EPC member states that currently include France, Germany and the United Kingdom, will accept granted European Patents in any one of English, French or German—the three official languages of the European Patent Office, while states such as Croatia, Denmark, Iceland, the Netherlands and Sweden will accept documentation in English.

Each of these approaches limits the need of governmental authorities responding to party demands for services, specifically in the case of secured lending, the creation and registration of a security interest, and in the case of enforcement of a judgment, the recognition of a foreign judgment, to give attention to the substance of the underlying matter. In the case of patent filings, the diminished requirement of translation reflects the increased reliance of national patent authorities on the European Patent Office. Accordingly, each of these approaches implies less need for translation so as to enable governmental authorities to provide the necessary service. Neither approach is suitable for implementation unless the corresponding prerequisite is sufficiently satisfied. In the case of secured lending, the prerequisite is the sophistication of the relevant parties, both (i) the transaction parties and other potential creditors and (ii) the courts that will be called upon to resolve competing claims. In the case of full faith and credit to foreign judgments, the prerequisite is the trust of the foreign legal system's integrity. However, once the relevant prerequisite is adequately satisfied, these approaches allow party choice of language to be respected in greater measure, and in so doing, they lighten the burden of conforming to a requirement of using a particular language in order to interact with a governmental agency, be it a registry official or a court. Interestingly, however, in the event of a dispute before a court concerning a patent accepted under the London Agreement without translation into a national official language of that court, translation of the patent would likely be required at the time of the dispute, thus resulting in a useful delay in respect of incurring the burden of translation, but not its definitive avoidance.

4. *Supranational law making:*

a. Europe unleashed?

What the European Union does within its borders to harmonize and unify the law of its Member States relevant to transnational commercial and financial deals has broad significance also outside of Europe. Its influence has now come to rival the significance of United States (and English) law for such transactions. The sources of this increased profile of the European Union include the number, linguistic range, and cultural and legal heterogeneity of the European Union Member States, as well as their commercial importance and of course the existence of significant European Union law relevant to transnational commercial and financial deals. The relevance of this law to international unification and harmonization efforts derives from its application to intra-Union transactions, its applicability to transactions in ways that extend beyond the confines of the European Union (of which European Union competition law is a prime illustration), and its role as a source of inspiration for international unification and harmonization of law efforts generally.

The European Union is more than the sum of its Member States, by virtue of its supranational institutions endowed with executive, legislative and judicial powers and their ability to make decisions in a wide range of instances that are not subject to individual Member State veto. However, the distinction between what falls within the subject matter competence of the European Union and that of its Member States remains a sensitive point. Relative to harmonization of law with respect to contracts, a European Community Commission staff report observed some years ago that the focus of the European Community's motivation was to achieve "a genuine internal market" with "a common law-enforcement area in which all citizens can assert their rights not only in their home country but also in other Member States."[368] In that instance, the Commission staff highlighted the European Community's primary focus as the development of the common market, not the inter-relation of the European Union (of which the European Community was a component and into which it is now subsumed) and the rest of the world.

An increased role of the European Union in international harmonization of law efforts outside the Union's internal market would have many implications, including relative to language. Even absent such increased engagement, the European Union is a significant force in global harmonization and unification of law efforts, whether or not it chooses to assume a role as an active partner. The European Union's infrastructure for translation and diffusion of legal texts through and to its Member States and their legal institutions and actors, the sheer size of its internal market and the heterogeneity of the legal systems included within it, assure this significance for the European Union. The European Union, with its twenty-seven Member States and now, pursuant to the Lisbon Treaty fully subsuming the European Community, constitutes a significant economic space within which parties to commercial and financial contracts can in increasing measure define the terms of their agreements without the burden of having to confront and work around un-harmonized mandatory provisions of national law.

Because the European Union publishes its normative materials in its twenty-three official languages, its extensive normative materials relative to transnational commercial and financial deals are generally available in a language readily accessible to any given party to such a transaction. The additional benefit and force of the European Union's linguistic diversity is that many of its official languages are also employed elsewhere in the world. Notably, each of English, French, Portuguese and Spanish is among its official languages, and each of them is spoken by more people outside of Europe than within it.

(1) European Union authority

The relative roles of the European Union and its Member States in harmonization of law initiatives that extend outside the European Union are established by provisions of the Treaty on European Union and the Treaty on the functioning of the European Union (formerly known as the Treaty establishing the European Community, and initially known as the Treaty of Rome establishing the European Economic Community), as well as case law of the European Court of Justice construing them. Consistent with the challenge of multilateral coordination inherent to improving the coordination of disparate national approaches to private law generally and private international law in particular, European Union law recognizes the importance of European Union action relative not only to the issue of establishing its internal market, but also the relationships between that market and the private international law of the rest of the world. It does so, however, with considerable attention to the continued relevance of the ongoing diversity of its Member States' legal systems and the approaches specific to the legal systems of each. Relevant European Union law reflects a balance of such law's provision for "subsidiarity" and for an exclusive Union competence for external relations relative to subject matters for which European Union rules have been adopted.

Article 5 of the Treaty on European Union defines the principles of conferral, subsidiarity and proportionality. Article 5 affirms that the Union may act only within the limits of the competences conferred upon it in the European treaties by the Members States and to attain the objectives set forth in those treaties. It further affirms that European Union action as to areas not within its exclusive competence be in accord with the principle of subsidiarity, which mandates that the lowest effective level of government deal with any issue. In particular, it affirms that the Union shall act if the objectives of a proposed action cannot be sufficiently achieved by Member States, but rather, "by reason of the scale or effects of the proposed action," can be better achieved at the Union level. Article 5 further asserts, under the principle of proportionality, that the content and form of Union action shall not exceed what is necessary to achieve the objectives of the treaties.

The European Court of Justice has been quite clear that the European Community, now fully subsumed into the European Union, has had exclusive competence, to the exclusion of any competence of its Member States, to undertake obligations with non-Member States that would affect common rules adopted by the European Community. Hence, whether responsibility for multilateral initiatives to harmonize law with states that are not members of the European Union falls to a Member State or the European Union institutions, depends on whether the harmonization initiative concerns a subject matter for which the European Union has already adopted common internal norms. Only to the extent that the harmonization initiative is outside the Union's exclusive competence because the Union has not already adopted common internal norms, or perhaps because under the principle of proportionality the treaties' objectives can be attained without full arrogation to the Union of the responsibility for carrying forward the participation in the multilateral initiative, does there remain space for the direct involvement of the Member States.

The clarity as to the European Union's exclusive competence to undertake obligations with non-Member States arose in the context of a 1971 decision of the European Court of Justice, when the European Economic Community remained limited to its six founding members of France, Germany, Italy and the three Benelux countries of Belgium, Luxembourg and the Netherlands. The controversy concerned the role of the Community institutions, relative to the Member States, in the establishment of standards of road safety pertinent to truckers moving goods across the borders of various European states, including the initial Member States of the European Economic Community. The European Court of Justice held that:

> "In particular, each time the Community, with a view to implementing a common policy envisaged by the Treaty, adopts provisions laying down common rules, whatever form these may take, the Member States no longer have the right, acting individually or even collectively, to undertake obligations with third countries which affect those rules."[369]

In a fashion typical of the Court's politically savvy approach, this bold statement of Community power was tempered by the

Court's ultimate conclusion that the challenged position of the Council was in fact justified. That position concerned how to handle the completion of negotiations commenced years before by the Member States of the Community and other European states through the United Nations Economic Commission for Europe for the finalization of a "European agreement concerning the work of crews of vehicles engaged in international road transport". Thus, in its ruling the Court validated each of the competing concerns of the European Community Commission, which had challenged the Council position, and the European Community Council. The Court validated the Commission's point in bringing the action to challenge what the Commission perceived as a Council failure to protect Community prerogatives. However, the Court also validated the Council's concern that an agreement concerning safety standards to be observed by truck drivers moving freight in and out of the Community not be jeopardized by wrangling over the proper Community procedure to be followed. For the long run, the Court's declaration of the principle of exclusive Community competence to undertake obligations with third countries that affect European Community rules is an enduring significance of its ruling for the European Union.

Recently, the European Court of Justice revisited the issue of the European Community's exclusive competence to undertake obligations with third countries that affect European Community rules. The subject matter of the Court's ruling was the new Lugano Convention—intended to extend the substance of Regulation no. 44/2001 concerning the recognition and enforcement of judgments to non-EC Member States Iceland, Norway and Switzerland, plus Denmark, the French overseas territories and the Netherlands Antilles and Aruba.

In its recent ruling, the European Court of Justice explained the purpose of the Community's exclusive competence in the context of determining that the negotiation and conclusion of the new Lugano Convention falls entirely within the sphere of exclusive competence of the European Community. The Court explained that the purpose of the exclusive competence is:

> "primarily to preserve the effectiveness of Community law and the proper functioning of the systems established by its rules, independently of any limits laid down by the provision of the Treaty on which the institutions base the adoption of such rules."[370]

The Court further explained that:

> "a comprehensive and detailed analysis must be carried out to determine whether the Community has the competence to conclude an international agreement and whether that competence is exclusive. In doing so, account must be taken not only of the area covered by the Community rules and by the provisions of the agreement envisaged, insofar as the latter are known, but also of the nature and content of those rules and those provisions, to ensure that the agreement is not capable of undermining the uniform and consistent application of the Community rules and the proper functioning of the system which they establish."[371]

In light of the extensive European Union rules pertinent to transnational commercial and financial deals, there are clearly areas as to which an exclusive European Union competence can be inferred to address harmonization of commercial and financial law not only inside the European Union, but also as between the European Union and the balance of the world.

(2) Logistics of European Union action

The provisions of each of the Treaty on European Union and the Treaty on the functioning of the European Union (formerly known as the Treaty establishing the European Community) relative to Member State coordination of foreign policies also have implications for the allocation of roles between Member States and the Union in respect of international harmonization of law efforts. Each of the two treaties provides architecture for the participation of European Union institutions in such efforts. And, together the two treaties offer the possibility of the accomplishment of harmonization of law within the Union via the adoption by the Union of international agreements with states and international organizations outside the Union.

The Lisbon Treaty reforms the Treaty on European Union to fully define the European Council, and to provide for a President of the European Council[372] and a High Representative of the Union for Foreign Affairs and Security Policy (who will also serve as a Vice-President of the Commission and as Secretary-General of the Council). The European Council is comprised of the Heads of State and Government of the Member States as well as the President of the European Council and the President of the Commission, and except as otherwise expressly provided by the Treaty on European Union, is to make decisions by consensus. The European Council elects its President by qualified majority voting to serve a two and a half year term. The High Representative for Foreign Affairs and Security Policy is elected by a similar mechanism, with the further proviso of approval by the President of the Commission.[373]

How the President of the European Council and the High Representative for Foreign Affairs and Security Policy will embrace the topics of harmonization of law and attention to the role of language in transnational commerce as instruments of the European Union's foreign policy within their scopes of action remains to be seen. Although such officials clearly have the discretion to focus on such topics, the Commission is likely to remain the lead institution of the European Union in respect of participation in harmonization of law initiatives involving states outside the Union. The Council and the European Parliament will also remain influential.

The Treaty on the functioning of the European Union provides that agreements to be made between the Union and one or more states or international organizations are in general to be negotiated by the Commission following Council authorization, and approved by the Council following proposal by the Commission.[374] The European Parliament is to have the opportunity to voice its input prior to Council approval of an agreement, and in cases which would involve modifications of Community acts adopted by the cooperation procedure among the Community institutions including the Parliament, as well as cases which would have important budgetary implications for the Community, the Parliament's assent is required.[375] In general, the Council is to decide by qualified majority vote, although when the agreement covers a subject matter as to which unanimity is required for the adoption of internal rules, unanimity of the Council is also required for the adoption of the agreement.[376] Unanimity of the Council is also required when the Community by these procedures exercises its power to enter into agreements with states "establishing an association involving reciprocal rights and obligations, common action and special procedure." [377]

Accordingly, the procedural consequences of a European Union determination to participate in an international harmonization of law initiative by negotiation and adoption of a treaty to which the European Union itself would be a party are to involve each of the principal European Union institutions in the process. The Commission would lead the negotiations. The assent of each of the Council and the Parliament would likely be required because of the impacts on existing European Union legislation and perhaps implications for the Union budget as well.

Moreover, the European Court of Justice might be involved by virtue of a request for its opinion as to whether the European Union is empowered to enter into the treaty, just as its jurisdiction was invoked and in response it rendered its binding opinion in the recent landmark case discussed above concerning the extension of Regulation no. 44/2001. In some instances it would likely be unclear whether the particular initiative of harmonization of law would fall within the subject matter for which unanimous Council action is required, in essence a unanimous vote of the heads of state and government of the Member States, or within the subject matter for which qualified majority voting of the heads of state and government comprising the Council would suffice. The Court of Justice would likely be called to rule in such matters, and it has been a consistent advocate for the proposition that Community action (that now by virtue of the Lisbon Treaty would be European Union action) should be taken on the basis of the Treaty ground that requires the least onerous voting threshold of the Member States.

In some instances the operation of the Treaty provisions on the competence of the European Union could impede, rather than promote, the active engagement of European Union Member States in general international harmonization of law efforts. This result would derive from the existence of the exclusive jurisdiction of the Union as a result of the existence of internal Union measures regulating the relevant subject matter. Such exclusive jurisdiction, combined with the determination in any instance of a requirement of unanimity of the European Union Member States to reach an agreement with states outside the Union, would enable any European Union Member State to veto progress in the harmonization of relevant law with third states. What renders this risk less acute is that the treaty provisions for the organization of European Union and Member State efforts to harmonize law are not, however, limited to the provisions which address the logistics of the negotiation and the making of treaties by the European Union. The Court of Justice's longstanding orientation to examine with care the basis for any assertion that a Community (now European Union) activity requires Member State unanimity likewise constrains this risk.[378]

Member States have broad obligations to collaborate with European initiatives. These obligations are the glue that may hold the European Union together as an effective force in international harmonization of law initiatives also outside the European Union. Provisions of the Treaty on European Union speak directly to the obligation of the Member States to collaborate with each other and the Union, and corresponding mandate that the Council and the High Representative ensure compliance their performance of this obligation. The Treaty on European Union provides that:

"The Member States shall support the Union's external and security policy actively and unreservedly in a spirit of loyalty and mutual solidarity and shall comply with the Union's action in this area.

The Member States shall work together to enhance and develop their mutual political solidarity. They shall refrain from any action which is contrary to the interests of the Union or likely to impair its effectiveness as a cohesive force in international relations."[379]

In addition, there is provision for the Council to adopt "common positions". Their significance is that:

"The Council shall adopt decisions which shall define the approach of the Union to a particular matter of a geographical or thematic nature. Member States shall ensure that their national policies conform to the Union positions."[380]

Lastly,

"1. Member States shall coordinate their action in international organisations and at international conferences. They shall uphold the Union's positions in such forums. The High Representative of the Union for Foreign Affairs and Security Policy shall organise this coordination.

In international organisations and at international conferences where not all the Member States participate, those which do take part shall uphold the Union's positions."[381]

The Treaty on the functioning of the European Union provides that the Commission is to maintain relations with international organizations, including the United Nations and its specialized agencies, the Council of Europe, the Organisation for Security and Cooperation in Europe, and the Organization for Economic Cooperation and Development.[382] Interestingly in light of this provision, neither the European Union nor its predecessor component, the European Community, has been or is a member of the United Nations. However, in light of the provisions of the Treaty on European Union relative to solidarity of the Member States, the weight of the European Union within the United Nations system is significant, as European Union Member States constitute more than an eighth of the votes in the General Assembly and, together with countries that are candidates for European Union membership, a third of votes in the Security Council.[383] Nonetheless, the European Union's lack of status as a General Assembly member has so far precluded its direct membership in significant forces for international harmonization of law efforts that are part of the United Nations system, such as UNCITRAL. The European Union is likewise not directly a member of key international organizations outside the United Nations system, for example, UNIDROIT, although the European Community has been a member of the Hague Conference on Private International

Law, a status to which the European Union accedes under the Lisbon Treaty.

Although the European Court of Justice has boldly declared the principle of exclusive Community (now European Union) competence, it has been cautious in finding specific instances of such competence. Likewise, the Council has yet to adopt a "common position" speaking to the role of the Member States and the position of the Union relative to harmonization of law efforts, either generally or with respect to some specific subject matter. In addition, the Council, Commission and European Parliament have not availed themselves broadly of the power to conclude international conventions with parties outside the European Union that harmonize law relevant to transnational commercial and financial deals. For example, the European Community did not become a party either to the New York Convention on Arbitration or to the Vienna Convention on the International Sale of Goods. The European Union so far remains outside these conventions notwithstanding that all of its members are party to the New York Convention, and all but four of its Member States are parties to the Convention on the International Sale of Goods.[384]

Accordingly, each of the principal European Union institutions, notably the Court of Justice and the Council, leaves space for a significant continuing role for individual Member States in the broad work of improving legal frameworks for transnational commercial and financial deals. The continuing heterogeneity of Member State legal systems relative to topics pertinent to transnational commercial and financial deals is itself a continuing challenge to the European Union's ability to find its voice in respect of broader international efforts to harmonize law relative to such topics. Nonetheless, the "constitutional" architecture by which the European Union Member States might, and in many instances would be required to, present themselves as a block, working through the Union institutions, with respect to questions of harmonization of law relative to transnational commercial and financial deals, is very much a reality. The consolidation of the European Union's Foreign Policy under the Lisbon Treaty offers further opportunity to reinforce this reality.

(3) Hague Convention on Choice of Court Agreements

The commencement of ratification of the recently proposed Hague Convention of June 30, 2005 on Choice of Court Agreements, so far ratified only by one state, Mexico, but signed by each of the European Community and the United States, offers an opportunity for European Union action in a topic of importance to efforts to harmonize private law pertinent to transnational commercial and financial deals.[385] The proposed Hague Convention would provide for respect of agreements by which parties to transnational commercial and financial deals specify an exclusive choice of court for resolution of disputes. It would also provide for the recognition of any resulting judgment by the courts of any state for which the Convention is in force. Notably in light of the discussion of the leverage of governmental authorities with respect to the establishment of priority claims in security interests in collateral for a loan, the Convention would not apply to the validity of entries in public registries, such as those necessary to establish a lien priority effective against third parties.[386] In essence, in this regard the Convention would maintain the current leverage of national authorities over matters pertaining to the constitution of priority claims against third party creditors in collateral left in possession of a borrower as security for the repayment of a loan.

Bringing the Convention into force also supports the autonomy of parties to transnational commercial and financial deals to manage the linguistic burdens associated with them. The ability of the parties to designate the jurisdiction whose courts will resolve their eventual disputes, with assurance that the courts of any relevant legal system will respect the designation, carries with it power relative to use of language. The power derives from the association of courts with the official languages in which they work. Selecting a court is also a choice to work with that court in the official language that the court employs.

The European Community participated in the negotiation of the new Hague Convention, through its membership in the Hague Conference on Private International Law, to which the European Union will now accede by virtue of the full incorporation of the European Community into the European Union. The general importance of this Hague Convention is that it may begin to bring the party incentives to choose arbitration, as contrasted with agreement on choice of a court as the forum for dispute resolution, into greater parity. The international consensus on the acceptability of arbitration is vastly greater than such consensus on the effectiveness of agreements on choice of a court for dispute resolution. In particular, there is far greater openness, as a result of the widespread ratification of the New York Convention, to the recognition of international arbitration awards than there is to the recognition of foreign judgments.

Greater parity in respect of agreements to arbitrate and agreements to use a particular court for dispute resolution has importance to the issue of language. This importance derives from the limitation that international arbitration is not a universal solution to challenges to respect of party preferences as to the language for conduct of transactions. Some kinds of transactions are simply not suited to arbitration. A lender, for example, is unlikely to agree to arbitration of its rights to foreclose following a borrower payment default. Instead, it will want to pursue collection against the debtor in whatever jurisdictions the debtor has available assets. The ability of a lender and a debtor who are parties to a cross-border financial transaction, to specify in advance in which jurisdiction's courts the question of whether a debtor default has occurred so as to entitle the lender to foreclose, enables them at the time of the grant of credit to forestall potentially complex litigation about which courts might have jurisdiction over an eventual dispute on the issue of default in repayment or in other terms of the loan agreement. Should the lender prevail on the question of its entitlement to foreclose and collect from the borrower, the Convention would further simplify the ensuing enforcement effort in the various states where the Convention would be in force and the borrower might have assets.

The ability of parties to agree on a choice of court for resolution of disputes between the parties, with the prospect of respect of that choice by other courts to which a disgruntled party might turn, further reinforces the parties' power of agreement with respect to language at the time of entering into transactions. Embedded within party agreement on choice of court is party agreement on the use of the language in which that court functions for purposes of resolving any dispute that might arise. The enforceability of party agreement on choice of court also signifies the respect of the parties' implicit agreement on choice of language.

Interest in ratification appears to exist in each of two critical participants in international harmonization of law efforts, the European Union and the United States.[387] Because of the Union's existing norms on recognition of judgments, dating back to the Brussels Convention and now embodied in its Regulation no. 44/2001, there is ample basis to support a conclusion that European Union measures have occupied the subject matter field within the Union. This result, under the European Court of Justice's case law discussed above, leaves to the European Union, rather than to its Member States, the ratification of the new Hague Convention. Indeed, the new Hague Convention contains express provisions for its ratification by the European Union as a "Regional Economic Integration Organisation". These provisions allow its ratification by the European Union, while preserving its application to agreements on choice of court and recognition of judgments even as to cross-border business involving solely the European Union's Member States.[388]

Although the European Union's ratification of the new Hague Convention would promptly apply its terms throughout the European Union, such ratification would rigidify in some measure the European Union's approach to recognition of party choices of forum for dispute resolution. The provisions of the Treaty establishing the European Community pursuant to which Regulation no. 44/2001 was adopted mandated unanimous assent of the Member States acting through the Council. Nonetheless, the European Community's applicable internal legislative process, which now addresses the issue of respect of party choice of court through Regulation no. 44/2001, allows the flexibility simply to adopt a new Regulation through the applicable European Union legislative process. In contrast, ratification of the new Hague Convention would imply an ongoing obligation to third party states, the modification of which would properly occur only with their assent.

In some measure, this is the issue that the United States faces when it ratifies a treaty like the Convention on the International Sale of Goods and also faces as it contemplates its own potential ratification of the new Hague Convention on Choice of Court. State law predominates as to commercial and property matters within the United States' federal system. An ongoing challenge of increased engagement by the United States in the international process of norm formulation is the interaction of federal commitments with the now traditional process of ongoing state update of substantive commercial, corporate and financial law in response to judicial decisions and changing business realities. This is part of the continuing challenge of conforming multilateral initiatives to local realities, in the United States and elsewhere, including the European Union.[389] The ratification of such a treaty by a federal country like the United States, or a supranational organization like the European Union, further federalizes, or supranationalizes, the relevant body of law, thereby limiting the opportunities of states or Member States, as the case may be, to serve as laboratories for new and alternative legal approaches perhaps more closely linked to local needs.

b. CPLP as an opportunity for language promotion, law reform and harmonization of law

The European Union as discussed above is the preeminent example of supranational law-making in multiple languages. As a further example of what can be achieved, the OHADA countries by treaty have given themselves a framework for establishment of a sophisticated and effective market space for commercial and financial deals, not only among themselves, but with the rest of the world as well. An incidental effect of this gift to themselves and the rest of *la francophonie* is the promotion of the sophisticated use of their *lingua franca*, French.

The *Comunidade dos Países de Língua Portuguesa* ("CPLP" – Community of Portuguese Language Countries) offers a potential further example of how improving on the present framework of private international law for transnational commercial and financial deals can offer not only economic benefits, but also assist in language promotion efforts. The CPLP countries present parallels to the OHADA countries, namely a shared *lingua franca* (French for OHADA, Portuguese for CPLP) that they wish to promote, a desire for increased commercial and financial dealings among themselves and the rest of the world, and the challenge of creating supportive legal frameworks.

They of course also present differences. The CPLP countries are more geographically-dispersed relative to each other than the OHADA countries, and there are greater disparities among them. Brazil in particular is an economic entity sufficiently large and insular to be slow to focus on the benefits of active embrace of international harmonization and unification of law efforts, particularly relative to the other Portuguese-speaking countries.[390] Moreover, the magnitude of economic disparity between Brazil and Portugal at the high end and some of the CPLP states only just emerging from extended periods of violence, for example, East Timor, is greater than that among OHADA states. Nonetheless, at least one provider of legal services currently seeks to address the CPLP states as a common Portuguese-language legal space in which cross-border commercial and financial matters can be managed through a unified team of lawyers sharing Portuguese-language skills and legal training.[391]

To reclaim the seventeenth century-legacy of Portuguese as a global language of commerce and exploration is promoted by simplifying and strengthening the legal framework for commerce and investment among the CPLP countries and with the rest of the world. This by no means diminishes the importance of diffusion of Portuguese-language television broadcasting to those in the CPLP countries and to other Portuguese-speaking communities scattered around the world, and the training and funding of language teachers as similarly important elements of promoting the Portuguese language.[392] The provision of adequate legal frameworks is especially important for the African states that are members of the CPLP and for East Timor. Like the OHADA states, they face an opportunity for greater participation in the benefits of transnational economic activity, but that is tempered by the challenge to provide an adequately-supportive legal framework.[393] OHADA itself is aware of the opportunities and needs for improved legal frameworks in the neighboring states of Africa. The pending amendment of its constitutive treaty to extend its working languages from exclusively French to Portuguese and English is clearly intended to capture the opportunity to provide them its developing framework.

If the OHADA model of legislating commercial law through treaty institutions is too aggressive for Portugal with its European Union obligations and for Brazil in view of its size and geographical remoteness relative to the other CPLP countries, perhaps a model law approach, commencing, for example, with the Portuguese text of the OAS model law on commercial transactions,[394] would serve as a feasible initial step. Incentives for such a first step include not only the benefits of harmonization of law among CPLP members and progress in respect of the rule of law in the CPLP members that are recovering from only recently concluded periods of prolonged, armed conflict. Brazil, as the largest member of the CPLP, could also benefit from improvement of its laws for secured lending.[395]

The CPLP could without modification of its existing institutions and governance structures commence a program of work focused on law reform through the adoption of model legislation. Such an approach would avoid any mandate for the use of Portuguese, which transaction parties might perceive as simply an obstacle to be worked around by investing resources in the various techniques sketched above. The approach instead would be to create a legal framework in Portuguese that works well on its own and that accepts whatever language parties may choose for the conduct of their transactions. Such an approach would offer the CPLP countries the prospect of what the OHADA countries are already well on their way to achieving. Indeed, were such a model law injected into OHADA itself as a Uniform Act, it would contribute to greater alignment of OHADA with the CPLP countries as a whole. A proposal in this sense from the CPLP countries would also contribute to a greater measure of parity of Portuguese with French in the context of OHADA.

NOTES TO CHAPTER VII

350. *See* text *supra* at section V.B.

351. Michael P. Vandenbergh, *The New Wal-Mart Effect: The Role of Private Contracting in Global Governance*, 54 UCLA L.R. 913 (2007).

352. *See, e.g.* Franco Ferrari, ed., THE CISG AND ITS IMPACT ON NATIONAL LEGAL SYSTEMS (2008); Louis Del Duca and Patrick Del Duca, *Selected Topics under the Convention on International Sale of Goods (CISG)*, 106 DICKINSON L.R. 205 (2001); Louis Del Duca and Patrick Del Duca, *Internationalization of Sales Law - Practice Under the New Convention on International Sale of Goods - A Primer for Attorneys and International Traders (Part II)*, 29 UCC L.J. 99 (1996); Louis Del Duca and Patrick Del Duca, *Practice under the Convention on International Sale of Goods (CISG): A Primer for Attorneys and International Traders (Part I)*, 27 UCC L.J. 331 (1995). Emmanuel S. Darankoum, *La pérennité du lien contractuel dans la vente commerciale OHADA: analyse et rédaction des clauses*, 35(115) RECUEIL PENANT 500 (2005), in an analogous vein offers thoughtful practical advice to lawyers and merchants working with the uniform law of OHADA on commercial sales.

353. *Supra*, note 311.

354. *See, e.g.* the sites of Pace Law School (cisgw3.law.pace.edu), UNIDROIT (www.unilex.info), and UNCITRAL ("CLOUT" database—www.uncitral. org/uncitral/en/case_law.html). The American Society of International Law's ELECTRONIC INFORMATION SYSTEM FOR INTERNATIONAL LAW (www.eisil.org) further exemplifies the power of the internet as an inclusive tool for diffusing international law resources.

355. http://www.cisg.law.pace.edu/cisg/countries/cntries-China.html, citing Court of Cassation, First Civil Chamber, arrêt no. 389 of April 2, 2008 (*Logicom SA v. CTT marketing Limited et autre*), *available at* www.courdecassation.fr.

356. Treaty on the functioning of the European Union, art. 267 (*ex* art. 234 TEC, *ex* art. 177 Treaty of Rome).

357. Case C-213/89 *supra* note 153.

358. *See* text *supra* at note 324.

359. *See* text *supra* at section VI.B.

360. American Law Institute, PRINCIPLES OF COOPERATION AMONG THE NAFTA COUNTRIES (2003) (lead volume of additional volumes on each of Canada, Mexico and United States as part of the ALI's project entitled "Transnational Insolvency: Cooperation among the NAFTA Countries").

361. *See* www.uncitral.org/uncitral/en/uncitral_texts/insolvency/1997Model_status.html.

362. *See* text *supra* at note 56.

363. Adopted Nov. 16, 2001, entered into force April 1, 2004, http://www.unidroit. org/english/conventions/mobile-equipment/main.htm.

364. *Id.*, art. 33.

365. *Id.*, articles 57 and 58.

366. OJ L 143/15 (April 30, 2004), as amended by Commission Regulation (EC) no. 1869/2005 of Nov. 16, 2005 L 300/6 (Nov. 17,2005).

367. *See* www.epo.org.

368. Commission of the European Communities, *Green Paper on the conversion of the Rome Convention of 1980 on the law applicable to contractual obligations in to a Community instrument and its modernization*, COM(2002) 654 final (Jan. 14, 2003).

369. Case 22/70 (*Commission v. Council ("ERTA")*), [1971] ECR 263, at ¶17.

370. Opinion 1/03, [2006] ECR I-42, ¶131.

371. *Id.* at ¶133.

372. Treaty on European Union, art. 15.

373. *Id.*, art. 18.

374. Treaty on the functioning of the European Union, art. 207, 218 (*ex* art. 300 TEC).

375. *Id.*

376. *Id.*

377. Treaty on the functioning of the European Union, art. 217, 218(8) (*ex* art. 310 TEC, 300(2) TEC). New article 218(8) omits the unanimity requirement for agreements with international organizations previously present under article 300(2) TEC.

378. Case 242/87 (*Commission v. Council (Erasmus)*), [1989] ECR 1425 (Court of Justice examines carefully whether Council action could be justified without recourse to a Treaty provision that required unanimous Member State consent).

379. Treaty on European Union, art. 24(3) (*ex* TEU art. 11(2)).

380. *Id.*, art. 29 (*ex* TEU art. 15).

381. *Id.*, art 34 (1), (*ex* TEU art. 19, first paragraph).

382. Treaty on the functioning of the European Union, art. 220 (*ex* art. 302 TEC).

383. *See* www.europa-eu-un.org.

384. *See supra* note 311 and www.uncitral.org.

385. On the Convention on Choice of Court Agreements and its status, see www. hcch.net. *See also* Ronald A. Brand, *A New Role for Litigation in CISG Contracts: The 2005 Hague Choice of Court Convention*, in Harry M Flechtner, Ronald A. Brand, and Mark S. Walter, eds., DRAFTING CONTRACTS UNDER THE CISG 149-166 (2008).

386. Convention on Choice of Court Agreements, *supra* note 385, art. 2(2)(p). *See* text *supra* at Section IV.C.

387. *See* James Podgers, *Convention Inches Ahead: ABA champions U.S. ratification of agreement to recognize judgments of foreign courts*, ABA J. 60 (Dec. 2007).

388. Convention on Choice of Court Agreements, *supra* note 385, articles 29 and 30.

389. *See* Amelia H. Boss, *The Future of the Uniform Commercial Code Process in an Increasingly International World*, 68 Ohio State L.J. 349 (2007).

390. Eduardo Grebler, *The Convention on International Sale of Goods and Brazilian Law: Are Differences Irreconcilable?*, 25 J. Law & Commerce 467 (2005-06), addresses Brazil's delay in adopting the Vienna Convention.

391. www.mirandalawfirm.com.

392. José Manuel Matias, *Que fazer com a nossa língua?*, Instituto Internacional da Língua Portuguesa, http://www.iilp-cplp.cv/index.php?option=com_conte nt&task=blogcategory&id=16&Itemid=69.

393. *See* Harry G. Boardman, Africa's Silk Road: China and India's New Economic Frontier, The International Bank for Reconstruction and Development / The World Bank 176-77, 223 (2007).

394. *See also* United Nations Commission on International Trade Law (UNCITRAL), *Security Interests: Draft Legislative Guide on Secured Transactions* 1, 3-24 (12-16 Feb. 2007), *available at* http://daccessdds.un.org/doc/UNDOC/LTD/ V06/585/73/PDF/V0658573.pdf?OpenElement; Spyridon V. Bazinas, *UNCITRAL's Work in the Field of Secured Transactions*, 36 UCC L. J. 67-88 (2004).

395. Silva *et al.*, *supra* note 245 at 16, endorse adoption by Brazil of the OAS model law as a desirable reform.

Map Nine

A sketch of the distribution of select language families across Europe, drawn from www.eurominority.eu

■ Romanic
■ Celtic
■ Slavic
■ Germanic
□ Uralic

Map Nine - Distribution of Select Language Families Across Europe

VIII. LANGUAGE AS EMPOWERMENT

L anguage, and more particularly a sophisticated approach to language, can serve as a fulcrum of empowerment relative to transnational commercial and financial deals for both transaction parties and governmental authorities. It can open opportunities for greater participation in such transactions, and it can empower those who engage in them to better understand and define their transactions. Likewise, it can empower stakeholders with an interest in improved frameworks of law and of governmental institutions for support of transnational commercial and financial deals to achieve those frameworks. To consider language in this fashion, offers the prospect of new opportunities of participation in transactions and of accomplishment of law reform.

The stakeholders of interest include those who conduct transnational business and those who might do so were it less burdensome to conduct. In each instance, stakeholders also include those who benefit from more efficiently-provided goods, services and infrastructure. Employing language as a fulcrum to advance reform, in particular, offers benefits to parties now excluded because of linguistic and other hurdles.

The stakeholders of interest, however, are by no means limited to those with a strictly economic interest in transnational business. Stakeholders of interest include governments and those further interested in the benefits of the rule of law. Unilateral governmental actions intelligently formulated with reference to facilitating, rather than mandating use of language, and multilateral initiatives that establish coordinated frameworks within which respect for party choice of language is encouraged, promote the conduct of cross-border transactions within, rather than outside, the norms and institutions of legal systems. By doing so, they further promote and reinforce the integrity and vitality of such legal systems, as well as the use of the associated official languages.

Narrowly viewed, language is a choice of transaction parties, a peremptory mandate by governmental authorities for interactions with such authorities, and a troublesome filter through which to achieve understanding. Indeed, in the course of negotiating, structuring, documenting, performing and enforcing a transaction, language is all of these things between parties, as well as among parties and the governmental authorities with which one or more parties may interact.

More broadly viewed, language is an opportunity. Facilitation of language use, rather than mere imposition of peremptory mandates to use an official language in the interactions with governmental authorities that inevitably are associated with a commercial or financial deal that crosses borders, lowers barriers to transactions, and diminishes the need to work around, rather than through, governmental institutions. It enables more transactions, more effectively, to be consummated, and it opens the prospect of participation in transnational commerce and finance to speakers of a target language otherwise subject to marginalization. Recognition of these benefits can motivate stakeholders to invest in multilateral efforts to reform law, through unification and harmonization, with a focus on overcoming existing linguistic barriers that burden international commerce and finance.

The approaches here suggested, that address unilateral consideration of reducing linguistic burdens and pursuit of multilateral law reform initiatives with attention to the power of language, offer the prospect of tangible improvements to the legal frameworks through which transnational commerce and finance occur. Applying these approaches to national law reform efforts, as for example France, acting unilaterally, has recently done with respect to non-possessory liens in moveable and intangible property, and to international harmonization of law initiatives, be they through treaty-making, coordinated governmental measures including model laws, supra-national legislation, formulation of sector-specific practices, international restatements of the law, and the like, works to diminish the concerns of parties and governmental actors that each may have varying expectations as to the agreed and permissible terms of a transnational commercial or financial deal. Such application also minimizes the distortions and costs confronted by parties as they otherwise seek to work around governmental impositions that they find troublesome.

Like any other collective human endeavor, the dynamic of developing and embracing good law on the part of governmental actors and transactional parties will vary as a function of who else participates in them from time to time. Both transactional interests and governmental parties will likely be well-served not only to seek to participate in models and frameworks that appear the most dynamic at any given moment, but also to collaborate most closely with the currently most dynamic actors in the process.[396] Actors who appreciate the importance of language to transnational commerce and finance as a fulcrum of empowerment for all concerned, are more likely to be effective than others. To be blunt, any of a brilliantly drafted international convention which never takes effect because not ratified by a sufficient number of states, a model law never enacted, or an insightful restatement of the law ignored by parties and courts alike, runs the risk of being a sterile exercise, at best and optimistically justified as an intellectual inspiration for future reform efforts. Actors who harness the enthusiasm of those who speak a language to use that language are more likely to see tangible responses to initiatives to improve legal frameworks for transnational business.

The opportunities to be derived from intelligent consideration of the role of language in interactions with governmental authorities relative to transnational commercial and financial deals are intensified by the evolution of the European Union and other supranational organizations such as OHADA. The development of such organizations, among many other implications, challenges any notion that the United States can effectively contribute to international efforts to unify and harmonize relevant law without actively engaging in dialog that involves such organizations and without considering the vitality of the topic of language to transnational commerce and finance.

Even the most enlightened and dynamically-implemented initiatives to improve legal frameworks for transnational commerce and finance will fail to eliminate all divergences in expectations of parties and governmental authorities as they interact in the course of transaction formulation and eventual enforcement. Language and conflicting perspectives on language are an inherent part of these divergences. Accordingly, there will remain ample margin for legal experts, typically lawyers acting on behalf of transaction parties, and judges resolving disputes either directly or in the context of determining how to respond to an arbitral award or foreign judgment, to define through their collective work product the effective bounds of party autonomy and governmental mandate.

Perhaps some day the Wilsonian dreams of coordinated world governance associated with the institution of the League of Nations will be substantially realized. However, even if this transpires, human nature and cultural diversity would likely leave in place the domain between party autonomy and governmental mandate, a domain for astute transactional structuring and definition of choice of law and mechanisms and fora for dispute resolution. Such structuring and definition of deals will unfold in view of the continued lack of a perfect match between what legal systems impose on transnational commercial and financial deals under conflict of law norms and how parties prefer to conduct their transactions.

The heretic monk in Umberto Eco's THE NAME OF THE ROSE (*Il nome della rosa*) spoke all languages, shifting with each word to another language, with the consequence that he made limited and indeed often no sense to anyone. His version of multilingualism severely constrained his ability to communicate. Parties to transnational commercial and financial deals do indeed readily flout external pressures seeking to direct their choice of language in which to conduct business. However, their heresy in the face of such pressures does not extend to frustrating their ability to communicate with each other. Parties to significant transnational commercial and financial deals generally have the good sense to make choices about the language in which to conduct their business that are supportive of such business.

A policy of promotion of a language is likely more effective if it is based on facilitating the choices of transaction parties about what language to use in dealings among themselves. What limited leverage exists in the hands of governmental authorities to affect party choice of language derives from the necessity of interactions by one or more of the parties with governmental authorities in connection with making, performing or enforcing the deal. Minimizing the linguistic burdens of such interactions facilitates transnational commerce and finance. In addition to minimizing burdens on the parties, such an approach recognizes the inherently problematic aspect of efforts to control use of language. One author has elegantly phrased the reality of regulation of language as follows:

> "Language traditionally has emerged as stronger than any law purporting to control it, like a butterfly escaping from its chrysalis in colors impossible to predict and flying in unknown directions."[397]

As parties to transnational commercial and financial deals seek to negotiate, structure, document and render enforceable their understandings, consciousness of the context in which they are working should extend to the possibility of constraints on choice of language and how such constraints might be encountered in contacts with governmental authorities for purposes of first structuring and eventually enforcing their transactions. Legal systems, in the context of globalization, that wish to preserve or impose constraints on the content of transnational commercial and financial deals should be cognizant of the limitations in their ability to do so. Inartfully pursued, such constraints may simply stimulate the creativity of lawyers and their clients to construct transactions in ways that remove as much as practicable the essence of such transactions and their enforcement from the imposing legal system's jurisdiction. Rather than focus on constraints of elusive application, governmental authorities, transaction parties and other stakeholders in the rule of law are best served to bind the creativity of those who transact across borders with the passions for language and communication. Creativity and communication are keys not only to constructing the individual deals that cumulatively comprise transnational commerce and finance, but also to improving the legal frameworks that serve them.

NOTES TO CHAPTER VIII

396. Ann E. Carlson, *Iterative Federalism and Climate Change,* 103 NORTHWESTERN U. L. REV. 1097 (2009), illustrates the functioning of "iterative federalism" relative to air emission regulation, observing that recognizing the leadership capability at any given time of specific states or groups of states, *e.g.* California, can be a productive alternative to the poles of devolution and centralization. Thus, relative to legal frameworks supportive of transnational commercial and financial deals, particular states, groupings of states, and international supranational organizations may from time to time be "hot spots" of innovation and leadership on particular topics, and accordingly worthy of greater investment of effort and resources.

397. Curran, *supra* note 29, at 696.

SELECT BIBLIOGRAPHY

Books and Articles

José E. Alvarez, INTERNATIONAL ORGANIZATIONS AS LAW-MAKERS (2005)

American Law Institute, PRINCIPLES OF COOPERATION AMONG THE NAFTA COUNTRIES (2003)

Oren Bar-Gill, Michal Barzuza & Lucian Bebchuk, *The Market for Corporate Law*, 162 J. INSTITUTIONAL & THEORETICAL ECONOMICS 134 (2006)

George A. Bermann, 54 *Bilingualism and Translation in the U.S. Legal System: a Study of the Louisiana Experience*, AM. J. COMP. L. 89 (supp. 2006)

Pierre Birnbaum, THE HEIGHTS OF POWER: AN ESSAY ON THE POWER ELITE IN FRANCE (1982)

Harry G. Boardman, AFRICA'S SILK ROAD : CHINA AND INDIA'S NEW ECONOMIC FRONTIER, The International Bank for Reconstruction and Development / The World Bank (2007)

Michael Joachim Bonell, *Soft Law and Party Autonomy: The Case of the UNIDROIT Principles*, 51 LOYOLA LAW REV. 229 (2005)

Thierry Bosly, Thierrry Lohest, Gilbert Nyatanyi & Vincent Moyhy, *Belgium* in INTERNATIONAL SECURED TRANSACTIONS (2005)

Amelia H. Boss, *The Future of the Uniform Commercial Code Process in an Increasingly International World*, 68 OHIO STATE L.J. 349 (2007)

Ronald A. Brand, *A New Role for Litigation in CISG Contracts: The 2005 Hague Choice of Court Convention*, in Harry M. Flechtner, Ronald A. Brand & Mark S. Walter, eds., DRAFTING CONTRACTS UNDER THE CISG (2008)

Charles H. Brower II, *Investor-State Disputes Under NAFTA: The Empire Strikes Back*, 40 COLUM. J. TRANSNAT'L L. 28 (2001-2002)

Edward Brunet, Richard E. Speidel, Jean E. Sternlight & Stephen H. Ware, ARBITRATION LAW IN AMERICA: A CRITICAL ASSESSMENT (2006)

Hal Burman, *Private International Law*, 43 THE INT'L LAWYER 741 (2009)

Mauro Bussani & Ugo Mattei, *Preface* in Mauro Bussani & Ugo Mattei, eds., OPENING UP EUROPEAN LAW: THE COMMON CORE PROJECT TOWARDS EASTERN AND SOUTH EASTERN EUROPE (2007)

Carlos Calvo, 1 LE DROIT INTERNATIONAL THÉORIQUE ET PRATIQUE (4th ed., 1887)

Paulo Canelas de Castro, *A Comunidade dos Países de Língua Portuguesa — Para um Discurso Jurídico sobre a sua Identidade e um seu Programa de Acção*, in COLÓQUIO DE DIREITO INTERNACIONAL: COMUNIDADE DOS PAÍSES DE LÍNGUA PORTUGUESA (2003)

Thomas E. Carbonneau, *Linguistic Legislation and Transnational Commercial Activity: France & Belgium*, 29 AM. J. COMP. L. 393 (1981)

Ann E. Carlson, *Iterative Federalism and Climate Change* 103 NORTHWESTERN U. L. REV. 1097 (2009)

Jack J. Coe, Jr., *Transparency in the Resolution of Investor-State Disputes — Adoption, Adaptation, and NAFTA Leadership*, 54 U. KAN. L. REV. 1339 (2005-2006)

Richard L. Creech, LAW AND LANGUAGE IN THE EUROPEAN UNION: THE PARADOX OF A BABEL "UNITED IN DIVERSITY" (2005)

Vivian G. Curran, *Comparative Law and Language*, in Mathias Reimann & Reinhard Zimmermann, eds., THE OXFORD HANDBOOK OF COMPARATIVE LAW (2007)

Emmanuel S. Darankoum, *La pérennité du lien contractuel dans la vente commerciale OHADA: analyse et rédaction des clauses*, 35(115) RECUEIL PENANT 500 (2005)

José A. de Bonilla Pella, *Spain* in INTERNATIONAL SECURED TRANSACTIONS (2003)

Isabelle de Lamberterie, Georges Rouhette & Denis Tallon, (eds.), LES PRINCIPES DU DROIT EUROPÉEN DU CONTRAT: L'EXÉCUTION, L'INEXÉCUTION ET SES SUITES (1997)

Bruno de Witte, *Language Law of the European Union: Protecting or Eroding Linguistic Diversity?* in Rachael Craufurd Smith, ed., CULTURE AND EUROPEAN UNION LAW (2004)

Bruno de Witte, *Regional autonomy, cultural diversity and European integration: the experience of Spain and Belgium*, in Sergio Ortino, Mitja Žagar & Vojtech Mastny, eds., THE CHANGING FACES OF FEDERALISM: INSTITUTIONAL RECONFIGURATION IN EUROPE FROM EAST TO WEST (2005)

Paulina Dejmek, *The EU Internal Market for Financial Services–a Look at the First Regulatory Responses to the Financial Crisis and a View to the Future*, 15 COLUM. J. EUR. L. 455 (2008-2009)

Louis Del Duca, *The Accelerating Pace of Common Law and Civil Law Convergence in A Global Society—Harmonization and Subsidiarity in the Twenty-First Century*, 42 U. Texas Int'l. L.J. 625 (2007)

Louis Del Duca & Patrick Del Duca, *An Italian Federalism?— the State, its Institutions and National Culture as Rule of Law Guarantor*, 54 Am J. Comp. L. 799 (2006)

Louis Del Duca & Patrick Del Duca, *Selected Topics under the Convention on International Sale of Goods (CISG)*, 106 Dickinson L.R. 205 (2001)

Louis Del Duca & Patrick Del Duca, *Internationalization of Sales Law - Practice Under the New Convention on International Sale of Goods - A Primer for Attorneys and International Traders (Part II)*, 29 UCC L.J. 99 (1996)

Louis Del Duca & Patrick Del Duca, *Practice under the Convention on International Sale of Goods (CISG): A Primer for Attorneys and International Traders (Part I)*, 27 UCC L.J. 331 (1995)

Patrick Del Duca, *The Rule of Law: Mexico's Approach to Expropriation Disputes in the Face of Investment Globalization*, 51 UCLA Law Rev. 35 (2003)

Patrick Del Duca, *Uniform law, federated jurisdictions and an example from U.S. and EEC securities regulation* in Int'l Uniform Law in Practice 470 (UNIDROIT, 1988)

Patrick Del Duca & Rodrigo Zamora Etcharren, *Mexico's Secured Lending Reforms*, 33 UCC L.J. 225 (2000)

Doing Business in Brazil (The International Bank for Reconstruction and Development / The World Bank, 2006)

Jian En Ci, *Desen volvimento da Localização e Modernização do Direito Comercial de Macau* 6 Perspectivas do Direito (1999)

Nelson Enonchong, *The Harmonization of Business Law in Africa: Is Article 42 of the OHADA Treaty a Problem?*, 51 J. African L. 95 (2007)

Franco Ferrari, ed., The CISG and its Impact on National Legal Systems (2008)

Heywood W. Fleisig & Nuria de la Peña, *Argentina: Cómo las Leyes para Garantizar Préstamos Limitan el Acceso a Crédito* (Center for the Economic Analysis of Law, 1996)

Marc Frangi, *État, langue et droit en France*, 119 Revue du Droit Public 1607 (2003)

David J. Gerber, *Reading the Map of European Private Law: Language and Knowledge in Contemporary Comparative Law*, in Mauro Bussani & Ugo Mattei, eds., OPENING UP EUROPEAN LAW: THE COMMON CORE PROJECT TOWARDS EASTERN AND SOUTH EASTERN EUROPE (2007)

Michael D. Goldhaber, A PEOPLE'S HISTORY OF THE EUROPEAN COURT OF HUMAN RIGHTS (2007)

Eduardo Grebler, *The Convention on International Sale of Goods and Brazilian Law: Are Differences Irreconcilable?*, 25 J. LAW & COMMERCE 467 (2005-06)

Aline Grenon, *Major Differences between PPSA Legislation and Security over Moveables in Quebec under the New Civil Code*, 26 CANADIAN BUS. L.J. 391 (1996)

Vivian Grosswald Curran, *A Comparative Perspective on the CISG*, in Harry M. Flechtner, Ronald A. Brand & Mark S. Walter, eds., DRAFTING CONTRACTS UNDER THE CISG (2008)

Werner Heisenberg, THE PHYSICAL PRINCIPLES OF QUANTUM THEORY (1930, Carl Eckart & Frank C. Hoyt, trans.)

Manley O. Hudson, *Languages Used in Treaties*, 26 AM. J. INT'L L. 368 (1932)

Introducing the Bar of England and Wales, American Lawyer Media and the Bar Council of England and Wales (Oct. 2007)

Ana Luisa Izquierdo & Manuel González Oropeza, *Indigenous Autonomy in Mexico*, 45 VOICES OF MEXICO 17 (1998)

Friedrich K. Juenger, *The Problem with Private International Law*, 37 SAGGI CONFERENZE E SEMINARI (Centro di studi e ricerche di diritto comparato e straniero, Rome, 1999)

Nicholas Kasirer, *Lex-icographie mercatoria*, 47 AM. J. COMP. L. 653 (1999)

Julio A. Kelly, *Argentina* in INTERNATIONAL SECURED TRANSACTIONS (2003)

Eva-Marie Kieninger, *Evaluation: a common core? Convergences, subsisting differences and possible ways for harmonization*, in Eva-Marie Kieninger, ed., SECURITY RIGHTS IN MOVABLE PROPERTY IN EUROPEAN PRIVATE LAW (2004)

Heinz Kloss, THE AMERICAN BILINGUAL TRADITION (2nd ed., 1998)

Jenning Kohlberger, *Using Principles of International Law to Reshape American Legislation of State Official English Laws*, 29 J. OF LEGISLATION 253 (2003)

Boris Kozolchyk & Dale Beck Furnish☐, *The OAS Model Law on Secured Transactions: A Comparative Analysis*, 12 SOUTHWESTERN J. OF LAW AND TRADE IN THE AMERICAS 101 (2006)

Antonio La Pergola & Patrick Del Duca, *Community Law, International Law, and the Italian Constitution*, 79 AM. J. INT'L L. 598 (1985)

Marie Landick, *French courts and language legislation*, 11 FRENCH CULTURAL STUDIES 131 (2000)

Ole Lando & Hugh Beale, (eds.), THE PRINCIPLES OF EUROPEAN CONTRACT LAW PART I: PERFORMANCE, NON-PERFORMANCE AND REMEDIES (1995)

Mitchel Lasser, *The European Pasteurization of French Law*, 90 CORNELL L. REV. 995 (2005)

Seth Lerer, INVENTING ENGLISH, A PORTABLE HISTORY OF THE LANGUAGE (2007)

Julian S. Lim, *Tongue-Tied in the Market: The Relevance of Contract Law to Racial-Language Minorities*, 91 CAL. L.R. 579 (2003)

Maïnassara Maïdagi (Justice of the Common Court of Justice and Arbitration of OHADA), *Le défi de l'exécution des décisions de justice en droit OHADA*, 35 (116) RECUEIL PENANT 176 (2006)

José Manuel Matias, *Que fazer com a nossa língua?*, Instituto Internacional da Língua Portuguesa, http://www.iilp-cplp.cv/index.php?option=com_content&task=blogcategory&id=16&Itemid=69

James R. Maxeiner, *Uniform Law and its Impact on National Laws — Limits and Possibilities: Uniform Law and its Impact on National Laws Limits and Possibilities*, MEMOIRS OF THE INTERNATIONAL ACADEMY OF COMPARATIVE LAW, GENERAL AND NATIONAL REPORTS OF THE FIRST INTERMEDIATE CONGRESS, THE IMPACT OF UNIFORM LAW ON NATIONAL LAW: LIMITS AND POSSIBILITIES, 2009, *available at* www.ssrn.com

Campbell McLachlan, Laurence Shore & Matthew Weiniger, INTERNATIONAL INVESTMENT ARBITRATION: SUBSTANTIVE PRINCIPLES (2007)

Marcello Messori, *I problemi del settore italiano del risparmo gestito*, ASSOGESTIONI WORKING PAPER 2008/4 (July 2008), *available at* www.assogestioni.it

Pierre Meyer, *La sécurité juridique et judiciaire dans l'espace OHADA*, 35 (116) RECUEIL PENANT 151 (2006)

Joaquim T. de Paiva Muniz & Ana Tereza Palhares Basilio, ARBITRATION LAW OF BRAZIL: PRACTICE AND PROCEDURE (2006)

Joseph S. Nye, Jr., SOFT POWER: THE MEANS TO SUCCESS IN WORLD POLITICS (2004)

Félix Onana Etoundi, *Les Principes d'UNIDROIT et la sécurité juridique des transactions commerciales dans l'avant-projet d'Acte uniforme OHADA sur le droit des contrats*, X UNIFORM LAW REVIEW / REVUE DE DROIT UNIFORME 683 (UNIDROIT 2005-4)

Mark Pagel, *Human language as a culturally transmitted replicator*, 10 NATURE REVIEWS GENETICS 405 (June 2009)

Antonio R. Parra, *The Development of the Regulations and Rules of the International Centre for Settlement of Investment Disputes*, 41 THE INTERNATIONAL LAWYER 47 (2007)

James Podgers, *Convention Inches Ahead: ABA champions U.S. ratification of agreement to recognize judgments of foreign courts*, ABA J. 60 (Dec. 2007)

James D. Prendergast, *Secured Real Estate Mezzanine Lending (with Form)*, THE PRACTICAL REAL ESTATE LAWYER 35 (March 2007)

Mathias Reimann, *Comparative Law and Private International Law* in Mathias Reimann & Reinhard Zimmermann, eds., THE OXFORD HANDBOOK OF COMPARATIVE LAW 1363 (2007)

Lucy Riall, GARIBALDI: INVENTION OF A HERO (2007)

Encarna Roca Trias, *The Process of Codifying the European Legal System*, in Mauro Bussani & Ugo Mattei, eds., OPENING UP EUROPEAN LAW: THE COMMON CORE PROJECT TOWARDS EASTERN AND SOUTH EASTERN EUROPE 101 (2007)

Arthur Rosett, *UNIDROIT Principles and Harmonization of International Commercial Law*, 1996, *available at* www.unidroit.org

Peter H. Schlechtriem, *25 Years of the CISG: An International* lingua franca *for Drafting Uniform Laws, Legal Principles, Domestic Legislation and Transnational Contracts*, in Harry M. Flechtner, Ronald A. Brand & Mark S. Walter, eds., DRAFTING CONTRACTS UNDER THE CISG (2008)

Hyon B. Shin with Rosalind Bruno, *Language Use and English-Speaking Ability: 2000*, CENSUS 2000 BRIEF (Oct. 2003)

Jordan Siegel, *Can Foreign Firms Bond Themselves Effectively by Renting US Securities Laws?*, 75 J. FINANCIAL ECONOMICS 319 (2005)

Harry C. Sigman, *Security in movables in the United States – Uniform Commercial Code Article 9: a basis for comparison* in Eva-Marie Kieninger, ed., SECURITY RIGHTS IN MOVABLE PROPERTY IN EUROPEAN PRIVATE LAW 54 (2004)

Sergio Spinelli Silva Jr., Daniel Calhman de Miranda, Camila Leal Calais and Katerine Yuka Tsuchitori, *Brazil* in INTERNATIONAL SECURED TRANSACTIONS (2007)

Jan Smits, *The Draft-Common Frame of Reference for a European Private Law: Fit for Purpose?*, 15 MAASTRICHT J. EUR. & COMP. LAW 145 (2008)

Ezra N. Suleiman, POLITICS, POWER, AND BUREAUCRACY IN FRANCE: THE ADMINISTRATIVE ELITE (1974)

Ruth Sullivan, *The Challenges of Interpreting Multilingual, Multijural Legislation*, 29 BROOKLYN J. INT'L L. 985 (2004)

Christopher Tanner, *Law-Making in an African Context: The 1997 Mozambican Land Law*, FAO LEGAL PAPERS ONLINE #26 (March 2002)

Michael P. Vandenbergh, *The New Wal-Mart Effect: The Role of Private Contracting in Global Governance*, 54 UCLA L.R. 913 (2007)

Eugene Volokh, *Correcting Students' Usage Errors without Making Errors of Our Own*, 58 J. LEGAL EDUCATION 533 (2008)

Neil Walker, *Postnational constitutionalism and the problem of translation*, in J.H.H. Weiler & Marlene Wind, eds., EUROPEAN CONSTITUTIONALISM BEYOND THE STATE (2003)

George Weber, *Top Languages: the World's 10 Most Influential Languages*, LANGUAGE TODAY 12 (Dec. 1997)

Cases

Brazil
Superior Tribunal de Justiça–2004, REsp 151079/SP–*Recurso Especial* 1997/0072063-2

Canada
Lefebvre (Syndic de); Tremblay (Syndic de), [2004] 3 S.C.R. 326, 2004 SCC 63

Ouellet (Syndic de), [2004] 3 S.C.R. 348, 2004 SCC 64

Re Manitoba Language Rights, [1985] 1 S.C.R. 721

United Mexican States v. Metalclad Corporation, 2001 BCSC 664 (British Columbia Sup. Ct. May 2, 2001)

European Court of Justice
Case 22/70 (*Commission v. Council ("ERTA")*), [1971] ECR 263

Case 120/78 (*Rewe-Zentral AG v. Bundesmonopolverwaltung fur Branntwein ("Cassis de Dijon")*), [1979] ECR 649

Case 242/87 (*Commission v. Council (Erasmus)*), [1989] ECR 1425

Case 379/87 (*Groener v. Minister for Education and the Dublin Vocational Education Committee*), [1989] ECR 3967

Case C-213/89 (*The Queen v. Secretary of State for Transport, ex parte: Factortame Ltd and others*), [1990] ECR I-2433

Case C-281/98 (*Angonese v. Cassa di Risparmio di Bolzano*), [2000] ECR I-4083

Case C-366/98 (*Criminal proceedings against Yannick Geffroy and Casino France SNC. Reference for a preliminary ruling: Cour d'appel de Lyon – France*), [2000] ECR I-6579

Case C-361/01P (*Cristina Kik v. Office for Harmonisation in the Internal Market (Trade Marks and Designs) (OHIM)*), [2003] ECR I-8283

Opinion 1/03, [2006] ECR I-42

France

Conseil Constitutionnel, Decision no. 94-345 of July 29, 1994, J.O.R.F. of Aug. 2, 1994, at 11240

Conseil Constitutionnel, Decision no. 99-412 of June 15, 1999, J.O.R.F. of June 18, 1999, at 8964

Cour de Cassation, chambre commerciale, financière et économique., arrêt no. 1500 of Dec. 19, 2006, *SARL DIVA v. Caisse fédérale du crédit mutuel du Nord de la France*

Cour de Cassation, First Civil Chamber, arrêt no. 389 of April 2, 2008 (*Logicom SA v. CTT marketing Limited et autre*)

Italy

Corte costituzionale, judgment nos. 348, 349 of Dec. 22, 2007, GAZZ. UFF. of Oct. 31, 2007

Spain

Tribunal Constitucional – Pleno, Sentencia no. 46 of Feb. 28, 1991

United States

Amgen, Inc. v. Hoechst Marion Roussel, Inc., 339 F.Supp. 2d 202 (D.Mass. 2004)

Carbon Black Export, Inc. v. The Monrosa, 254 F.2d 297 (5ᵗʰ Cir. 1958), *cert. dismissed*, 359 U.S. 180 (1959)

Gaskin v. Stumm Handel GmbH, 390 F.Supp. 361, 366 (D.N.Y. 1975)

Home Insurance Company v. Dick, 281 U.S. 397 (1930)

Lau v. Nichols, 414 U.S. 563 (1974)

MCC-Marble Ceramic Center, Inc. v. Ceramica Nuova D'Agostino, S.P.A., 144 F.3d 1384 (11ᵗʰ Cir. 1998), *cert. denied*, 526 U.S. 1087 (1999)

Meyer v. Nebraska, 262 U.S. 390 (1923)

Ramos-Baez v. Bossolo-Lopez, 240 F.3d 92, 94 (1ˢᵗ Cir. 2001)

The Bremen v. Zapata Off-Shore Co., 407 U.S. 1 (1972)

Treaty, Model Law, Restatement and Other Materials

ALI/UNIDROIT Principles of Transnational Civil Procedure

Commission of the European Communities, *Communication from the Commission to the Council, the European Parliament, the European Economic and Social Committee and the Committee of the Regions: A New Framework Strategy for Multilingualism*, COM(2005) 596 final, Nov. 22, 2005

Commission of the European Communities, *Green Paper on the conversion of the Rome Convention of 1980 on the law applicable to contractual obligations in to a Community instrument and its modernization*, COM(2002) 654 final, Jan. 14, 2003

Conclusions of the Colloquium at Ouagadougou (Burkina Faso), Nov. 15-17, 2007, *The Harmonisation of Contract Law within OHADA, available at* www.unidroit.org.

Convention on Choice of Court Agreements

Convention on the Recognition and Enforcement of Foreign Arbitral Awards - "New York" Convention

Council of Europe, *Explanatory report, European Charter for Regional or Minority Languages, available at* http://conventions.coe.int/Treaty/en/Reports/Html/148.htm

European Charter for Regional or Minority Languages

European Convention on Human Rights

Joint declaration of the Government of the People's Republic of China and the Government of the Republic of Portugal on the question of Macao (1987)

Organization of American States, *Model Law on Secured Lending*

Protocol to the Lisbon Treaty on the Application of the Charter of Fundamental Rights of the European Union

Restatement, Second, of Contracts (1981)

The Inter-American Convention on the Law Applicable to International Contracts

Traité portant Révision du Traité relative à l'Harmonisation du Droit des Affaires en Afrique, signé à Port-Louis (Ile Maurice), le 17 Octobre 1993

Traité Relatif à l'Harmonisation en Afrique du Droit des Affaires, signed at Port-Louis (Mauritius), Oct. 17, 1993

Treaty of Lisbon amending the Treaty on European Union and the Treaty establishing the European Community, signed at Lisbon, Dec. 13, 2007, fully ratified November 2009

Treaty on European Union

Treaty on the functioning of the European Union

UNIDROIT Principles of International Commercial Contracts

United Nations Commission on International Trade Law (UNCITRAL), *Security Interests: Draft Legislative Guide on Secured Transactions* (Feb. 2007), *available at* http://daccessdds.un.org/doc/UNDOC/LTD/V06/585/73/PDF/V0658573

United States Department of Justice, *Guidance to Federal Financial Assistance Recipients Regarding Title VI Prohibition Against National Origin Discrimination Affecting Limited English Proficient Persons,* 67 Fed. Reg. 41455 (June 18, 2002)

Vienna Convention on the International Sale of Goods

INDEX

F

G

Guinea-Bissau, 101.
*See Organisation pour
l'Harmonisation en Afrique du
Droit des Affaires* (OHADA)
Gujarati, 69

H

Hague Conference on Private
International Law, 208, 262-
263, 265
Hague Convention, on choice
of court agreements, 196–197,
264–268
harmonization of law efforts,
16–17, 197–201
    accommodation and, 37–43
    European Union and, 55–56
    "soft power" and, 37
Hawaii, 68–69, 71
Heisenberg's uncertainty
principle of quantum
mechanics, 215
Hindi, 11, 69
Home Insurance Company v. Dick,
178–179, 181–182
hypothec, 79

I

implementation, international
norm, 241–244
incentives, 32–34
INCOTERMS, 17, 215–216, 219
India, 49
integration. *See* development of
legal frameworks
Inter-American Court for
Human Rights (Mexico), 58
Inter-American Specialized
Conferences on Private
International Law (CIDIP),
208–209

inter-creditor agreements, 184–
186
International Center for the
Settlement of Investment
Disputes (ICSID), 191
International Chamber of
Commerce, 220
international conference model,
207–213
International Organization
for the Unification of
Private International Law
(UNIDROIT), 17, 134, 187,
212–213, 217–219, 245
Ireland, 42
Italian, 10
    certification, 123
    European Union
    institutions and, 120
    language status, 103–104
    spoken in U.S., 69
    spoken in Switzerland, 95
Italy, 40–43, 85, 136–137
    *Commissione Nazionale
    per le Società e la Borsa*
    (CONSOB), 40–41
    Italian Code of Civil
    Procedure, 137
    Italian Constitutional
    Court, 130–131
    multiple official languages
    in, 154–157
    notarization, 156-157
    securities law, 160
    status of Italian in, 103–104
    UCITS ("Undertakings for
    the Collective Investment
    in Transferable
    Securities"), 40
Ivory Coast. *See Organisation
pour l'Harmonisation en Afrique
du Droit des Affaires* (OHADA)

J

Japanese, 69

K

Korean, 69

L

laissez-faire, 65–67. *See also* United States

language. *See also* transactional language choices

diffusion of, during European colonial era, 49

as empowerment, 275–280

problems resulting from miscommunication, 1–5

recognizing linguistic diversity, 37–39

world language, 10

language status

European Union and language rights, 116–133

French, 88–103

Italian, 103–104

Portugese, 104–111

Spanish, 111–116

Latin, 13

lawyers, linguistic skill of, 33–34

League of Nations, 278

legal systems

party incentives to structure transactions in multiple legal systems, 32–34

successful regulation for transnational commercial/financial deals, 23–25

legal systems, understanding of, 1–5

Lerer, Seth, 13

Ley de Política Lingüística, 115

lex mercatoria, 23–25

lien priority, 26–29

lingua franca, 49

linguistically-neutral forum, 195–197

Lisbon Treaty, 116–118, 126–131, 221, 227, 253, 258–264. *See also* European Union

litigation

divergent parameters of party autonomy relative to courts and security interest registrars, 30–32

English and *laissez-faire* approach of U.S., 71–73

translation, 1

London, image of, 51

London Agreement, 250

Louisiana, 61

Lugano Convention, 223, 256

Luxembourg, 41–42

European Charter for Regional or Minority Languages and, 133

securities law, 160

status of French in, 88–89, 96

Luxembourgeois (*Letzeburgesch*), 96

M

Macao, 104–107

Mali. *See* Organisation pour l'Harmonisation en Afrique du Droit des Affaires (OHADA)

Manitoba, 97

N

O